INDIGENOUS AUSTRALIANS AND THE LAW

Cavendish
Publishing
(Australia)
Pty Limited

INDIGENOUS AUSTRALIANS AND THE LAW

Edited by
Elliott Johnston QC,
Martin Hinton,
Daryle Rigney
of the Flinders University of South Australia

Cavendish
Publishing
(Australia)
Pty Limited

First published in 1997 by Cavendish Publishing (Australia) Pty Limited,
Governor Phillip Tower, Level 53, 1 Farrer Place, Sydney,
New South Wales 2000

Australia Cataloguing in Publication Data
Indigenous Australians and the law
1. Aborigines, Australian – Legal status, laws etc
I Hinton, Martin II Johnston, Elliott III Rigney, Daryle
342.940872

ISBN 1 876213 21 3

Printed and bound in Great Britain by
Biddles Ltd, Guildford and King's Lynn

CONTRIBUTORS

Frank Brennan, SJ, AO, a Jesuit priest and lawyer, is an Adjunct Fellow at the Australian National University in the Research School of Social Sciences, Honorary Visiting Fellow in Law at the University of New South Wales, the Director of Uniya, the Jesuit Social Justice Centre in Sydney, and a member of the Council of the Constitutional Centenary Foundation. He has written extensively on Aboriginal Land Rights and is the author of a number of books, including *One Land One Nation, Sharing the Country* and *Land Rights Queensland Style*, and is the co-author of *Finding Common Ground* and *Reconciling Our Differences*.

In 1996, he completed two years of studies and field trips in the Philippines, Cambodia, Uganda and the United States where he was a Fulbright Scholar at Georgetown University and the first Visiting Fellow at the Australia and New Zealand Studies Center. His current interests and commitments include Aboriginal rights, refugee rights, the bill of rights and constitutional reform, intercultural and inter-religious perspectives on human rights in East Asia.

Bruce Debelle has been a Justice of the Supreme Court of South Australia since October 1990. He graduated with an Honours Degree Bachelor of Laws from the University of Adelaide in 1961. He served for a period of 12 months as Associate to Sir Victor Windeyer, one of the Justices of the High Court of Australia. From 1978–83 he was a member of the Australian Law Reform Commission and, in those years, was the Commissioner in charge of the Commission's reference on Aboriginal customary law. In preparing his report, he has drawn extensively on the researches of the Commission and its report, The Recognition of Aboriginal Customary Laws, ALRC 31 (hereafter cited as 'ALRC 31') which was written after he had left the Commission. The author acknowledges his debt to his colleagues at the Commission and to all those Aborigines from whom he has learned so much when working on the reference.

In November 1982, he was appointed Queen's Counsel. He has served on the Executive of the Law Society of South Australia and of the Law Council of Australia. He has been President of the Law Society of South Australia and was President of the Law Council of Australia upon his appointment as Justice of the Supreme Court of South Australia.

Michael Dodson is Australia's first Aboriginal and Torres Strait Islander Social Justice Commissioner. The position of Aboriginal and Torres Strait Islander Social Justice Commissioner was created as a result of the Royal Commission into Aboriginal Deaths in Custody and the National Inquiry into Racist Violence. Born in the Northern Territory township of Katherine, Mick was educated in Katherine, Darwin and Victoria. He completed a Bachelor of Jurisprudence and a Bachelor of Laws at Monash University. He worked with the Victorian Aboriginal Legal Service from 1979–81, when he became a barrister at the Victoria Bar. He joined the Northern Land Council as Senior Legal Adviser in 1984 and became Director of the Council in 1990.

From August 1988 to October 1990 Mick was Counsel assisting the Royal Commission into Aboriginal Deaths in Custody. He has been a member of the Victorian Equal Opportunity Advisory Council, Treasurer of the North Australian Legal

Aid Service and a member of the Australian Institute of Aboriginal and Torres Strait Islander Studies. He is currently the Chair of the National Aboriginal Youth Law Centre Advisory Board. Commissioner Dodson was the Co-Deputy Chair of the Technical Committee for the 1993 International Year of the World's Indigenous People.

Mick's most direct contribution has been in the crafting of the text of the *Draft Declaration on the Rights of Indigenous Peoples*. Now that the *Draft Declaration* has left the Working Group on Indigenous Populations – on its way to the General Assembly – Mick will follow its passage through the United Nations system, endeavouring to preserve its integrity.

Justice John Doyle is the Chief Justice of South Australia. He obtained the degree of Bachelor of Laws from the University of Adelaide in 1966 and the degree of Bachelor of Civil Law from Oxford University in 1969. After being admitted as a barrister and solicitor of the Supreme Court of South Australia, he practised in the firm of Kelly & Co until 1977. He then joined the Separate Bar, which at that time comprised only about 25 practitioners. He took Silk in 1981 and continued to practise at the Bar until 1986 when he was appointed Solicitor-General for the State of South Australia. He was appointed Chief Justice of South Australia in May 1995. He was a member of the Council of the Law Society of South Australia from 1972–79, and a member of the South Australian Legal Services Commission from its formation in 1978 until 1986 (at which time he was Chairman of the Commission). He is also a member of the Council of Flinders University, South Australia, and since 1988, has been a Pro-Chancellor.

Elliot Johnston, AO, QC has been a Justice of the Supreme Court of South Australia, National Commissioner, Royal Commission into Aboriginal Deaths in Custody, member of the Laverton Royal Commission 1974–75, Associate Professor of Law, Flinders University of South Australia, and the inaugural Chairperson of the Aboriginal Legal Rights Movement of South Australia Inc.

Maria Lane is a member of the Ngarrindjeri Peoples. She is currently senior lecturer at the Underdale campus at the University of South Australia, in the Faculty of Aboriginal and Islander Studies, and Head of its Aboriginal and Islander Support Unit.

Jill McKeough is Associate Professor of Law at the University of New South Wales. Her area of specialisation is Intellectual Property which she teaches at both undergraduate and postgraduate level. She is a member of the Law Council of Australia's Intellectual Property Committee. Jill has also taught commercial law, legal system and torts and is Associate Dean for undergraduate students. Her publications include *Intellectual Property in Australia* and *Intellectual Property: Commentary and Materials*.

Tony Moore is an Associate Professor of Law, Flinders University, a lecturer and writer on property law matters since 1970, and member of the South Australian Residential Tenancies Tribunal.

Christopher Reynolds is a senior lecturer of law at Flinders University of South Australia, lecturer in the Department of Community Medicine, University of Adelaide. He is a barrister and solicitor of the South Australian Supreme Court and has a PhD in Community Medicine from the University of Adelaide.

Daryle Rigney is an indigenous person of the Ngarrindjeri Peoples. He is currently a lecturer at the Flinders University of South Australia, in the Yunggorendi, Aboriginal and Torres Strait Islander Education Programme. His area of specialisation is anti-racist education and racism in sport.

Andrew Stewart is Professor and Dean of Law at Flinders University of South Australia. Educated at Oxford University, he taught at the University of Adelaide and the University of Sydney prior to joining the new law school at Flinders in 1991 as a foundation staff member. In 1994, he was appointed to the chair in law and also became Dean.

His main teaching and research interests lie in labour and employment law, intellectual property and contract law. His books include *Labour Law: An Introduction and Intellectual Property in Australia*, and he has written numerous articles for Australian and international journals. In the field of intellectual property he is particularly interested in the area of trade secrets and confidential information and has worked with the National Tertiary Education Union and a number of individual universities to develop model policies on the ownership and control of intellectual property, within higher education institutions. We would like to thank Simon Morris for his invaluable research assistance, and Colin Golvan for helpful information about the Aboriginal flag dispute.

Irene Watson is an indigenous member of the Tanganekald Peoples. She is a lawyer currently writing a PhD thesis on indigenous law-ways.

Belinda Wells, LLB (Adel), LLM (Lond), teaches constitutional law and human rights at Flinders University. She was formerly Assistant to the Solicitor-General of South Australia and a senior legal officer with the Crown Solicitor's Office in South Australia. Ms Wells has also worked as a senior law reform officer for the Australian Law Reform Commission in Sydney, and for a commercial law firm in Adelaide.

ACKNOWLEDGMENTS

First and foremost our thanks are due to the many contributors to this work without whom it would simply not exist. We are also indebted to Yvette Taylor, Sue Manswer and Debbie Kuss of the Law School, Flinders University of South Australia, for their assistance in producing the manuscript and marshalling the various contributors. Lastly, we owe a vote of thanks to our publishers for their encouragement, support, and patience.

CONTENTS

CHAPTER ONE

PROLOGUE

This book is born of a shared sense of the responsibility we, as university teachers in a law school, shoulder in supporting the journey toward maturity as one nation, the journey toward reconciliation. It is the product of the close relationship between the school of law and Yunggorendi, the Aboriginal and Torres Strait Islander Education Programme at the Flinders University of South Australia. It has grown from a commitment not just to the education of indigenous lawyers, but to the liberation of our non-indigenous students by raising their consciousness and understanding of indigenous Australians. In this regard, like other law schools, we have encouraged teachers across the breadth of the LLB to consider the perspective of the indigenous people in all of their courses. And, in support of such teaching, we have developed an optional topic carrying the same name as this book. We find ourselves in entire agreement with the Chairperson of the Council for Aboriginal Reconciliation when he said:[1]

> Reconciliation is based upon the need to recognise the essential dignity of every person, the need to build a national commitment towards recognition of the just and equitable positions that the indigenous people of this country aspire to in the political, economic, cultural and civil domains.

We are very conscious of the fact that the average law student in South Australia is a person who has received a private education, whose family are financially comfortable, whose contact with indigenous people extends no further than superficial observations fuelled by perceptions grounded in stereotypes. We are wary of simply portraying the indigenous people as victims of a legal system introduced by and designed for the dominant culture. We are conscious of the fact that their own law continues to operate, to different extents, in different communities.

In this book we, with the assistance of the many contributors, endeavour to contextualise the study of law (by which we mean the processes of law and the administration of the law) and its impact upon the indigenous people. Also we have attempted to address the cultural clash of white and black Australia that is sometimes particularly visible in our legal system, whilst at other times forming the backdrop to its administration. Further, we have looked to the future asking wherever pertinent, can customary operate exclusively? If it cannot, can it be accommodated within the law of the dominant culture? And, if it cannot, is there some other means by which it may be vested with the respect that it must attract if the indigenous people and the dominant culture are to be reconciled? These questions we have asked of ourselves in the

1 Dodson, P, *Addressing the Key Issues for Reconciliation,* 1993, *Australian Government Printer,* a publication of the Council for Aboriginal Reconciliation, Preface.

knowledge that society is undergoing great change, and that the society of the indigenous people is undergoing even greater change.

The issue of racism in our institutions is of enormous concern and needs to occupy a prominent place in our research and writing, but of even greater concern is the limited level of understanding of the phenomenon of racism. While attention is often focused on the personal and visible racism in the administration of the law, and occasionally on institutional racism, little attention is paid to how the legal system itself is embedded in the history of racism and how the legal system may combat racism. White settlement was an act of invasion and conquest. That is history and cannot be undone. The white colonists brought with them a culture including a legal system that had good and bad qualities (one such bad quality being that it condoned invasion). It was natural and inevitable that white colonists would resort to their own legal system to govern relations between themselves. It was not inevitable but, given the conquest, historically likely that legal system would be used to govern relations between indigenous people. The consequence has been that the legal system of the indigenous people has been supplanted, and in some instances, obliterated. What counts as a legal system and what has been legitimated as a legal system in this country are not indigenous legal systems but imposed legal systems.

It is no longer satisfactory for the clash of cultures in our society to be resolves in favour of the dominant culture by virtue of its dominance. Reconciliation is all important.

In our opinion it is crucial to reconciliation that the lawyers we produce have some insight into the living culture of the indigenous people. Then it may become all the more apparent in the law that square pegs cannot be forced into round holes, and that the hole must be refashioned before there can, indeed, be a whole.

Accordingly, we have placed great emphasis in this book on the living culture of the indigenous people and how the law currently impacts upon that culture. Of necessity, therefore, many of the contributors to this book are indigenous people.

At the end of the day we hope that we have contributed something useful to reconciliation. We are not experts, just well-meaning contributors, and in saying that we are particularly mindful of the words of Brandeis J in *Olmstead v United States*:[2]

> Experience should teach us to be most on our guard when the government's purposes are beneficial ... The greatest dangers to liberty lurk in insidious encroachments by men of zeal, well meaning, but without understanding.

Understanding is the key, and it is our responsibility, to the extent that we are able, to ensure that our students take with them the will to understand.

2 277 US 438 at 471–488.

CHAPTER TWO

INDIGENOUS AUSTRALIANS AND THE LEGACY OF EUROPEAN CONQUEST: INVASION AND RESURGENCE

Maria Lane

INTRODUCTION

The intention in this introductory chapter is to lay before the reader a basic guide to the most valuable literary sources and basic historical changes concerning indigenous people in Australia: law and policy. Students need to be aware of the active responses which indigenous people have fashioned to the forces ranged against them over the past couple of hundred years and the changes which they have forced on successive governments.

The mind-sets which continue to portray indigenous people as either passive, or unchanging and unchangeable, or in some way doomed or out of step with contemporary society are in desperate need of demolition. Certainly most Aboriginal people in South Australia have never lost a sense of community and place, past and future, and the continuity of this sense and our distinctive historical experience will ensure the on-going construction of positive identities.

Major works and references

A lot of immensely important material is now available and which students should consult if they wish to do justice to the field. Most basically very detailed law-related bibliographies can be found in McCorquodale[1] and McRae *et al.*[2] McCorquodale also contains easily the best summary of all legislation affecting Aboriginal people, Act by Act. Some of the most important texts concerning Aboriginal people and the law apart from these include Egglestone,[3] Gale *et al*,[4] Hazlehurst[5] and the Aboriginal Law Bulletin initiated by Professor Garth Nettheim at the University of New South Wales. Hocking[6] provides a very comprehensive coverage of international law and its relation to Aboriginal human rights.

1 McCorquodale, J, *Aborigines and the Law: A Digest*, 1987, Canberra: Aboriginal Studies Press.

2 McRae, H, Nettheim, G, and Beacroft, L (eds), *Aboriginal Legal Issues: Commentary and Materials*, 1991, North Ryde: Law Book Company.

3 Eggleston, E, *Fear, Favour or Affection: Aborigines and the Criminal Law in Victoria, South Australia and Western Australia*, 1976, Canberra: ANU Press.

4 Gale, GF, Bailey-Harris, R, and Wundersitz, J, *Aboriginal Youth and the Criminal Justice System: The Injustice of Justice?* 1990, Melbourne: Cambridge University Press.

5 Hazlehurst, KM (ed), *Ivory Scales: Black Australians and the Law*, 1987, Kensington: NSW University Press.

6 Hocking, B (ed), *International Law and Aboriginal Human Rights*, 1988, North Ryde: Law Book Company.

For detailed analysis of traditional Aboriginal society, one should try to start with Berndt and Berndt,[7] Elkin,[8] or Maddock.[9] Bearing in mind the complexities of traditional society and the integration of law, kinship, land and belief, a student should dip into Edwards,[10] especially the articles by Meggitt, Sackett, Edwards, Hiatt, Stanner and the Australian Law Reform Commission. One of the best works ever written about traditional society is the work by Berndt and Berndt.[11] Suppressed for 50 years, this massive work deals with my own group, the Ngarrindjeri, owners of the land from Kingston to Tailem Bend to the southern suburbs of Adelaide, magicians, fighters and politicians. The compiling of Berndt's work is in itself a fascinating account of the conflict between justice and the law. The book is therefore a long-deferred victory for both the Aboriginal people as a whole and for the advantage of academic research.

As for general history and policy, by far the most comprehensive and sympathetic works would still be Rowley's.[12] His commentary is well worth browsing through to gauge the sincerity and compassion of a truly wonderful Australian, as well as his differentiation of law from justice.[13] We strongly encourage students to browse through the various bibliographies to gain a feel for issues and a familiarity with writers and their special research concerns. One of the most exciting aspects of this area of study is the range of new works being published every year – the empty spaces of Australian history and social critique are rapidly being filled.

A most useful start for any student, Aboriginal or non-Aboriginal, is provided by Mattingley and Hampton, the history of South Australia from Aboriginal perspectives.[14] Other writers are more identified with particular historical periods. For example, Reynolds[15] concentrates his historical research on the periods of initial 'contact', especially in the pastoral north, and the first couple of generations thereafter, the sorry outcomes of which are dealt with by Berndt and Berndt.[16] Hasluck, in a neglected work written in the late 1930s, has contributed a detailed history of 19th century policy in Western Australia.[17] Not a lot has been written to date concerning the terrible years of

7 Berndt, RM, and Berndt, CH, *The World of the First Australians: An Introduction to the Traditional Life of the Australian Aborigines*, 1964, Sydney: Ure Smith.

8 Elkin, AP, *The Australian Aborigines: How to Understand Them*, 1964, Sydney: Angus and Robertson.

9 Maddock, K, *The Australian Aborigines: A Portrait of their Society*, 1982, Ringwood: Penguin.

10 Edwards, WH (ed), *Traditional Aboriginal Society: A Reader*, 1987, South Melbourne: Macmillan.

11 Berndt, RM, and Berndt, CH, *A World That Was: The Yaraldi of the Murray River and the Lakes*, 1993, Carlton: South Australia Miegunyah-Melbourne University Press.

12 Rowley, CD, *Outcasts in White Australia*, 1970b, Ringwood: Pelican; *The Remote Aborigines* 1970c, Ringwood: Pelican; *A Matter of Justice*, 1978, Canberra: ANU Press.

13 Rowley, CD, *A Matter of Justice*, 1978, Canberra: ANU Press.

14 Mattingley, C, and Hampton, K (eds), *Survival in our Own Land: 'Aboriginal' Experiences in 'South Australia' since 1836*, 1988, Adelaide: Wakefield Press.

15 Reynolds, H, *The Other Side of the Frontier*, 1982, Ringwood: Pelican. Reynolds, H, *The Law of the Land*, 1985, Ringwood: Pelican. Reynolds, H, *With the White People*, 1990, Ringwood: Pelican.

16 Berndt, RM, and Berndt, CH, *End of an Era: Aboriginal Labour in the Northern Territory*, 1987, Canberra: AIAS (original 1946 report suppressed).

17 Hasluck, P, *Black Australians: A Survey of Native Policy in Western Australia, 1829–1997*, original 1942, 2nd edn, 1970, Carlton: Melbourne University Press.

the segregation policies and the use of State terror against indigenous people from the late 19th century until after the Second World War. However, apart from Rowley's works, Hasluck[18] details the unravelling of these policies and indigenous reactions to them in the prelude to the assimilation policies of the 1960s (for an alternative view see Biskup).[19] The period of the shift towards policy 'preparation' for assimilation is otherwise skimmed over but Gale[20] provides a contemporary account, one which alludes to much more agency on the part of Aboriginal people than they are given credit for even today.

Over the past 30 years, the quantity and quality of written material has increased immensely. Writers over those years dealing with the contemporary scene who would be strongly recommended (but not necessarily agreed with) include Reay *et al*,[21] Gale,[22] Franklin,[23] Lippmann,[24] Broome[25] and Brennan.[26] Apart from these works, journals have been initiated over the past 20 years, which students would also find very useful, and often much more up-to-date, eg *Aboriginal History*, the *Aboriginal Law Bulletin*, *Land Rights News* and the *Koori Mail* and other publications in health and education stand out.

BACKGROUND CONTEXT: PRIOR TO THE INVASION

Population

Generally, the earlier the estimates of pre-Invasion numbers the lower the figure (for example, Sir Joseph Banks' 150,000 early in the 19th century; Radcliffe-Brown's 252,000 in 1930; White and Mulvaney's 750,000 in the 1970s). With new evidence about the land's carrying capacity of its relative abundance and stability in pre-Invasion times, and the realisation that many areas could support permanent or semi-permanent villages along the major rivers and coasts, around the Lakes, in western Victoria and in the tropics, figures above one million are now seriously considered. Rowley[27] suggests a figure over three million.

18 Hasluck, P, *Shades of Darkness: Aboriginal Affairs 1925–1965*, 1988, Carlton: Melbourne University Press.

19 Biskup, P, *Not Slaves Not Citizens: The Aboriginal Problem in Western Australia, 1898–1954*, 1973, St Lucia: University of Queensland Press.

20 Gale, GF, *A Study in Assimilation*, PhD Thesis, 1964, Adelaide: Libraries Board of SA.

21 Reay, M (ed), *Aborigines Now: New Perspectives in the Study of Aboriginal Communities*, 1964, Sydney: Angus and Robertson.

22 Gale, GF, *Urban Aborigines*, 1972, Canberra: ANU Press.

23 Franklin, MA, *Black and White Australians: An Inter-Racial History 1788–1975*, 1976, South Yarra: Heinemann.

24 Lippmann, L, *Generations of Resistance: The Aboriginal Struggle for Justice*, 1981, Melbourne: Longman Cheshire.

25 Broome, R, *Aboriginal Australians: Black Response to White Dominance, 1788–1980*, 1982, North Sydney: Allen and Unwin.

26 Brennan, F, *Finding Common Ground: An Assessment of the Bases of Aboriginal Land Rights*, 1988, Ringwood: Penguin. Brennan, F, *Sharing the Country*, 1993, Ringwood: Penguin.

27 Rowley, CD, *A Matter of Justice*, 1978, Canberra: ANU Press.

From the perspective of social organisation, calculations can be derived fairly roughly from the numbers of language groups, or 'tribes', and the number of subsidiary groups, or 'clans', within them: my own clan, for example, the Talkindjeri-on, is one of 40 or so within the Jaraldi, which is one of the major groupings within the Ngarrindjeri 'nation' of the lower Murray Lakes, the Coorong and southern Fleurieu, one of the major 'tribal' groupings in southern Australia. The Jaraldi may have numbered 2000–3000 people before the Invasion and constituted, as they still do, one of 500 or more such inter-related groupings in Australia.

However, whether the original population was a quarter of a million, or one and a half million, or three million, the Invasion spelt catastrophic disaster for Aboriginal populations across the country, through European diseases (smallpox, venereal diseases, measles, tuberculosis and flu), murder and starvation, dispossession and *de facto* enslavement. This occurred on a scale and force relative to that of, but obviously not equivalent to, the Holocaust for the Jewish people in Europe. Early this century, the population had declined to barely 100,000 and even now has increased only by a threefold.

The broad details of dispossession, denial of sovereignty ('*res nullius*') and of systems of law and thereby any concept of land ownership ('*terra nullius*') are well-known and acknowledged nowadays by both the legal and academic worlds. So we will commence our historical and policy analysis after the wars of aggression had come to their sorry conclusion.

HISTORY AND POLICY

People are not merely passive quantities of product like potatoes. At any time, they may respond to their legal situation and changes to it in many unpredictable ways. They tend to expect to be involved, at least indirectly, in the making of policy and the administration of any law that concerns them. If such demands are either prohibited or ignored, as they have tended to be in the case of Aboriginal and Islander people, the people devise ways of coping with what they may see as impractical, unjust or absurd.

Policy may lag behind or lead changes in circumstances and in the law or, in fact, be anticipated by the people for whom it is designed. People often act in accordance with what they perceive as justice, regardless of the law of the day; policy and legislative changes may simply recognise *faits accomplis* rather than just initiate change. As Gale noted about the South Australian situation:[28]

> Although in practice the policy towards Aborigines and part-Aborigines in South Australia has altered in recent years, unlike most other States the law governing Aboriginal welfare has seen few changes. With a few amendments in 1939, the Aborigines Act of 1934, fundamentally the same as the Act of 1911, remains the legal basis of policy in this State.

28 Gale, GF, *A Study of Assimilation: Part-Aborigines in South Australia*, 1964, Adelaide: Libraries Board of South Australia, p 196.

Aboriginal policy and legislative change from 1836 until very recently has been even more problematic, in so far as it attempted to engage people against their will in changes that did not have their interests at their base, with manifestly no control by the people themselves over such shifts and on the basis of poorly estimated funding needs and imperfect understanding of social processes. The legal status of Aboriginal people has fluctuated accordingly.

Especially in the 19th century, when human rights were still the prerogative of white adult males with property, the relationship between the colonial and provincial governments and their Aboriginal subjects were marked by ambiguity and indecision. Thus reflecting the attitudes of pastoralists ('exterminate'), farmers ('use'), missions ('civilise and Christianise') and other groups and classes in South Australia at the time ('exclude').

More recent policies and legislative changes, mindful of the law pertaining to human rights, present their own range of unanticipatable responses to the express intentions of law-makers.

PRE-FEDERATION

Application of imperial law

From 1834, even before 'settlement', the colonial authorities had assumed the application of British law to the colonies, *re* 'Crown' land, common law and the rights of British subjects, and imperial and colonial statutes, eg the South Australia Act 1834 and Lord Stanley's Australian Wastelands Act 1842.[29] In practice, within weeks of the Proclamation, the law underwent discriminatory application to Aboriginal subjects: it became an offence to supply alcoholic liquor to any 'native', an offence which generally went unpunished, while the native concerned, who had not actually committed an offence, could be thrashed by the local constable and denied rations.

Nevertheless, schools were set up for Aboriginal children, in Adelaide and at Walkerville in 1839 and 1844 by Hindmarsh and Gawler respectively, in the conviction, which was justified, that Aboriginal people were educable, or, in the phrase of the time, able to be 'civilised and Christianised'. This success was not at all unique – early missions at Wellington Valley in New South Wales, at Ramahyuck in Victoria and at New Norcia in Western Australia, all quickly demonstrated the adaptability and initiative of Aboriginal people.

For example, the Native Institution and School at Black Town, west of Sydney, was so effective in reaching its goals, due to Governor Macquarie's passionate support, that one of its first students, Maria Lock, gained first place in a colony-wide examination in 1819 at the age of only 11.[30] She later married a convict who was assigned to her to

29 Cf Pike, D, *Paradise of Dissent: South Australia 1829–1857*, 1967, Carlton: Melbourne University Press.

30 Brook, J, and Kohen, JL, *The Parramatta Native Institution and the Black Town: A History*, 1991, Kensington: New South Wales University Press, pp 250–51.

serve out his sentence and went on to live a long and fruitful life with him until her death in 1878. However, such successes did not dissuade the pastoralists and others with a vested interest in Aboriginal 'failure to adapt', 'doomed adherence to primitive ways' and general 'ineducability', from eventually prevailing with their preferred policies of segregation and exclusion.

Colonial rule and self-government

For Aboriginal people conditions deteriorated after the granting of self-government. However, the imperial powers appeared to have extracted some guarantees on the civil rights of Aboriginal citizens and included the extension of the vote, within a generation; legislation imposed progressively more restrictions on civil rights, property rights, movement and residence over the next 80 years. Those were the years of tightening control, paralleled overseas by the strengthening of segregation and State terror in the southern States of the United States, the whittling away of African rights in South Africa, and indeed in all colonial territories, further watering-down of New Zealand's Treaty of Waitangi provisions (eg fishing rights) and the aggressive expansion of empire throughout the world, leading up to the First World War.

Students would be particularly interested in the changes in the application of forms of law at different policy phases throughout this period, especially in the areas of civil rights and rights of parents towards their own children. Basically every area of law was involved, even labour law, since for much of this period, Aboriginal people, men and women, were employed in rural industry and no award existed for agricultural labourers.

In the early years after the Invasion, policy was rarely well-developed and unambiguous, as observed by Macrae:[31]

> ... there was no clear-cut simultaneous national progression from one policy phase to another. Massacres could still be occurring in remote parts of a colony while protection was the order of the day in the more settled regions.

Much of State policy towards Aboriginal people and the consequent legal predicaments impinging on them becomes clearer if we differentiate *control* policies from what we might call enabling (or even empowering) policies. That is, those which impose the wishes and intentions of others, restrict, direct, constrain, shape, or otherwise attempt to channel the actions and options of Aboriginal people; and those which leave alone, allow to exercise basic liberal rights to life, liberty, assembly, and generally provide the full range of options available to everybody else.

I would maintain that the 'protectionist' or segregationist policies, early 'assimilation' policies and some forms of 'self-determination' and 'self-management' policies as well, could be unambiguously described as control policies, while enabling policies have actually been given very little room and time to operate[32] and, ironically, owe their

31 McRae, H, Nettheim, G, and Beacroft, L (eds), *Aboriginal Legal Issues: Commentary and Materials*, 1991, North Ryde: Law Book Company, p 9.

32 *Cf* Hollinsworth, D, 'The Control and Management of the Dispossessed: 1860–1894', 1984, Coursework material for Aboriginal Studies 2, pp 1–39.

existence to the broadened forms of assimilation, 'equal rights', or 'integration', policies from the mid-1960s onwards.

The Aboriginal people themselves have, since the early 1960s been the main actors in making one form of policy or another work to the extent that it has, in the context of what might be called constrained agency. People always have wills, minds and aspirations of their own; they are usually not just passive and fatalistic, allowing a sea of troubles to wash over them. On the other hand, neither are they in a world free of restrictions, constraints and parameters.

For most of South Australia's unhappy history, the legal position for Aboriginal people has usually been a complex package of just such restrictions. But we need to always keep in mind the varieties of indigenous responses to different policy and legal configurations for different groups in time, socio-political and geographic space, and in specific relationships, when we consider different policies ranged against indigenous people and their impact on indigenous legal status.

POST-FEDERATION POLICIES

Protection/segregation

In South Australia, after Federation, after the initial invasion and destruction of almost all independent political, economic, jurisdictional and social life for Aboriginal people,[33] provincial and colonial authorities, both hostile and sympathetic, found themselves with an unanticipated range of problems. That is, what to do about the people whose land and authority they had usurped (but which there could not possibly have been any intention to reinState). Colonial authorities back in Britain such as Lord Grey 'assumed ... that the Aboriginal [subject] still had [the] full rights of [a] legal-liberal society'.[34]

Although Hindmarsh and Gawler earnestly attempted to extend the modified rights and obligations of British subjects to Aboriginal people, and although the economy required and made extensive use of Aboriginal labour, the dominant thread in the policy passed, and the rule rather than the exception from 1836, tended towards the exclusion of Aboriginal people from the rest of society. For example, one of the first ordinances passed in 1837 made it an offence for Aboriginal people to drink, or for any person to offer an Aboriginal person any alcoholic beverage. This prohibition stayed in force until the early 1960s and was ineffectual the whole time.

In South Australia, after self-government and even more so after Federation in 1901, recourse to exclusion was relabelled 'protection', requiring the confinement, wherever and whenever possible, particularly of darker Aboriginal people to missions and stations. There they were under constant supervision and suffered from loss of freedoms. Therefore indigence created, over the generations, a hostile and dependent institutionalisation on the part of many inhabitants. At its zenith, from about 1880 to the 1950s, it was rationalised as necessary to:

33 *Cf* Rowley, CD, *Outcasts in White Australia*, 1970b, Ringwood: Pelican.

34 *Ibid*, p 136.

- protect public health and good order;
- to provide a pillow for a dying race;
- to manage and control an uneducatable and doomed population;
- conversely to train Aboriginal people for their selective transition into civilized society; and
- to justify the continuing dispossession of the original owners of the land.

In turn, Aboriginal people developed, alongside an understandable paranoia about white people, a myriad of ways of keeping away from whites, from avoiding just such dependence, of laughing at the absurdity of their situation. For example, on one occasion, at the height of one of the Social-Darwinist attacks on Aboriginal people in 1903, one Ngarrindjeri leader from Point McLeay, John Sumner, recounted at a meeting how he had once been accosted by a 'grinkari' while fishing on the banks of the Murray:

> The white gentleman said, 'Do you know what question I am going to ask you, young fellow?' I said, 'No.' He said, 'You are descended from a baboon monkey. I saw it in a book.' I replied, 'You get a monkey and put him alongside me, and ask us a question in your language, and if the monkey can answer you the same as I do, then I am descended from a monkey. Then you sit down alongside the monkey, and I will ask you a question in my language, and if you cannot answer it any more than the monkey, you are descended from the monkey'.[35]

Earlier, during the 1850s, Sumner had worked for white farmers and, in the 1860s and 1870s, had operated his own agricultural property. Nevertheless, along with other Ngarrindjeri, he was discouraged from leaving the mission after the 1880s and died there in 1905.

In the years post-Federation exclusionary legislation, States' rights and prerogatives dominated the problems faced by Aboriginal people. Again, we can discern the influence of other colonial/settler regimes and American southern States, eg the reactionary influence of early Apartheid in South Africa, segregation and exclusion in America and contemporaneous demands by sectors of South Australian society, especially its rural dominance, and the influence of the pastoralists on government lasted well into the 1960s. Nor should one forget the general ideologies around the turn of the century, which spawned the White Australia Policy (which was still being debated in 1970), Social-Darwinism and the Eugenics movement. Most chillingly of all, one should never forget that these policies were promoted almost as actively by sections of the left-wing in Australian politics as by the more conservative right-wing.

With the growth of racist repression, exemplified by use of the White Australia Policy against Asians of all nationalities, and the exclusion of indigenous people from Australian citizenship, one would have to speak of forms of State terror against Aboriginal people, and not just out on the pastoral frontier.[36] That behaviour was similar to that being used against black people in America at that time. For example,

35 Jenkin, GK, *Conquest of the Ngarrindjeri*, 1979, Adelaide: Rigby, p 254.

36 *Cf* Rowley, CD, *The Remote Aborigines*, 1970c, Ringwood: Pelican.

where hundreds of public lynchings were occurring every year with the connivance of the authorities and Booker T Washington was forced to choose between a new form of slavery or extermination, and therefore to plead for a place, no matter how menial, for the people whom he was seen to represent:[37]

> Casting down your bucket among my people ... you will find we shall stand by you with a devotion that no foreigner can approach ... In all things that are purely social we can be as separate as the fingers, yet one as the hand in all things essential to mutual progress.

How relevant to Aboriginal people was this 1895 'Atlanta Compromise' of Washington's – a trade-off of survival for inferior position and abridgement of rights, a capitulation infamous for the cynical (but highly ambiguous) slogan 'separate but equal'? One hundred years have passed since this catastrophic landmark, one which had repercussions for generations around the non-white world in all colonial and semi-colonial jurisdictions. Even in America, African-Americans are still living with its direct consequences, while simultaneously, others who have not learnt from history are setting out to re-enact it. To rephrase Marx: history repeats itself, the first time as tragedy, the second time as radical and New Age and post-modern chic.

Severe restrictions were placed on Aboriginal people after the turn of the century. Local councils were given powers to expel Aboriginal families; schools could bar Aboriginal children. From 1908, the Protector was given legislative powers to remove children from their parents and, in 1924, was ruled to be the guardian of all Aboriginal children under the age of 18.

Aboriginal men and women had been given the vote along with other South Australians. (The fact that Aboriginal women had the vote in South Australia before white women in Britain (1918), France (1929) and the United States (1920), typifies the hypocritical nature of the 'protection' policy, in that people who had had the vote in the 19th century now were to lose it in the 20th, on the grounds that they were not yet ready for it.) Aboriginal people across Australia were not counted as Australian citizens, nor could they enrol and vote unless they had done so in colonial times, until the Citizenship Act 1948.[38] In many parts of Australia they were discouraged from exercising this right until well into the 1970s, in fact, voting was not even compulsory for Aboriginal people across Australia until the 1980s.

In the South Australian Criminal Law Consolidation Act 1935 (No 1935/2252) perhaps the lowest point in discriminatory treatment was reached. It reaffirmed s 307 1876 Act: an Aboriginal sentenced to death for murder was to be executed at the scene of the crime and his body buried there 'or at such other place as the Governor may deem expedient'. That section was not repealed until *1971*.

And who could forget the symbol of segregation on missions: the cattle grid? Even in the 1970s, at the entrance to every mission in South Australia, one had to cross a cattle or sheep grid to meet people and one's own relations.

37 Washington, BT, *Up from Slavery*, 1967, New York: Airmont, pp 115–116. (Originally published in 1900.)

38 *Cf* Rowley, CD, *Outcasts in White Australia*, 1970b, Ringwood: Pelican, pp 392–94 for an fascinating consequence of this Act.

Legal inequality and 'the stolen generation'

One of the most far-reaching and blatant consequences of legal, economic and political inequality for Aboriginal people around the country was the separation of the children from their families, which occurred right up until the gaining of equal rights, no region was spared and has directly affected nearly one in six of all Aboriginal people. In some regions the proportion of children taken has been even higher, for some communities a good deal lower. Nevertheless, the rate was probably twice as high as the rate for white working-class children.

The reasons for these separations or removals were many and complex, to name just a few:

- many children would have been taken away for life from very early ages from caring, loving mothers and capable, supportive households, as a consequence of State government policies;
- many mothers died young or in childbirth and, with no unemployment benefits of any kind until 1969, widowed fathers were forced to ask for assistance for their children;
- many families became destitute when the breadwinners were put out of work, and disintegrated as a direct consequence;
- in the north, it was reported that pastoralists regularly had their 'part'-Aboriginal offspring taken away or adopted elsewhere to avoid any claims for paternity;
- during the Second World War, many children were evacuated from the north of Australia to the south and not reunited with their families afterwards;
- children conceived while husbands were away during the world wars or in jail were occasionally sent, or taken, away to children's homes;
- given the often appalling living conditions forced on Aboriginal people, families occasionally were simply unable to care for children. Infant mortality rates in some situations were, after all, amongst the highest in the world. Rates at Point McLeay, for example, were higher during the 1940s and 1950s than at any time under the old mission administration (1859–1915); and
- occasionally parental care was seriously impeded by alcoholism and domestic violence. Less often, parental mental illness induced by the hardships and desperations of living conditions (including alcohol consumption) forced authorities, sometimes with surprising reluctance, to take over responsibilities for the care of children.

Thus, the removal of children covered a complicated and varied spectrum from outright denial of any human rights at all to reluctant but essential taking into care for limited periods, from situations of outrageous illegality, and completely immoral and heartless deprivation, to situations of dire necessity. In resolving future compensation claims, it was likely that each case will have to be considered on its own terms, although the understandable emotions involved would make this approach difficult.

While many children were fostered only for short periods comparatively vast numbers of children from every part of Australia, throughout the years of segregation and 'protection', were permanently removed from their families to be raised (if they survived) in segregated homes and to be adopted into non-Aboriginal families. Many would have grown up with no idea of their Aboriginality at all. Others would spend their lives searching for their own birth-families. Such was one of the legacies of the oppression and discrimination forced on Aboriginal people right up until the Racial Discrimination Act 1975 and, in places like Queensland and Western Australia, well beyond.

Aboriginal deaths in custody

Commissioner Johnston QC found that almost half of the Aboriginal people whose cases were examined by the Royal Commission into Aboriginal Deaths in Custody had been, at some time or other, removed from their families. Given that many of the total number of cases involved people born and raised since the 1950s and 1960s, one has to wonder at both continuing welfare practices on the one hand, and living conditions and aspirations on the other.

ASSIMILATION

'Sameness' and equal rights

While segregation, the negation of self-determination in almost every way, was the rule throughout Australia, and in New Zealand and North America,[39] from the initial Invasion until almost the present, the other side of the same coin, assimilation for the few, has always been on the agenda but with much less emphasis. In South Australia, the first Governors (Hindmarsh and Gawler) and Protectors (Wyatt and Moorhouse) were concerned to attempt to absorb, or otherwise bring in as many 'suitable' Aboriginal people as was practicable, to overcome the chronic labour shortage of the first couple of decades of 'settlement'.

The now-dreaded assimilation policy was initiated in a vague, unco-ordinated way by a conference in Canberra attended by State and territory ministers for Aboriginal and 'native' affairs in April 1937. Such was the nature of social policy, however, that it had hardly got off the ground by the time of another national conference in 1951.

In fact, as Gumbert[40] remarked '... aside from some cosmetic changes, the new policy of assimilation was to bring with it very few reforms'. Rowley was even more dismissive:[41]

39 *Cf* Brown, DN, 'Native Americans and the Right of Self-Government in the United States,' in Renwick, W (ed), *Sovereignty and Indigenous Rights: The Treaty of Waitangi in International Contexts,* 1991, Wellington: Victoria University Press, pp 42–43.

40 Gumbert, M, *Neither Justice nor Reason,* 1984, St Lucia: University of Queensland Press, p 18.

41 Rowley, CD, *Outcasts in White Australia,* 1970b, Ringwood: Pelican, p 398.

> Obviously the assimilation policy was no more than a general term for what each government was doing anyway, up until 1961, since it was not until then that a common definition of assimilation was worked out and agreed to.

One wonders what specific evils, in the limited time that assimilation appeared to be in full force, could really be laid at its door rather than attributed to the winding down, which was hardly likely to be easy or swift, of earlier segregation and 'protection' policies. Those were certainly still operating in Queensland, at least up to the end of the 1970s.[42]

This raises intriguing questions about just what different people mean by the term 'assimilation', including some of the contributors to this book, and from whose point of view is the term defined, that of the outside observer or that of the insider subject? Assimilation, meaning living in some way like 'whitefellas', or next door to 'whitefellas'? Speaking English? Using money and having a job? Intermarriage? Getting an education? Trying to pass during the bad times? Not identifying even in the good times? These all mean different things to the people experiencing them than to people looking on from a distance. If you haven't walked the walk ...

Even in its limited form, assimilationist outcomes were intended at first for only a small minority, while the great majority were still to be confined and supervised. For example, Native Welfare Ordinances in the Northern Territory, devised in 1954, classified all 'full-bloods' as wards with extremely limited rights, while 'half-castes' were no longer classified as Aboriginal at all. Significantly, the first 'half-caste' graduates from high school and teachers' college occurred soon afterwards.

Assimilation is castigated these days as the summation of all that was evil in former policies, but often without a great deal of analysis, insight or consistency. However, at the time, the major impetus for a longer-term policy shift in the direction of assimilation as equal rights was provided by the Aboriginal people themselves, on two different, but related, fronts:

- through the 1930s Aboriginal groups in the Eastern States (significantly, staffed by Aboriginal men who were either ex-servicemen or ex-union men, or both and also familiar with the left-wing of politics) pressed for equal rights, using the word 'assimilation' in its most basic sense, to mean the same rights as other Australians, citizenship rights for all indigenous people. Aboriginal people across the country owe an eternal debt of gratitude to men like William Cooper, Bill Ferguson and Jack Patten, and women like Margaret Tucker and Pearl Gibbs; and
- since the Invasion itself, a population of mixed 'race' Aboriginal people (in most racist societies, offspring of the dominant and a subordinate group were socially allocated to that group) had been steadily growing in numbers, confounding theories of the dying out of the Aboriginal people and creating 'the half-caste problem'.

42 *Cf* FAIRA (Foundation for Aboriginal and Islander Research Action), *Beyond the Act,* 1979, Brisbane: FAIRA and Tatz. Tatz, C, *Race Politics in Australia: Aborigines, Politics and the Law,* 1979, Armidale: University of New England Publishing Unit.

At the 1937 conference, the anthropologist Norman Tindale provided a detailed report on this 'problem'. The consequent thrust of Stated policy intention in all States during the following 25 years concerned the solution to it. As well, one suspects, as trying to minimise contact between Aborigines who had been 'tainted' by contact with political troublemakers and Aborigines still in a 'pristine' condition. The policies usually centred on absorption into society through marriage of half-caste women to low-class white men, and confinement of 'part-Aboriginal' men to the missions, along with more severe restrictions on the rest of the Aboriginal population and dire penalties for any whites found 'consorting' with Aboriginal women.

This presented a slight contradiction in so far as what was expressly desired for 'part-Aboriginal' women was expressly prohibited for 'Aboriginal' women. A white man could be jailed for being near a woman whose friend, cousin or even sister he had been encouraged to consort with. (What the legal repercussions of a white woman and a 'part-Aboriginal' man being together might have been depended on the circumstances.) But as Gale suggested as late as 1964:[43]

> Government policy in South Australia is in an extremely difficult position. It is attempting to protect one section of the Aboriginal people and to absorb another with no distinct demarcation between the two. Its organisational base is autocratic yet it aims at encouraging democracy amongst its people.

One vital phenomenon which was consistently and completely overlooked in every analysis and yet concerned most of the Aboriginal population is the fact that 60% of all Aboriginal children over the past generation or so have had either a non-Aboriginal father (ie nearly 40% of all Aboriginal children born in South Australia) or a non-Aboriginal mother (ie totalling 20%). Almost invariably, the children of such unions are these days counted and are considered by the Aboriginal community and consider themselves proudly as Aboriginal, with the active concurrence of both parents. In this way, perhaps not without costs and tensions:

- the Aboriginal population is notionally boosted by some 40% each generation;
- both segregation and assimilation-as-absorption are defeated, but equal opportunity is enhanced. We still live in a fairly racist society;
- since, on balance, non-Aboriginal people have more access to power and knowledge, valuable social and cognitive connections are made; and
- some 10% of the non-Aboriginal population are brought into close and fairly lengthy contact with Aboriginal people through marriage, in-lawhood, cousinhood etc. Conversely, the great majority of the Aboriginal population has some on-going contact with non-Aboriginal people, warts and all.

Very few, if any, analysts know how to deal with this common and on-going phenomenon. For example, McConnochie[44] refers to it by the discredited term

43 Gale, GF, *A Study of Assimilation: Part-Aborigines in South Australia*, 1964, Adelaide: Libraries Board of South Australia, p 233.

44 McConnochie, KR, *Realities of Race*, 1973, Sydney: ANZ Book Co.

'miscegenation'.[45] None seem to be aware of how much it helped to force policy changes over the past 60 years especially in the south, which might partly explain the obsession of many writers with the most remote and inaccessible regions and communities in the north. One even suspects that, perhaps unconsciously, the hostility of many writers these days to assimilation policy is similar to a surrogate for intermarriage.

At the outbreak of the Second World War Aboriginal people were subject to even tighter restrictions, partly in fear that they would spy for the Japanese or Germans in the event of an invasion. News films were circulated about the links between some Lutheran missions in the Northern Territory and Nazi sympathisers in the Barossa, ample proof that Aboriginal people generally would be eager to spy for Hitler. By extension, indigenous people had to be supervised. Only a select few, at first, were issued with 'dog licences' to work away from 'missions' or join the armed forces.

Pronouncements about assimilation by the newly formed Aborigines Protection Board in 1939 and announcements about its fortunes over the next 20 years indicated that the introduction of such a new and profoundly impacting policy was, for implementers, more intention than immediate or even medium-term enactment or fulfilment. Further emphasised by the fact that the expectation that such a policy would take generations to implement effectively. In the meantime, for the majority of Aboriginal people, the prevailing legal situation remained one of segregation and control.

A contemporary re-interpretation of those years, apart from somewhat neglecting the active agency of the Aboriginal people themselves, conflated the evils of both continued segregation and supervision for the majority, and isolation and monitoring for the few, into one policy called 'assimilation', to which all of the evils of prior policies were also attributed. For example, the concentration of populations onto wasteland missions, the removal of children, cultural change and the prohibitions against traditional practices and the use of proper language, and the growing dependence on rations and other forms of welfare still existed. Most of these injustices were actually in full swing in the 19th century, well before 1937; and, worse still, some were still going on in the 1970s.

After the war, with the rapid increase of population on 'missions' (families of 10 and 12 children were the rule rather than the exception) the Aborigines Protection Board policy in South Australia accelerated the dispersal of young families across the settled rural areas of the State. Probably the majority of the Aboriginal population in Adelaide today descended from these families, rather than from those who migrated directly from mission to city in the last 30 years.

However, regardless of the legal situation, Aboriginal people came and went with some degree of 'illicit' freedom. Confined to, but dispersed throughout the countryside, most adults (ie all men and women over the age of 14) were employed by farmers and pastoralists in the south and the north. Perhaps without recourse to Aboriginal labour, the rural economy may never have been viable, never in South Australia's history. Certainly during the war, for example, every *single able-bodied person* from Point McLeay and Point Pearce, the two main southern stations were employed in farm labour away

45 Cowlishaw, G, Black, *White or Brindle: Race in Rural Australia*, 1988, Cambridge: Cambridge University Press, pp 3–4, 37–41.

from their homes. (Both Point McLeay and Point Pearce had ceased to be church-supported missions about 1915 and had been taken over by the State government.)

Necessarily, Aboriginal people moved frequently around the State, returning to the 'mission' and, almost by serendipity, maintaining much more cohesion with other people on and off the mission than the authorities would have been aware of.

By law, Aboriginal people were not allowed to stay overnight in Adelaide until about 1959, nor were they allowed to drink until the early 1960s. In fact, they often did both enthusiastically – some laws are less enforceable than others.

Following the Native Welfare Ministers' Conference in 1937, one of the few steps taken was to tighten up on Aboriginal freedom of movement through the confinement of Aboriginal people to reserves, stations and missions (mainly by the tactics of enforcing the Criminal Law Acts and local council powers) unless they had been exempted from the Aborigines Act 1939. If they were exempt they were given a certificate which was available only to hard-working, sober individuals and their immediate families, and only on condition that they break links with their birth-families on the missions, did not return, and kept their jobs.

Generally, only paler Aboriginal people acquired those 'dog licences', but in practice, those who kept away from both towns and missions, and those who secured exemption certificates and found work in country towns across the State, represented a network of safe houses – an archipelago in an hostile white sea. Friends and relations could show up at any hour of the day or night, stay a few days and move on to the next 'island'. That was the way in which Aboriginal people passed on news and maintained some integrity, while building a strong and enduring, *emergent*, range of Aboriginal identities.

From the early 1940s until the official policy collapsed under its own impracticability and was revised through the Aboriginal Affairs Act 1962 (No 1962/45). The policy of 'assimilation' signified the selective, tightly controlled assimilation of a few and the continued exclusion and tightly supervised segregation of the many.[46] In South Africa more honesty prevailed and a similar policy of selective inclusion in grossly inferior conditions and mass exclusion in appalling conditions was called 'apartheid'.

However, even s 20 of the 1962 Act required Aboriginal people having nowhere else to go apart from the 'mission' to agree to undergo 'training' and only at the completion of 'training' 'to the satisfaction of the Minister' were they allowed to leave the institution to live elsewhere. So paradoxically, 'assimilation' for many people meant 'confinement to the settlement'.

In practical everyday terms, assimilation did not touch the majority of Aboriginal people (a new cattle grid was installed at Point McLeay in the early 1970s, while negotiations were going on for self-management). Perhaps for most of the people in the more remote countryside, it still has not touched them, except in formal senses.

But we should not overlook the influence of political currents within Australia, or of anti-colonial independence and American civil rights movements from the late 1950s.

46 Rowley, CD, *The Destruction of Aboriginal Society*, original 1970a, 1986 edition also cited, Ringwood: Pelican, Chapter 17, esp pp 320–21.

Encouraged by these overseas developments, the first major nationwide indigenous organisation, the Federal Council for the Advancement of Aborigines and Torres Strait Islanders (FCAATSI) first took to the political stage in the early 1960s. The Freedom Ride through northern New South Wales in 1965 galvanised many Aboriginal people from one side of Australia to the other. It also shocked non-Aboriginal people into the realisation that, in the year of the publication of Donald Horne's book, *The Lucky Country,* segregation kept Aboriginal people from using public facilities in their own country.

The scene was set for the 1967 referendum, to force the Commonwealth to take control of Aboriginal affairs from the States, and to count Aboriginal people for the first time as Australians. In hindsight, it was an indictment on Australian attitudes and indigenous powerlessness of the time that such a referendum was even held with indigenous people as mere spectators, should equal rights be subject to the whims of an electorate in this way?

Commonwealth involvement was mandated by the 1967 referendum – a three-person Office of Aboriginal Affairs was set up, which evolved rapidly into a full Department of Aboriginal Affairs (DAA) from the earliest days of the Whitlam government. With the close co-operation of the South Australian Dunstan government and direct responsibility for Aboriginal Affairs in the Northern Territory, the DAA quickly developed consultation and representation mechanisms in response to insistent calls for equal rights, land rights and indigenous control of indigenous affairs.

In many ways, the DAA's 20 years of existence (its functions were taken over substantially by Aboriginal and Torres Strait Islander Commission (ATSIC) in 1991),[47] were a chronicle of a struggle for control over indigenous affairs between the bureaucrats who devised the policies and procedures and the people whom the policies and procedures were supposed to serve. However, in the process the DAA arguably accelerated the pace of change in policy practice and irreversibly placed control of its direction in indigenous hands.

The Commonwealth Racial Discrimination Act 1975 at last brought formal (non-discriminatory) equality to indigenous people. Some 40 years after the 1937 conference this legislation represented the culmination of formal assimilation and, in turn, was the keystone on which the *Mabo* judgment of June 1992 was based. Without formal equality before the law and the right to one's property (which came with the formal banning of discrimination) even in Queensland, the case could never have been brought to court.

Self-determination, self-management and sovereignty

One of the human rights, the exercise of which formal equality enables, is the right to be self-determining within the bounds of the law, ie to eat, drink, read, to live, sleep, travel wherever you like, to speak, fight, associate, love and live with whomever you like. Those rights actually encompass what was usually called a policy of 'integration'.

47 See Rowse, T, 'The Revolution in Aboriginal Affairs', March 1990, *Australian Society*, p 16 and Rowse, T, 'ATSIC's Heritage: The Problems of Leadership and Unity in Aboriginal Political Culture', January 1991, *Current Affairs Bulletin*, pp 11–12.

Nobody could be forced to assimilate if that meant to exercise one's equal rights in any of these ways. Nobody could be forced to exercise one's rights, that was one of our human rights! If such assimilation implied the right to associate with whomever one liked, for whatever legal purpose one liked, a fully functioning assimilation policy could provide the basis for either integration or self-determination at an individual or supra-individual level.

A United Nations declarations affirmed the rights of all people to self-determination.[48] However, as Roberts remarked on O'Donoghue's citation of the Federal government definition as being '... Aboriginal communities deciding the pace and nature of their future development as significant components within a diverse Australia':[49]

> (Roberts): ... this in effect limits the exercise of self-determination to what is compatible with the interests of the Australian State. Successive Australian governments have rejected the view that self-determination includes the right of Aboriginal people to decide their political status and the exploration of political options such as self-government and Aboriginal sovereignty.[50]

Different meanings attach themselves to the term 'self-determination' from one writer to another and often by the same writer. For example, Young[51] appeared to understand the term to mean not much more than community consultation and deliberation about crucial decisions, such as how to keep the camp clean. Generally, writers and Aboriginal leaders understood the term to refer solely to group self-determination in community, region, State or national aggregates. In reaction to the last possibility, the Fraser government tended to move away from the term and favour 'self-management' instead, which quite explicitly limited autonomy to what O'Donoghue delineates above.

However, the possibilities afforded by self-determination (versions of which, as was demonstrated above, have been available informally since the culmination, paradoxically, of the assimilation policy) have fuelled perceptions of opportunity to:

- seek autonomy to develop the complete self-management of communities;
- to extend such forms of self-determination towards self-government and even sovereignty; and
- alternatively and/or simultaneously, to seek full equity for:
    - the people as a whole,
    - individuals, or
    - various combinations of almost all of the above.

48 *Cf* Crawford, JR, 'Outside the Colonial Context', in Macartney, WJA, Macartney (ed), *Self-Determination in the Commonwealth*, 1988, Aberdeen: Aberdeen University Press, p 1.

49 O'Donoghue, L, 'One nation: promise or paradox?', speech at the National Press Club, 20 May 1992, Canberra: ATSIC Publication, p 7.

50 Roberts, D, 'Self-determination and the Struggle for Aboriginal Equality', in Bourke, C, Bourke, E, and Edwards, B (eds), *Aboriginal Australia: An Introductory Reader in Aboriginal Studies*, 1994, St Lucia: University of Queensland Press, p 212.

51 Young, E, 'Self-Determination of Australian Aborigines', in Macartney, WJA (ed), *Self-Determination in the Commonwealth*, 1988, Aberdeen: Aberdeen University Press, pp 82–89.

Forms of self-determination were formally introduced in South Australia from the late 1960s, evolving fairly rapidly into more concrete, locality-focused and less nationally-oriented forms such as self-management.

Generally, the preoccupation has been with small, remote communities and almost invariably one major factor has been overlooked, a factor which, one would have thought, was the *sine qua non* of self-determination in such a form (indeed in any form). All communities, no matter how big or small, needed a range of services and functions performed. The smaller and more remote a community, the more skills required by each person and the more skilled each person has to become. The reverse was usually assumed, ie small and remote communities did not require high levels of skill. That itself fed the perception of the viability of the self-management of such communities, since the Aboriginal people there were almost invariably unskilled, especially in those functions which a small community needed: teacher, nurse, administrator, mechanic (vehicle, generator, pump, plane, various equipment), pilot, store-keeper, accountant etc, skills which almost invariably could not be learnt on the job, or even by distance education, and skills which almost invariably were being applied by non-Aboriginal people in those communities.

As a result there were unarticulated problems with remote community self-management. At the level of discourse, it constricted the notion of self-determination. At the level of practice, it condemned Aboriginal people in such places to either stay, as unskilled spectators of their 'own' affairs (not a single remote South Australia or North Territory Aboriginal community had a secondary school at which even basic clerical training could take place); or move to the nearest major town and either live on its fringes, or somehow get a decent education, which was still an extremely unlikely occurrence for ex-mission or ex-community people, or either to move back to home communities or further into urban society. It was no coincidence that living conditions were the worst in Australia in such places and not amongst Aboriginal people in the cities. Of the 7,000 or so university graduates across the country, perhaps fewer than 100 were living and working in remote or small communities.

Self-management

Almost simultaneously with the expansion of rights and more active involvement of the State under the Walsh and Dunstan Labour governments of the mid-1960s, community councils were set up, partly to 'train for assimilation', and partly to train Aboriginal people in managing their own affairs in those on-going communities. Substantially, for the great majority still living in government settlements in the late 1960s, the option of moving away did not arise. For them, in many aspects, the old segregation policy gave way easily to the new self-management policy *de facto* rather than *de jure* without any necessary intermediate stage of assimilation. That would have been the case even more so for more remote, non-English-speaking communities.

As Robbins[52] and Howard[53] demonstrated over the last couple of decades there has been a consistent, almost irresistible, tendency to transform (or subvert, depending on one's point of view) what was supposed to be a vehicle for positive development and change into merely one more machine for managing welfare policies, precisely the rationale for the control policies of the past.

From the early 1970s, in another manifestation of self-determination, that dealing with nationwide representative, deliberative and potentially administrative organs emanating from the people themselves, a range of national representative bodies were initiated which culminated in the Aboriginal and Torres Strait Islander Commission (ATSIC) in March 1991. Certainly, the latter organisation promised immense opportunities to enable indigenous organisations and individuals to achieve their legitimate aspirations.

Self-government

In the United States, as a result of the efforts of John Collier, Indian Commissioner under Roosevelt, many Indian groups reorganised in reaction to the policies of termination and assimilation in force up to the 1930s and re-established tribal governments.[54] Marshall J had, in 1831, recognised native entities as 'domestic dependent nations' with whom the United States could, and in fact was required to, enter into treaty negotiations with, entities within States but not of States, and thereby not required to pay either State or federal taxes (but also not entitled to financial support from either source). Much of those directives were observed more in their breach over the next century but strengthened by Collier's work in cleaning out the Augean stables of the dreaded BIA (the Bureau of Indian Affairs), tribal governments entered into active arrangements with both the Nixon and Reagan administrations to develop inter-governmental relations and boost their economies.[55] Currently however, the Republican-dominated legislatures in America are dismantling these initiatives. Self-government is sometimes a fragile flower.

In Australia, the Anangu Pitjantjatjaraku, or Pitjantjatjara Council, has sometimes been characterised as exercising some form of self-government. It was certainly true that it possessed more powers, funding and responsibilities than most local governments serving similar numbers of people (about 2,000). However, given the distances, homogeneity of population and plethora of government bodies, converted almost without any personnel change into 'community organisations', with the odd Pitjantjatjara face and office-holder, self-government was perhaps a slight and

52 Robbins, EJ, 'Self Determination or Welfare Colonialism: Aborigines and Federal Policy-making', unpublished PhD thesis, 1994, University of South Australia, pp 389–97.

53 Howard, MC, 'Australian Aboriginal Politics and the Perpetuation of Inequality' (1982) 53 *Oceania*, 82–100.

54 *Cf* Kelly, LC, *The Assault on Assimilation: John Collier and the Origins of Indian Policy Reform*, 1983, Albuquerque: University of New Mexico Press.

55 Brown, DN, 'Native Americans and the Right of Self-Government in the United States,' in Renwick, W (ed), *Sovereignty and Indigenous Rights: The Treaty of Waitangi in International Contexts*, 1991, Wellington: Victoria University Press, pp 41–47.

unintentional misrepresentation: white hands doing what white hands used to do, but with 'community consultation', may not represent such a drastic change from the days of segregation, just one with better manners and resources.

In 1990, former Premier Dunstan called for a separate form of local government for Aboriginal communities and for 'special laws'.[56] He suggested long-term training strategies (*cf* the 'traineeship' strategy of the early 1960s), especially in financial management, land capability surveys and a range of other measures which had supposedly been in place for many years. He concluded that some of his own initiatives 'policies of self-determination and self-management, introduced in the 1970s, have generally been unsuccessful' (see above).

Other rationales for group self-determination

Philpott[57] suggested that one of the grounds for self-determination, all other conditions being favourable, was provoked by the threat of genocide or harm to a group. However, was there a current threat to Aboriginal people? Or instead, was there evidence of government concern and intent, even action, to reduce and eliminate such threats, for example through the Racial Discrimination Act 1975 and current racial vilification legislation? As we move towards 2001, the republic and reconciliation, we shall see the result. Perhaps nothing is completely irreversible: the US Supreme Court has just allowed the Ku Klux Klan to set up a cross outside the Ohio State legislature building. But such things couldn't happen here, could they?

Self-determination is not a simple issue, there are a host of matters that have hardly been raised, let alone analysed and deliberated. Below are just a few:

Group v individual rights?

Would ascriptive group rights entitle a group to be tyrannical over its individual members? If so, how can such rights be supported against those of individuals they are supposed to encapsulate? Can a group exercise a right to be tyrannical over smaller groups within it? And so on, down to the level of a dyad (two people): can one person morally dominate another in the interests of the dyad? If the answer is no to any of these questions, one aspect of the notion of group rights conceived in this way is badly flawed.[58]

If such rights were to be sanctioned only if they could be kept democratic, in the sense that individuals could retain the individual rights of citizens of the encompassing polity, doesn't this simply allow for individual expression of self-determination, and thereby, on the one hand, allow for conflict between individual and group rights, while on the other, remove any particular need for group rights: individuals could freely come together whenever they desired?

56 Brinkworth, J, 'Dunstan urges separate Aboriginal local government', *The Advertiser*, Thursday, 29 March 1990, p 2.

57 Philpott, D, 'In defense of self-determination' (1995) 105 *Ethics*, 369.

58 *Cf* Watson, I, 'International Year for Indigenous Peoples 1993', *Kaurna Higher Education Journal*, pp 57–61.

On the other hand, if individuals were to surrender their 'majority' rights in order to come under a regime of 'minority' or group rights, wouldn't this arrangement have to be completely voluntary from the outset, with a continued right to exit or reversion? If the threat of exit were to hang over every group decision where would be the validity, the stability and continuity needed for the group to exercise power over its affairs?

Paradoxically, the rights and duties of voluntary members of an incorporated body may therefore be more binding, and the entity therefore more stable than an entity based on group rights. Majoritarianism is a much stronger basis from which to conduct business than unanimity and much more likely to reflect the reality of diverse opinion and interests, while minoritarianism, as protection for the rights of a minority from tyranny by the majority, could also be safeguarded more easily.

More practically, can the disappointing voter turn-out for ATSIC elections (especially in the cities), sometimes as low as 20%, be the basis for a strengthening of group rights over Aboriginal individuals' civil rights? Can such a small proportion of the 'group' have legitimation even in the eyes of its supposed constituents? Wouldn't a legitimate body have to gain, not necessarily the support, but at least the involvement of a majority of its declared constituency? And aren't the restrictions on ATSIC – that they currently have no responsibility for policies which might control or direct any Australian citizen of indigenous ancestry – precisely a consequence of the continued rights of such people as Australian citizens?

If there were individual rights, would they tend to be fissive or fusive? In other words, are they so divisive that they would have to be surrendered to protect the sanctity of the group? But surely anything but the voluntary surrender of such rights would be unconstitutional. What is better in the short and long run, the surrender of individual human rights to the group and trying to move the group in a democratic direction, or strengthening of individual human rights and trying to move fellow free individuals towards strong, voluntary groupings and organisations?

What would be the process of initiating group rights? How could any government turn this proposition into a reality without the full concurrence and the right of exit of all people involved who would have to freely and consciously surrender such of their individual rights as might conflict with those of the group? And to what extent could any Australian government agree to alter, ie diminish, the individual rights of some of its (indigenous) citizens and their subordination to those of groups which are self-determining and inaccessible to political pressure?

Special rights?

A premise of many of those proposing constitutional change in Australia is that indigenous people are, by virtue of 40,000 years or more prior ownership of every bit of the continent and their uncompensated dispossession of it, an illegal extinction of a complex but valid form of sovereignty and through their need for cultural preservation, are entitled and, in fact, require, special rights enshrined in the nation's supreme legal instrument. It could be that the High Court decision in *Mabo* was a recognition of the superiority, or at least the priority, in law of prior indigenous ownership over Crown claims and that this is precisely what the current native title legislation was intended to enact.

Certainly, the notion of the Crown or the State being the landowner from whom everybody else held their land has been called into question since the signing of the Magna Carta. King Charles I had similar trouble with the governors of Virginia and Rhode Island at the beginning of his reign when he attempted to export this feudal right from his native Scotland. At the time of Phillip's landing in Sydney Cove such a right did not exist even in England, although it had been used in conquered territories such as Scotland and Ireland. But as Philpott insists, a State does not 'own' land (except, obviously for land which it is using for explicit purposes and has abstracted from the whole by purchase or agreement) but acts as 'trustee' or 'agent' for it (and therefore, presumably, has a fiduciary relationship with the 'principals', the owners of the land, a position taken by Toohey J in his dissenting opinion in *Mabo*). In Philpott's words: '... a State governs, not owns; it's a matter of government, not land ... a government serves the people on the land it governs.'[59]

It follows that, if native title is commonly recognised in legal systems, and now in the Australian system as well, no special right in land is required. However, it also follows that compensation is due to all who can demonstrate some loss of patrimony by virtue of the dispossession of their lands, if such land cannot be returned. (Incidentally, it surely follows also that people do not have to demonstrate some continuing, loving, caring, nurturing attachment to land that they claim. Non-Aborigines do not have to demonstrate such attachment in order to retain ownership, judging by the devastation being wrought by the cattle and timber industries at present.)

If the restoration of sovereignty may not be an option (but see below) for most indigenous people in Australia, then it must follow that some compensation is owing to them, at least on this ground alone. As well, unless it can be demonstrated, perhaps by sociologists, that cultural change would have occurred as a 'natural' consequence of the Invasion and Dispossession, then some recompense is due to all indigenous groups and individuals whose cultural practices have been so fundamentally modified. Whether some special rights should thereby be enshrined in the constitution, with the subsequent alteration of any relevant legislation, is worth some thought.

Finally, whether special rights are due solely because of indigeneity, is a sore point with many indigenous people. Many simply cannot bring themselves to contemplate equality (signifying some sort of common identity) with non-indigenous people. We are not non-indigenous and often resent the loss of distinction that a common identity, even that as Australians. For example, in relation to the complex political situation in Fiji, Dr Tagupa concludes (not that I fully agree with him):[60]

> One of the primary obstacles to resolution of rights asserted by Aboriginals against the national State is common citizenship with non-Aboriginal groups. State policy on the Westminster model is contrary to any sanctioned form of differences in the legal

59 Philpott, D, 'In defense of self-determination' (1995) 105 *Ethics* 320.

60 Tagupa, F in Renwick, W (ed), *Sovereignty and Indigenous Rights: The Treaty of Waitangi in International Contexts*, 1991, Wellington: Victoria University Press, pp 143–44.

treatment between commonly-situated citizens. Any Aboriginal claims based on precedents in existence prior to the establishment of the national State and common citizenship of all its people must necessarily confront such assumptions.

SOVEREIGNTY AND INDEPENDENCE

Is indigenous sovereignty viable as a policy option? Or, has it been lost forever, the territory to which it once related irrevocably occupied and transformed? If full, uncompromising, self-reliant independence is intended across the whole country one single obstacle would frustrate such an aspiration:

- the presence of 17 million non-Aboriginal people who are not likely to pack their bags and return to Europe or Asia. If a more modest proposal is intended, circumscribing a territory and a major portion of Australia's indigenous population, (presumably in the north and remoter areas of the country), then any demand for sovereignty is still compromised by hard realities:
  - the poor economic viability of much of the land;
  - the vast distances across the territory to be administered;
  - the remarkable lack of institutions and facilities to promote the development of the skill and resource base needed. For example, from Cooktown to Broome and down to the Bight, in half of the land mass of Australia, only one university operates, the Northern Territory University in Darwin; major indigenous education centres are running at Batchelor, Alice Springs, Broome and Thursday Island, but these are thousands of kilometres apart; and
  - the simple fact, easily testable, that the great majority of indigenous people, particularly in the south, would not be interested in packing their bags and leaving their own country, careers, friends and lives behind.

Sovereignty at an even more modest level, that of independence of existing indigenous communities where they are, becomes progressively less viable, given the spatial fragmentation, lack of major service centres and lack of indigenous expertise, barely a single secondary school on any indigenous community in Australia, and Year 12-level graduates from those extremely rare, across a vast area of the country. This is hardly an sensible option to devote one's efforts to.

Proposals of the Aboriginal Provisional government in Hobart are rarely concrete or practical. The restoration of sovereignty seems to be a formal demand predicated on the undeniable *technicality* that indigenous sovereignty was extinguished without the consent of indigenous people.

If not sovereignty and independence but 'softer' forms of autonomy, to what extent are issues of Aboriginal politics autonomous from the main concerns and currents of Australian policy generally? To what degree is such (interest in) autonomy lasting or realistic in the context of Australian public policy and political activity, federal and State? Is there a general and common indigenous interest in autonomy?

Aboriginal magistrate and University of New England Chancellor, Pat O'Shane, always a passionate advocate for Aboriginal rights and no slouch when it comes to radical proposals, expresses strong misgivings about the practicalities of self-determination, for example:[61]

> ... the total Aboriginal population of Australia numbers less than 250,000; that population is scattered in small communities across the country; there is little or no sense of being a cohesive community of indigenous people (notwithstanding that they raise common demands, such as land rights); a very substantial proportion of the Aboriginal population now lives in urban areas ...

Many would reluctantly agree with O'Shane on these grounds, as well as her conclusion that if self-determination was seriously sought by the masses of Aboriginal people:[62]

> ... long ago there would have developed a strong, cohesive, co-ordinated movement of people, with a clearly and strongly articulated political platform, the force of which would be difficult for governments and the rest of the Australian community to resist. That has not happened, and in my assessment of things, will not.

Nor has there been, or is likely to be, a major shift in the population back to rural communities. In view of the consistent decline of 2% per annum in the rural share of the Aboriginal population over the past 20 years, I would have to support O'Shane in tentatively suggesting that, on balance, at present, self-determination in the sense of political independence for the majority of indigenous people in Australia, is not likely to be viable.

Depressingly, O'Shane's final comments also ring too true: that corruption and incompetence amongst many of the elite and those who monopolise organisational control, especially of the financial disbursement and employment selection mechanisms, could, in the long run, prove to be the downfall of any development towards self-determination:[63]

> ... there are small coteries or cohorts of our own people within such organisations who, having acquired the skills of their erstwhile masters, then use those skills to exploit the ignorance and continuing disempowerment of their people. In the mouths of such people, calls for self-determination ring hollow indeed. For my money, though, self-determination is no longer a valid demand–if it ever was. Rather, the demand must be for empowerment. THAT is the way ahead.

Perhaps in the future, if:

- indigenous communities and some hypothetical potentially self-determining region encompassing them could become economically viable, according to some agreed calculus;

61 O'Shane, P, 'Aborigines' future rests with empowerment', *The Weekend Australian*, 22–23 April 1995, p 30.

62 *Ibid.*

63 *Ibid.*

- such a region could feasibly be governed as a single entity, notwithstanding the immense diversity of custom, language and aspirations within it, and probably distance as well;
- there could be enthusiastic and general agreement on the forms of deliberative, decision-making, administrative, cultural, economic, social and political institutions;
- the rural communities could either bring about the education of their own young people where they are, or attract, voluntarily, large numbers of skilled and educated indigenous people from the cities, so that institutions could be staffed and functions carried out by indigenous people (unless, of course, it has been decided that self-determination and the large-scale need for non-indigenous expertise are compatible, a prospect which is probably quite objectionable to indigenous people with expertise);
- the bulk of the educated indigenous workforce, based in the cities, feel that their contributions might at last be valued by the communities and that indigenous people have moved on from the mindset which dichotomises 'education' and 'community', or 'education' and 'work', and got away from the notion that education is a meaningless activity only for children, and work means unskilled employment, for which you do not need education;
- educated people are allowed to participate fully in the decision-making of community, regional and other deliberative bodies in an atmosphere of mutual respect rather than hierarchy;
- the major problems of distance, resources and inconvenience could be neutralised; and
- the advantages of community life outweigh the freedom and attractions of urban living and working, then–

self-determination, even sovereignty, may be feasible. As time passes, however, each of these factors fade into the mists of regret.[64]

A TREATY?

O'Shane, with her characteristic iconoclasm, is extremely sceptical of the notion of a treaty.[65] I would concur with her observation that it has never had much support from indigenous people, who suspect that it deflects attention from the substance of issues of social justice for the sake of international cosmetics. She suggests that it has, in fact, divided any Aboriginal leadership and in turn has allowed for the exploitation of these differences.

Almost invariably in similar situations, treaties have been drawn up with the surrender of sovereignty as a precondition: between the American colonies and native

64 *Cf* Brennan, FSJ, *Sharing the Country*, 1993, Ringwood: Penguin.

65 O'Shane, P, 'A Treaty for Australians?', in Renwick, W (ed), *Sovereignty and Indigenous Rights: The Treaty of Waitangi in International Contexts*, 1991, Wellington: Victoria University Press, pp 147–55.

American 'tribes' or 'nations',[66] between the English monarch and the Maori rangatiratangas[67] and between the British Crown and African entities of all sorts, from small groups to States. The assumption of the day, according to Renwick[68] seemed to be that the right to State sovereignty was a European concept and prerogative unknown in non-white polities, subject to the written word and the backing of a standing army.

If not sovereignty, what would need to be in a treaty? Aboriginal people almost invariably suggest the recognition of their land rights, and compensation for whatever land cannot be returned. Having lost both sovereignty and land, however, many people suggest that a constitutional amendment, backed up by something a bit more substantial, should set out the special relationship that indigenous people have with the entity now called Australia. To this extent, group rights could be enacted which do not in any way represent a trade-off of individual rights and thus an abridgement of individual self-determination. Again, *Mabo* and the native title legislation have obviated some of this rationale.

The anguished question must then be asked. If not segregation, assimilation or self-determination, then what?

Again, everyday life for many indigenous people may provide the answer. As agents in the framing of legislation for their own lives they are living and shaping their destinies in terms of none of these absolutes but in the real world with its problems, opportunities, tragedies and achievements. Real life necessarily prevails over assertion, theory and chance observation. A generation of city-based Aboriginal people, living cheek-by-jowl with non-indigenous people, working, marrying, studying, playing and fighting with them, have remained Aboriginal, the dire predictions of segregationists have not materialised; but nor have the outcomes predicted by those who feared assimilation, and those who still fear it.

What are the options for Aboriginal people, particularly in urban areas, away from discrete communities; by what policies and practices are Aboriginal people currently attempting to make the best of their circumstances?

Self-determination in the first instance allows for individual self-expression. This is implied in the United Nations declarations, as well as most writing on the topic. But, with the abolition of formal restrictions on Aboriginal rights as Australian citizens, by definition the absence of any discriminatory pressures and constraints allowed, *enabled,* Aboriginal people, for the first time, to live as they liked within the commonly experienced constraints of budget, location and so on. But certainly nobody has forced us to live identical lives to white people. And we will certainly never have identical histories or genealogies!

---

66 *Cf* Brown, DN, 'Native Americans and the Right of Self-Government in the United States', in Renwick, W (ed), *Sovereignty and Indigenous Rights: The Treaty of Waitangi in International Contexts,* 1991, Wellington: Victoria University Press, pp 31–47.

67 *Cf* Sorrenson, MPK, 'Treaties in British Colonial Policy: Precedents for Waitangi' in Renwick, W (ed), *Sovereignty and Indigenous Rights: The Treaty of Waitangi in International Contexts,* 1991, Wellington: Victoria University Press, pp 22–30.

68 Renwick, W (ed), *Sovereignty and Indigenous Rights: The Treaty of Waitangi in International Contexts,* 1991, Wellington: Victoria University Press, p 9.

Of course, our budgets have been considerably more constrained than those of the average white person, our locations have been usually vastly less favourable and our knowledge of opportunities and how to seize them vastly poorer than that of the average white person. But, in a political, policy sense, and in a legislative sense, we are free. The choices, constrained now by recent history and its dreadful heritage, (but no longer by explicit and discriminatory policy) and framed by the liberal-individualist principles of a capitalist State, were and still are ours, modified by a range of affirmative action programmes initiated by the Department of Aboriginal Affairs.

These programmes have had mixed results, but initiatives in tertiary education, for example, have been phenomenally successful:

- graduate numbers across the country have been doubling every *four* years since the early 1950s; in fact, the doubling rate has accelerated;
- of the 6–7,000 indigenous university graduates, almost every one has found immediate employment (mostly in urban areas and usually in mainstream organisations) and their numbers are rising by about 15% each year; and
- across the country, some 7–8,000 indigenous students are enrolled at any one time at universities, the vast majority in mainstream awards; 4,500 *started* courses this year.

Currently, some 8% of the adult indigenous population are either university graduates or qualified tradespeople, an increase from 1% in 1970. In conversation, it is clear that the vast majority of these qualified people would respond favourably if they received the call from Aboriginal organisations, but it rarely comes.

CONCLUSION

So, liberal and individualist, rather than openly racist, parameters currently channel the scope of aspirations for Aboriginal people in urban areas and, in so far as they represent the outlines of a policy, could fairly inherit the term 'integration'. In a theoretical sense, this comes part way between assimilation and group self-determination, in that it operates when people are both left alone (as much as anybody can be in today's world) free from discriminatory restrictions, and indirectly provided with various supports to take advantage of a range of opportunities on an individual basis.

This then shapes, for better or for worse, the framework of activity which predominates in urban areas and which is likely to prevail, no matter what official policies are adopted.

It is revealing that the notion of integration, or individual self-determination, is treated as a pariah, yet how can one deny Aboriginal people standard liberal rights? Doesn't the freedom to choose still include the freedom to choose to associate, for the full possible range of purposes, with other Aboriginal people? By extension, doesn't it thus always contain the possibility of mobilising for whatever level of self-determination can be freely constructed?

What I am therefore suggesting is that, in the broadest sense and mindful of the anguish and tragedy in Aboriginal people's lives over the past 200 years, Aboriginal people themselves have, in barely a generation:

- partly (by no means completely) defeated the iniquitous segregation or protection policies;
- forced the adoption of, and partially transcended, wholesale 'assimilation as equal rights' policies, the first range of enabling options to be presented to Aboriginal people in those 200 years;
- in practice, created a range of options including forms of individual self-determination, one of which is integration;
- developed a complex range of organisational structures, national, urban and rural, from the local to the national levels, opening up possibilities for a range of forms of self-management, group self-determination, self-government and autonomy, even some opportunities for sovereignty; and
- substantially begun the creation of our own base of expertise, should it ever be called on, at whatever level of self-determination.

We have also opened up the possibility to press towards the reconciliation of Aboriginal and non-Aboriginal aspirations in the near future. Reconciliation is surely necessary, inevitable and desirable, on terms that recognise the justice of the indigenous people's claims to what land they can regain and compensation for what they can not. Recompense is necessary for the extinction of sovereignty and the rich and varied forms of human existence that our ancestors devised, and reparation for the genocidal treatment to which, in living memory, the hegemonic Anglo-Celtic State subjected them and us.

CHAPTER THREE

MOVING THE BOUNDARIES AND UNDOING THE RESTRICTIONS[1]

Daryle Rigney

INTRODUCTION

The aim of this paper is to explore a pro-active approach to social justice and the rights of indigenous peoples. It asserts that we need to move beyond merely making legal institutions safe and accessible places for Aboriginal and Islander people. It argues that there need to be ways of engaging legal institutions and their communities, including law schools and their students, in the struggle against injustice.

The Council for Aboriginal Reconciliation in *Towards Social Justice?: An Issues Paper*[2] makes the point that it is almost 10 years since the Australian Law Reform Commission delivered its recommendations for the incorporation of customary law into the Australian legal system. In those 10 years not one of the recommendations has been implemented. Only recently has the Office of Indigenous Affairs, Department of the Prime Minister and Cabinet, prepared a review of the implementation of the recommendations as a result of an acknowledged need to examine legal and governmental responses to the report following developments such as the National Inquiry into Racist Violence in Australia, the Royal Commission into Aboriginal Deaths in Custody (RCIADIC) and the High Court's decision in *Mabo v Queensland (No 2)*.

The Council's paper also raised the issue of the failure to recognise Aboriginal and Torres Strait Islander peoples as the indigenous peoples of this country in the Australian constitution. The right to have our identity and our indigenality acknowledged and respected is an important factor in the sociopolitical dynamics of contemporary Australian society. More often than not the recognition of difference and the recognition of our knowledge as legitimate and valid are unsatisfactory. This situation occurs even though Australia as a modern liberal state claims to protect and promote the rights of indigenous communities to be and to exist.[3] The recognition of difference and the right to be, however, varies from those seeking the recognition and that which is ultimately given. This reality 'poses a public policy challenge'[4] that Australian governments have struggled to come to terms with.

Recent developments in South Australia surrounding the protection of Ngarrindjeri women's rights at Hindmarsh Island demonstrates the chasm between recognition and

1 Title taken from Langton, M, *Well I heard it on the radio and saw it on the television ...*, 1993, North Sydney: Australian Film Commission.

2 Council for Aboriginal Reconciliation, '*Towards social justice?: An issues paper*', 1994, Canberra: ACT.

3 Salee, D, 'Identities in conflict, the Aboriginal question and the politics of recognition in Quebec', (1995) 18(2) *Ethnic and Racial Studies* 278.

4 *Ibid.*

realisation of rights for indigenous people. The comments of Michael Dodson, Commissioner of the Aboriginal and Torres Strait Islander Social Justice Unit, Human Rights and Equal Opportunity Commission would seem to ring true:

> This fine legal system fails to protect our rights in virtually every area of our lives[5] [and]
>
> Does an imposed patriarchal legal system have the right to override the cultural and spiritual laws that Aboriginal women have been honouring for thousands of years?[6]

The Federal Court's decision to overturn Minister Robert Tickner's protection of Hindmarsh Island suggests that a 'hierarchy of rights, a hierarchy of knowledge'[7] exists and that indigenous rights are at the bottom of that hierarchy. Dodson goes on to say that the gap between the rhetoric and the reality is not an isolated incident and suggests there are two reasons for this. Firstly, there is a deficiency in the capacity of existing laws and mechanisms to protect the rights of indigenous people. Secondly, there is a lack of full recognition of indigenous rights including the legitimisation and practice of indigenous knowledge. However, knowing that the current system is inadequate and that there is a gap between the rhetoric and the reality does not answer the problems of my people, the Ngarrindjeri.

Following Langton's approach, therefore, I would hope to 'move the boundaries and undo the restrictions rather than make prescriptions'.[8] I am not arguing for a complete rejection of the invaders' British cultural inheritance. I am arguing against the use of that invaders' colonial inheritance which ensures the construction and maintenance of racist, classist and gendered power, and monocultural dominance. It is clear that colonial domination suppresses, transforms or destroys the practices of the colonised and there must be a process of decolonisation if improvements are to be made in the lives of indigenous people.

UNDERSTANDING AND RESISTING RACISM

To achieve the goal of this paper and engage the legal fraternity in the struggle against racism there is a need to explore the concepts of resistance, racism and colonisation which underlie the approach advocated.

Moore compellingly argues that common contemporary thought surrounding injustice in general, and racism more particularly, is dominated by two distinct images. The first image is of helpless, innocent, suffering victims who invite 'responses of protection and charity'.[9] However, 'charity makes children of the oppressed'[10] and in

5 Dodson, M, 'Adequacy of protection for the rights of indigenous peoples' (1995) 19(2) *Aboriginal and Islander Health Worker Journal* 19.

6 See footnote 5 above.

7 *Ibid.*

8 Langton, M, *Well I heard it on the radio and saw it on the television ...*, 1993, p 7.

9 Moore, B, 'Resisting racism through religious education' (1994) 10(10) *Religious Education Journal of Australia* 13.

10 *Ibid.*

no way challenges or changes power relationships which are 'the root cause of the problem'[11] and, in fact, such a response dehumanises and robs these people of their dignity. The second image is of the challenging, compelling, courageous and determined political activist–the freedom fighter who sends out an invitation to join the struggle.

Further to the common images and understandings of oppression is what Moore calls 'the working definition of racism'. This definition locks racism in with the attitudes and values of racists and argues that if you are able to change peoples' attitudes you are resisting racism and working towards the elimination of racism in society: [12]

> Racist attitudes are the products, rather than the causes, of racism because racism is an historical and political movement, which did not grow out of ignorance or prejudice, but was the result of an attempt to legitimate the use of power to dispossess particular groups of people.

The politics of the representation of Aboriginality and ways of knowing are problematic and of great concern because the social construction of the concept 'race' became the foundation of the racist movement to differentiate between people and determine a hierarchical order for people.[13] Racism consists of constructed and targeted groups of people for systematic oppression. This systematic oppression is achieved through a process of racialisation of behaviours, attitudes, culture and social formations. Racism as a political and historical movement, therefore, ensures that every aspect of Australian society is racialised. The racialisation of Australia operates at many levels in our society including within the legal system. Archbishop Desmond Tutu when speaking of the process of racialisation in South Africa asserted:[14]

> ... one thing that racism means to black people is the denial of a right to vote or to participate in the process of making the laws which govern our lives.

In Australia, indigenous people were returned the right to vote and are able to participate in the process of making laws. Studies on law and colonialism, however, 'demonstrate the power of the state to reshape the social order, suggesting the dominance of this form of law over other normative orders'.[15] This is by no means the whole picture because even as the process of 'racialising' law continues it is also a site of ongoing struggle. Indigenous people have resisted and accommodated such laws and the creation of customary law itself is an ongoing collaborative process.

---

11 *Ibid.*

12 *Ibid.*

13 See Guillaumin, C, *Racism, Sexism, Power and Ideology*, 1995, London: Routledge; Montagu, A, *Race, Man's Most Dangerous Myth: The Fallacy of Race*, 1974, London: Oxford University Press; Moore, B, 'The politics of racism as a category of radical social analysis in South Africa', paper presented at International Conference on Racism: Aboriginality, Ethnicity and Gender in Australia, Canada, New Zealand and USA, Sydney, December 9–11, 1993 (1993a); Winant, H, *Racial Conditions: Politics, Theory, Comparisons*, 1994, Minneapolis: University of Minnesota Press.

14 Desmond Tutu in Moore, B (1993a) p 15.

15 Merry, S, 'Legal pluralism' (1988) 22 *Law and Society Review* 879.

As Salee notes:[16]

> Promoters of the Aboriginal cause have no trouble using the laws and institutions of the colonisers, the courts in particular, to assist their own struggle [*sic*].

This should not be a surprise though because the 'racialising' of social institutions by dominant societies allows no other recourse for indigenous peoples to voice our aspirations and claims.

In addition racism 'racialises' language and culture where racist concepts such as 'race', 'half-caste', 'urban' and 'remote' are built into language to interpret experience and thus influence action. Also, the cultural artifacts of society – television, radio, books, art and academic writing etc – legitimate and validate the colonisers' experience and understanding. From this position indigenous culture is framed and contained as something from the distant past and there is no allowance for the evolution and adaptation of our customs and practices. Thus denying them authenticity as a legitimate basis for indigenous rights. Our contemporary customs and practices, in all their diversity, act as our 'ideological mooring'[17] points. Any attempts to delegitimate or invalidate indigenous rights, including the right to recognise and practice customary law, on the basis of a constructed deculturalisation or acculturalisation argument 'only reflect[s] strategies of power used by the bearers of dominant sociopolitical institutions'.[18]

The process

Given the view of the nature of racism and the racialisation of law outlined above, the question is how do we continue the resistance movement and intervene in the continuing racialisation process? Moore identifies three main processes for resisting racism which he terms raising consciousness, making contact and taking action.

Consciousness raising

Consciousness raising is about raising the awareness and understanding of racism. It is about rejecting a 'victim' approach constructed for us as indigenous peoples' which locks us into seeing ourselves as victims. As Barney Pityana in Moore argues:[19]

> ... seeing the oppressed as suffering, helpless victims puts them where the oppressors want them to be. Here they pose no real threat. Their salvation depends on the generosity and magnanimity of the oppressor.

The emphasis must be on resistance activities that go beyond understanding racism at the attitudinal level. Resistance activity must also tackle the racialisation of our social formations, our behaviours and our culture and ideology including language and

16 Salee, *op cit*, p 292.

17 *Ibid.*

18 *Ibid*, p 293.

19 Moore, B (1993b) p 74.

knowledge. Bird acknowledges that the political system does not operate in a vacuum and is effected by political, social and economic forces operating in society. Law as a process, therefore, cannot be studied except in its cultural, material and political setting.[20] She further states that to study law and not take account of these factors would create a false representation of law as neutral, impartial and apolitical. Resistance in legal education therefore, means more than producing lawyers who are able to identify legal issues and then apply the existing law to it. It means producing lawyers who are able to critically challenge taken for granted, seemingly common sense, understandings of the law in order to actively confront racism within any community.

Making contact

The processes for confronting racism should not occur in isolation from existing anti-racist traditions and groups but in collaboration in order to strengthen and empower the resistance movements.

The next step in the anti-racism process, therefore, involves making contact with and listening to the resistance groups within the community. By making contact, consciousness raising is an ongoing occurrence for both indigenous and non-indigenous people. It is as essential for indigenous people to connect with their history, their understanding and their knowledges as it is for non-indigenous people to hear the voice of the 'other'. It is clear though that the rhetorical recognition of the voice without meaningful recognition of indigenous customary law, as a basis for shifting the boundaries of 'law', serves to continue the marginalisation and oppression of the rights of indigenous people.

Taking action

Taking action means becoming actively involved in the struggle against oppression and racism. Racism will not go away because we might be able to change the attitudes of racists nor will it disappear because we are able to recognise its more sophisticated forms including the racialisation of our social formations. It requires engaging in political action that is informed by an understanding of racism as a political and social movement which subjugated indigenous knowledges and traditions. This means selecting and planning resistance actions, implementing resistance actions and evaluating resistance actions. At this point the question then becomes what can you do to support the struggle against racism.

An indiginist response to the struggle against racism

My aim when I started to write this paper was to explore a pro-active approach to social justice and the rights of indigenous people. The intention was also to develop the readers understanding of racism as an ideological construction in order to provide the basis for undoing the restrictions and shifting the boundaries.

20 Bird, G, *The Process of Law in Australia: Intercultural Perspectives*, 1988, Sydney: Butterworths.

I will attempt to shift the boundaries through a description of some aspects of law in Ngarrindjeri society. This requires some discussion of what is Ngarrindjeri law and how it was engendered in my community. Mudrooroo is undoubtably correct when he states that indigenous ideology understands that all our indigenous laws come from the Dreaming.[21] The law was taught and reinforced daily by a variety of means including music, dance, song, storytelling, community responsibilities and interpersonal interactions. In the words of Marcia Langton:[22]

> The Aboriginal ancestors travelled the country during The Dreaming, the creative period from the time immemorial. They established the code of life which today is called The Dreaming or The Law.

The narratives of the Dreaming encoded our behaviours, attitudes, culture and social formation as well as describing how the physical environment came to be. It enshrined the relationship between indigenous people and the land and it is in the land that the law is found.[23] For example, a Ngarrindjeri narrative *Ngurunderi* provides for us the explanation for our being, the land and its formation, the flora and fauna and the rules for living. *Ngurunderi* gave us our weapons for war and our instruments for hunting as well as instituting all the rights and ceremonies practised by our community. These practices and signs are the basis for customary law in Ngarrindjeri society and form the framework for living.

Another illustration of how narratives hold law is seen in the story of *thukkeri*. *Thukkeri* is a narrative about two Ngarrindjeri men fishing for the best and most delicious bream fish, known as thukkeri in Ngarrindjeri language. The men are very successful and soon fill their canoe but as they paddle in to shore they see a stranger in the distance. The men are greedy and do not wish to share their catch so they cover the fish with reed mats. As they come closer to the stranger he said, 'Hello brothers, I haven't eaten anything today. Can you spare any fish?' The men say they cannot because they only caught a few fish and these are needed for their wives, children and the old people. The stranger stands for a long while before turning and walking away. He then suddenly stops and turns to the men saying, 'You lied. There are plenty of fish in the canoe and because you are so greedy you will never enjoy those *thukkeri* again'. After the stranger has walked away the men take the mats off and begin to gut the fish but soon find that the delicious *thukkeri* are now so full of sharp thin bones that they cannot eat them. Upon returning home the men are shamed because they can no longer feed their families. They then tell the old people of the events who reply that the stranger was really the creator *Ngurunderi* who was now punishing the Ngarrindjeri forever because of the greed of the two men.

21 Mudrooroo, *Us Mob*, 1995, Sydney: Angus and Robertson.

22 Report of the World Council of Churches, *Justice for Aboriginal Australians*, 1981, Sydney: Australian Council of Churches, p 13.

23 See Mudrooroo, *op cit*.

The purpose of this narrative is to remind us that *Ngurunderi* is the law giver of Ngarrindjeri society. The narrative reinforces this message and teaches us a lesson. The narrative also reminds us of rules for living including:

- the need to care for and respect others and the environment – the men forgot to take only the fish needed to supply food for the family;
- the consequences of bad behaviour greedy – men are punished for lying and not sharing;
- roles and responsibilities within the extended family;
- the effects upon the entire community – Ngarrindjeri people can no longer enjoy eating the *thukkeri* because they are now too bony.

While not mentioned in my edited account the full narrative also includes detail on:[24]

(i) the natural environment:
- detailing Lake Alexandrina including landmarks, local plants and the best fishing spots;
- making use of the natural environment;
- characteristics of the *thukkeri* including shape of the skeleton, colour and likely location; and

(ii) the spiritual world:
- *Ngurunderi* is always watching to see that people obey the laws;
- spirit ancestors enforce the law – *Ngurunderi* punishes the men for not sharing by making the fish bony.

The process of racialisation however ensured that Ngarrindjeri law would struggle to survive. The narratives which once governed life in my community were slowly but surely eroded, undermined, suppressed or obliterated. A campaign of targeted systematic racialisation of Ngarrindjeri law and other social formations including our system of government, the *Tendi,* which was a democratically elected body that acted as a kind of parliament as well as law court, was undertaken.

It is clear that law in post-Invasion society is not based on any indigenous practices. There is a fundamental difference between Westminster law based on common law (law made by judgments being followed by precedents), legislative law (law made by Parliament), and Ngarrindjeri law as determined in the Dreaming. The confidence of the invaders as to the superiority of their social formations and their law ensured a racialised legal system which served the interests of the invaders to the detriment of indigenous people. This foundation continues to shape what counts as law today and is a major factor in the repeated denial of indigenous human rights particularly in relation to land ownership.

24 Education Department of South Australia, *Thukkeri: a Ngarrindjeri Dreaming Story: Years R–3*, 1988, Adelaide: Education Department of South Australia.

CONCLUSION

Indigenous people today do participate in a racialised society. At the moment there is no other choice. This means we are participating in the social systems that are instrumental in our own oppression. Is there a future, though, for reclaiming an indigenous legal system?

About the possibility for reclamation Mudrooroo says:[25]

> There is a general consensus among the magistrates that there was not room in Australia for two laws, so that indigenous law could only be cited to plead mitigating circumstances. This position is borne out by a government report in 1994 on Aboriginal customary laws. It is worth quoting its recommendations:
>
> - Aboriginal customary law should be recognised, in appropriate ways, by the Australian legal system;
> - such recognition must occur against the background and within the framework of the general law;
> - the creation of new and separate legal structures should be avoided unless the need for these is demonstrated;
> - in most instances, codification or direct enforcement are not appropriate forms of recognition nor is the exclusion of the general law desirable.

Following invasion it was obvious that the Westminster system of government and law would not accord indigenous systems of government and law recognition as legitimate and valid forms of social organisation. The legacy has seen legislation enacted to support the foundation of a colonial empire which was not concerned with protecting indigenous people and our rights. These events are a matter of history and while we cannot undo history, we can make history. Let us work towards an authentic reconciliation by accepting the challenge to shift the boundaries and undo the restrictions.

25 Mudrooroo, *op cit*, pp 109–110.

CHAPTER FOUR

THE HEALTH OF INDIGENOUS AUSTRALIANS

Christopher Reynolds

> An Aboriginal baby born in 1980 will be four times more likely to die before the age of one. As a child he or she will be, on average, 20 times more likely to be diagnosed as having chronic upper respiratory tract infection ... 'he will suffer a small handful of illnesses in one body'. As an adult this person will be at least 13 times more likely than his European peer to go blind (mostly from preventable causes) and 20 times more likely to have a diabetic condition ... He will die, on average, at least 20 years before his European counterpart.[1]

> Our societies are complex and interrelated. Health cannot be separated from other goals. The inextricable links between people and their environment constitutes the basis for a socio-ecological basis for health.[2]

INTRODUCTION

Imagine a large public teaching hospital located nearby to a law school. People are being born, others are dying. The corridors are full of hurrying clinicians, nurses and patients on trolleys. The casualty department is hectic, its staff busy treating the victims of injuries or sudden events such as stroke or heart attack. Its wards are full of patients suffering from a range of diseases. If indigenous Australians are being treated (and they are far more likely to be admitted to hospital than other Australians for a variety of conditions including infectious and parasitic conditions, injuries and respiratory problems),[3] it is likely that the staff will be seeing a range of diseases, many of which their lecturers would have told them had been eradicated from mainstream Australia decades ago. In the far quieter corridors of a law school it is also 'business as usual', lectures and tutorials are given and cases are read and argued through. Students grapple with theories and speculate what the law is and sometimes what it might be.

It is easy to keep these two images separate and unconnected in our minds. It is easy to explore the issues that present themselves as important in law schools and to consider them as though they existed in isolation or, at best, within a rigidly defined boundary. Yet the things that go on in hospitals and the things that this says about the health of the Australian community and specific groups within this community have much to tell us as lawyers about many of the things we see as *lawyers' problems*. Why do indigenous Australians experience so much more sickness than other Australians? Does it just happen, or does it tell us something about the opportunities and life choices that the

1 Reid 1979, cited in Davis, A, and George, J, *States of Health*, 2nd edn, 1993, Sydney: Harper and Roe, p 78.

2 Ottawa Charter for Health Promotion.

3 Indigenous Australians are twice as likely to be hospitalised as other Australians. See Australian Institute of Health and Welfare, *Australia's Health 1992*, 1992, Canberra: AGPS.

former experience, both of which are a product of past events and having to survive in a community dominated by an alien non-indigenous culture. More generally, patterns of disease tell us much about how we are succeeding as a community in providing equality of opportunity for all. They provide us with the chance to be critical about what is in our community and the way that we order our social structure and to speculate on what *might* be. As lawyers we should grasp the opportunity to explore the questions that a different but related view, such as that of the health practitioner, present for us to consider. An exploration of pivotal social indicators including health will help us to more effectively contextualise the specific questions that we pose as lawyer's questions (such as the issue of land rights or reform of the public intoxication laws). It is for this reason that a chapter on health appears in a book that is centrally about law.

If we take the indigenous Australian community as a specific group and focus on their health we find that they suffer from a vastly higher burden of sickness and premature mortality than the rest of the Australian community. It is a burden of disadvantage and adversity that adds to the other burdens that are described in this book particularly the over-representation of indigenous people in the criminal justice systems.

Two things follow from this fact. Firstly, we might conclude that in the late 20th century indigenous Australians miss out in a variety of ways, but this is simply to do no more than 'report the facts' and to state the obvious. Secondly, we might go further and conclude that health and legal status are linked by antecedent causes: namely, the things that contribute to a poor legal outcome also contribute to a poor health outcome. We need to explore this second proposition not simply because it links the issues of health and law, but because it takes us beyond the stage of simply parroting the dismal data on indigenous health and legal outcomes, on a journey that tries to discover some of the causes of these data and with it the hope that Australian policymakers might set reforms in place that would provide a meaningful form of equal opportunity for indigenous Australians.

HOW DO WE APPROACH THIS QUESTION? THE PROBLEM OF THE 'ABORIGINAL HEALTH PROBLEM'

Policymakers bring many ideas to bear on the questions of Aboriginal health but overall, it is presented as a deeply problematic area. We need to consider the nature of these ideas. It is too easy to see the issue of indigenous health as though it were a permanent and inevitable legacy of our colonial past or the inevitable product of the meeting of European cultures with a far more ancient and materially less endowed culture. This is particularly the case where health is strongly influenced by personal or group behaviour as is the case with alcohol or tobacco use. It is important that we see indigenous health not as some inevitable and unalterable product of the past but as something that indigenous communities can take charge of and improve. In many respects, indigenous Australians can indeed take charge of their own health. The fact that many do not, in the same way that many European Australians do not, is the result of a series of individual choices and structural issues. In the case of indigenous Australians these issues are profound and all need to be addressed. They include the particular questions of very poor or non-existent public health services (such as water and sewerage) in so many of their outback communities. But, they also include the more general questions of poverty, unemployment and alienation which directly flows as a bleak legacy of dispossession. Most importantly, we need to recognise that vast improvements can be made now to indigenous health at an individual, community and population level. In particular, we need to avoid an explanation of indigenous ill-health that sees no way forward until the edifice of reconciliation is completely in place.

In brief, we must recognise that there are many things that we can do now, which generally involve the provision of proper sanitation and infrastructure, the easy access to health services, targeted health promotion campaigns and improved living conditions. We should do these things while also recognising the way in which the history of European and indigenous relations in this country has very powerfully diminished the latter's possibilities for health and happiness and their access to the opportunities that European Australians expect as a matter of course.

We must also be wary of a determinist approach which at least partially seeks to explain indigenous ill-health by suggesting that the indigenous community is genetically more susceptible to Western diseases or lifestyles. This kind of explanation lends itself to conclusions that the indigenous community is more affected by alcohol than Europeans for genetic reasons and that the indigenous 'alcohol problem' is, first and foremost, a physiological problem rather than a social issue.

Of this way of thinking, Moodie has written:[4]

> Views have been put forward that there is an Aboriginal 'racial' susceptibility of predisposition to tuberculosis, severe measles, middle ear disease, diabetes, epilepsy, lactose intolerance, ascorbic acid deficiency, alcoholism and so on. None of these views has withstood careful, critical analysis of the available data, particularly in view of the environmental, nutritional and behavioural stresses present, and their physiological and immunological consequences; these are more than enough to account for the observed differences in disease manifestations in the Aboriginal and non-Aboriginal populations ... The case for racial susceptibility remains, at best, unproven.

There is an obvious danger in biological determinism. It allows an approach to indigenous health that sees different health outcomes between the European and indigenous Australians as the fixed, inevitable and expected outcome of their differing physiology. The poor health of indigenous people thus becomes something that simply 'is' rather than something which can be changed.

With these preliminary ideas in mind, we should now consider the extent of indigenous ill-health in Australia.

4 Moodie, PM, 'Medical aspects of Aboriginal health' (1977) 6 *Australian Family Physician* 1309–17 (cited in Saggers, S, and Gray, D, *Aboriginal Health and Society*, 1995, Sydney: Allen and Unwin, p 5). For a further discussion of this areas see generally Saggers and Gray, Chapter 1.

Indigenous health in Australia: a historical perspective

The indigenous Australians were well adapted to the variety of climatic conditions in Australia, their communities resilient enough for them to have survived as a group for over 40,000 years. Over this period, they experienced a very different pattern of health than they now have. Saggers and Gray argue that chronic diseases were probably not a feature of their lives, if only because the life expectancies of hunter gatherers is usually low.[5] Specific diseases such as trachoma (an eye disease) and yaws (a spirochaete infection) and injuries more generally were conditions that affected communities prior to their contact with Europeans. As with other cultures, indigenous communities in Australia developed specific explanations for these diseases and illness such as sorcery that at first glance contrast strongly with late 20th century European explanations.[6]

As far as can be said, the years following 1788 saw the onset of new health problems for the communities that made earliest contact with the Europeans. The best recorded was the 'Great Sickness' of 1789. Watkin Tench, commander of the marines that arrived with the First Fleet, and an insightful reporter of the first few years of the settlement, wrote of this in the following terms:[7]

> An extraordinary calamity was now observed among the natives. Repeated accounts brought by our boats of finding bodies of the Indians [indigenous Australians] in all the coves and inlets of the harbour ... On inspection, it appeared that all the parties had died a natural death: pustules similar to those occasioned by the smallpox, were thickly spread on the bodies; but how a disease, to which our former observations had led us to suppose them strangers, could have introduced itself and spread so widely, seemed inexplicable.

The nature of the disease and its circumstances – was it smallpox, and if so where did it come from, and was it accidentally or intentionally released – has never been settled. Tench dismissed the possibility that it might have been a deliberate infection from the white settlers as to be 'so wild as to be unworthy of consideration'. Whatever the nature of the disease, there seems to have been evidence from oral accounts and evidence of mass burial sites that it radiated out from Sydney cove following known trade routes along the rivers. If the disease was caused by the European settlers, it was merely the precursor of a variety of destructive diseases which must have caused untold damage among the indigenous communities. Thus, infections such as measles, which were potent killers among 19th century European communities in Australia were even more destructive to the indigenous communities exposed to them because the latter had no existing patterns of immunity.[8]

---

5 At p 35.

6 Reid, J, *Sorcerers and Healing Spirits: Continuity and Change in an Aboriginal Medical System*, 1983, Canberra: ANUP.

7 Tench, W, *Sydney's First Four Years*, 1976, Sydney: Library of Australian History, p 146.

8 Curson, P, *Times of Crisis*, 1985, Sydney: Sydney University Press.

There were also dietary changes for those communities brought within the net of white civilisation. Hunter–gatherers, their traditional lands expropriated for sheep and cattle, became mendicants, dependent on a diet of carbohydrates such as flour and sugar and tobacco doled out by missionaries and government agents. In this way, disease and the more general patterns of ill-health joined the destruction of indigenous communities and their culture as the price to be paid for colonising and exploiting the resources of Australia over the past 200 years. There is one extremely telling marker that indicates the size of that price. It is the decline of the indigenous population after 1788. Estimates of the 'pre-European contact' population vary greatly, and they can only be estimated in general terms.[9] Estimates of the pre-1788 population range from the anthropologist Radcliffe-Brown's calculation in 1930 of 300,000 to the economic historian Noel Butlin whose more recent calculation was around a million.[10] If the figure is seen as somewhere over half a million, it went into decline and by 1888 it was estimated at 200,000, by 1921 it was said to be 70,000 (which included people of 'mixed race' – ie with indigenous and non-indigenous parentage)[11] and the view was prevalent that indigenous Australians were a dying race. In 1938, for example, Daisy Bates, the amateur anthropologist who spent much of her life among indigenous Australians, wrote of her experiences in a book she called *The Passing of the Aborigines.* While the decline in population has been arrested (the current population is said to be around 230,000) the picture that it presents is one of the premature mortality of individuals and the decimation of communities as alienation from traditional values and dispossession became widespread. This tragic process has been described in so many regions of Australia whenever competition for water and pasture put traditional interests in conflict with the European interests. The destruction and decline of the indigenous population was not even seen by the policymakers of the time as problematic, but rather as the inevitable price of development.

INDIGENOUS HEALTH TODAY

The burden of ill-health continues: the health of indigenous Australians is far worse today than that of the Australian population overall. The most telling statistic is life expectancy, or the number of years that a child born in any one year can expect to live. Life expectancy rates for Australians are quite high compared with the rest of the world. Males can expect to live for approximately 73 years and females for approximately 80

9 It is one of the profound flaws in our Constitution that the indigenous communities were made invisible by it – they were written out of the document by s 127 which provided that:

> In reckoning the numbers of the people of the Commonwealth ... Aboriginal natives shall not be counted.

It was not changed until the 1967 referendum. In the light of this kind of official thinking it is probably not surprising that the historical data should be so sparse.

10 See the discussion in Dingle, T, *Aboriginal Economy: Patterns of Experience,* 1988, Sydney: McPhee Gribble, pp 21–22.

11 See Vamplew, W, *Australians: Historical Statistics in Australians: a Historical Library,* 1987, Sydney: Fairfax, Syme and Weldon, p 30 and the *Australian Encyclopaedia,* vol 1, 1965, Sydney: Grolier, p 87.

years. These figures broadly compare with life expectancy figures in other developed countries such as in Europe, Japan and North America.[12] However, the life expectancy for indigenous Australians is far lower. Generally an indigenous child can expect to live some 20 years less than a non-indigenous child. Life expectancy for indigenous Australians is higher if they live in urban centres and lower if they live in the country. This is the broadest picture we can take of indigenous health. In practice, indigenous life expectancy is the result of many adverse health outcomes along the age spectrum.

Being born and surviving the first few weeks is a hazard experienced by babies in all communities. We measure the size of this risk as the *infant mortality rate* or the number of deaths that occur within this period compared with every 1,000 live births. In colonial Australia, these rates were extremely high by present standards. Until the turn of the century, it was typical to have over 100 deaths per 1,000, sometimes as high as 130. Variations in the rate were partly explained by epidemics of enteric disease which were prompted by the poor sanitation and hygiene of cities in 19th century Australia. By the first decades of the 20th century, the infant mortality rate began to fall and continued to fall gradually until by the 1980s, it was about 10 deaths per 1,000 births.[13] This tenfold reduction in risk over the century is a testament to the improvements that have been made in Australia to, firstly, public health status in the sense that our environments are healthier and safer, and also to medical services which can respond promptly to birthing complications when they occur.

But, these improvements have not been shared equally among the Australian community. Infant mortality among indigenous Australians is much higher than the general rate. Instead of 10 deaths per 1,000, rates for indigenous communities range from 20 to 30 deaths per 1,000. This reflects both their relative isolation from specialist health services and the problems of their general health. Yet, these figures, high as they are, are substantial improvements on the infant mortality rates of only 30 years ago. In the 1960s infant mortality in indigenous communities in Queensland and the Northern Territory were still around the level of the 19th century, suggesting that they had been completely untouched by any of the progress which European Australians took for granted over this century.

As people progress through life they face risks of disease and death from a variety of causes. When these risks for male Australians are compared with the risks for male indigenous Australians, they also show markedly increased rates for most common causes of death or sickness. For example, indigenous Australians are more than twice as likely as the rest of the community to die of heart disease or stroke; nearly four times more likely to die though injury or poisoning; nearly six times more likely to die of a respiratory disease; eight times more likely to die of a mental disorder and 28 times more likely to die from an infectious or parasitic disease. Similar elevated risks also exist for

12 See Priest K *et al*, *South Australian Health Statistics Chartbook*, 1993, Adelaide: SAHC, p 30.

13 See Vamplew, W, *Australians: Historical Statistics in Australians: A Historical Library*, 1987, Sydney: Fairfax, Syme and Weldon, p 58.

female indigenous Australians.[14] The extent of these over-representations may be debated but they are sufficiently aired in the press (under headlines such as *Outback blacks face 'Fourth World' lifespans*)[15] for Australians to be familiar with them, and seemingly accepting of them.

More particularly, these figures are well known to most students of health studies and to all policymakers. They demonstrate vast differences in health status but they are not simply explained away as the problem of 'being indigenous'. Within the Australian community generally, there are markedly different health outcomes determined by social and occupational status. It is well established that people, whether indigenous or non-indigenous, who are poor or unemployed or who have minimal levels of education are more susceptible to premature death and illness.[16] Indigenous Australians are the extreme of a social gradient that places the greatest burdens of ill-health on the poorest and most powerless members our community.

Some problems: structures and bad responses

Indigenous Australians are generally poor and largely unemployed. In regional areas, paid work is hard to find and the stigma of being 'Aboriginal' compounds the problem. Their communities are often in isolated parts of Australia which present particular difficulties in the provision of running water and safe and efficient methods of disposing of sewage. These are vast structural problems that impact vastly on indigenous health. For example, an ATSIC (Aboriginal and Torres Strait Islanders Commission) survey reported that in 1991, 311 communities had a water supply which does not meet National Health and Medical Research Council Australian health guidelines. Deficiencies in water quality affected nearly 15,000 people. Over 34,000 indigenous Australians experienced a water shortage problem. By comparison, access to clean and reliable water is simply an expected part of almost all urban Australian lives, so much so that we are profligate users of it. In addition to this problem other essentials for good health are also in short supply in the remote communities. Medical services are intermittent and food expensive. For example, in the supermarkets of Cape York, a lettuce is said to cost $4, meat $16 a kilogram and two litres of milk as much as a packet of cigarettes.[17] In these circumstances advice about good nutrition or personal hygiene, however important, is largely pointless.

To these specific problems, we can also add the more general problems of inadequate waste disposal, lack of electricity and remoteness of almost all community services.[18] In so many ways, proper health and services and public health infrastructure

14 See Thomson, N, 'A review of Aboriginal health status', in Reid, J, and Trompf, P, *The Health of Aboriginal Australia*, 1991, Sydney: HBJ, Chapter 2. See also Thomson, N, 'Trends in Aboriginal foetal and infant mortality 1972–1988' (1990) 14 *Aboriginal Health Information Bulletin* 31–37.

15 *Weekend Australian* 24–26 June 1995, p 7.

16 See, for example, McMichael, AJ, 'Social class and mortality in Australian Males 1985' 9 *Community Health Studies*, pp 220–30 and the *South Australian Health Statistics Chartbook*, pp 15–17 (see footnote 11).

17 Nelson, B, 'Once, too, were warriors', *Weekend Australian* 11–12 February 1995, p 25.

18 ATSIC, *Indigenous Australia Today*, 1994, Canberra: ATSIC, pp 10–11.

are simply not being provided to indigenous communities. It has been estimated by one indigenous health group that the cost of remedying the deficient infrastructure throughout indigenous communities is $2.5 billion.[19] Not surprisingly, government funding for these kinds of programmes comes nowhere near this figure. Also, indigenous Australians have not been targeted by the health promotion campaigns aimed at Australians more generally. One example is tobacco consumption which has long been recognised as a potent cause of ill-health in Australia, attributable to some 17,000–20,000 premature deaths per year. Some 25–30% of all Australians smoke but the rate among indigenous Australians is substantially higher than this, amounting to some 50% across the whole population,[20] yet for many years they were not targeted by the anti-smoking campaigns and remained largely invisible despite being the group in most need of these efforts.

In other respects, we wrongly and badly problematise aspects of indigenous ill-health. Alcohol consumption is a case in point; it is the *visible* aspect of indigenous alcohol consumption – in the public parks across Australia – that presents itself most graphically as the 'problem' of indigenous Australians and alcohol and it is reflected in the huge over-representation of indigenous Australians who are detained under the public drunkenness offences or their 'decriminalised' alternatives.[21] Yet, what kind of problem is it? Alcohol consumption in indigenous communities is less than it is in Australia generally. Less than 50% of indigenous Australians drink alcohol more than once a week while nearly 40% describe themselves as non-drinkers.[22] In cases where alcohol is consumed in potentially dangerous circumstances by indigenous Australians it must also be seen against the background circumstances of the drinkers. A number of theories have been offered that attempt to understand the issue of alcohol consumption by indigenous Australians. These are surveyed by Ernest Hunter and include a number of 'ways of seeing' including the argument that alcohol can be understood as a symbol of cohesion or a bond between indigenous drinkers with its own ritualised function, or a response to the displacement of indigenous males from their position of social dominance – by and large more of the social security cheques were made out to women (in the form of supporting mothers' benefits and family allowances) giving women a greater effective power in the communities than males. Alcohol has also been traditionally seen as an example of the powerlessness and anomie experienced by indigenous communities.[23] Whichever model is considered, excessive alcohol consumption is a potent cause of sickness and premature mortality for many indigenous

19 See the entry 'Health policy' in Horton, D (ed), *The Encyclopaedia of Aboriginal Australia*, 1994, Canberra: Aboriginal Studies Press.

20 Australian Bureau of Statistics, *National Aboriginal and Torres Strait Islander Survey 1994*, 1995, Canberra: ABS, p 22.

21 See South Australia Attorney General's Department, *Decriminalising Drunkenness in South Australia (Research Bulletin No 4)* 1986, Adelaide: Government Printer and also (1995) *Australian* 12 April, p 3 'Wiluna sergeant ordered to "clean the streets up"'.

22 Australian Bureau of Statistics, *National Aboriginal and Torres Strait Islander Survey 1994*, 1995, Canberra: ABS, p 13, 38% reported as not having consumed alcohol within the past 12 months.

23 Hunter, E, *Aboriginal Health and History*, 1993, Cambridge: Cambridge University Press, Chapters 5 and 7.

Australians. It is also a cause of poverty, particularly where it is sold at vastly inflated prices. For example, Hunter reports that in the Kimberlys, a bottle of rum 'could fetch as much as $200 around pension day'.[24]

The official response to the 'problem' of indigenous drinking has been to see it more as an issue of public order rather than one of public health. Legislation, which first focussed on prohibition now focuses on 'dry areas' and restrictions on where alcohol can be consumed. The offences of public drunkenness have long focused on indigenous Australians because their drinking was more visible – it occurred in public places such as parks and foreshores – and is seemingly more threatening to the community at large than – for example, a non-indigenous, middle-class picnic or barbecue, where large amounts of alcohol might also be consumed. For whatever reason, we know that indigenous Australians are routinely detained for alcohol-related offences, to such an extent that the policing must be seen as focused on them and appears to be the main official response to the issue. This is not a rational response to the problems of alcohol among the indigenous communities. Dry areas simply shift the 'problem' of indigenous drinking to other areas, while locking up indigenous drinkers exacerbates the issue adding the very significant risk of suicide and further alienation to the risks of the alcohol itself.[25]

What is to be done: what are the important issues?

What are the issues; what needs to be done to turn around the dismal health data that for so long has effected the lives of so many indigenous Australians?

> At a meeting in Darwin last year [1994] to discuss priority areas [in indigenous health] one group put forward land, stress, grief and trauma, dispossession, lifestyle, alcohol and drugs and nutrition. The other put forward cardiovascular disease, cancers, mental health and injury.[26]

It is not difficult to guess which group sought which solution. Traditional Australian health responses focus on particular health issues, in this case, those which are known to be problematic to the indigenous community. While the indigenous group saw the pattern of ill-health as symptomatic of a greater and more profound problem. In this view, specific diseases are the sequels of more fundamental questions such as grief and dispossession and are expressions of communities long under stress. It is difficult, however, to know how to address these issues. It is even more difficult to assert with confidence that they will be addressed in the future.

So, what is to be done? Many things need to be done; there is firstly the basic issue of resources; more money needs to be spent on indigenous health. Indigenous Australians are 1.5% of the Australian community; they are also the 1.5% that has the

24 Hunter, 1993, *op cit*, p 100.

25 The Royal Commission into Aboriginal deaths in custody found that in cases where deaths occurred in police custody, the deceased were three times more likely to have been detained for drunkenness than any other offence. (See the 'Royal Commission into Aboriginal deaths in custody' National Report, vol 1, 1991, Canberra: AGPS.)

26 Forbes, F, 'Live black die hard' *Australian*, 31 March 1995, p 13.

greatest health needs overall. Yet, spending on indigenous health amounts to 1.26% of the total Commonwealth health budget. On these figures, no one can accuse the Commonwealth of throwing money at the problem! Governments can alter their priorities to make the provision of sanitation, adequate housing and proper services, especially in rural areas, a far higher priority than it appears to be at present. Housing is an example; indigenous homelessness and overcrowding is vastly higher than that for non-indigenous Australians. At 1.5% of the population they represent 22% of homeless Australians.[27]

The Australian community has to accept that government spending in this area must be vastly increased but, there is no evidence that it will do this. When asked why, after 11 years of Labour Government, the situation for indigenous Australians was still so bad, the then Minister for Health, Graham Richardson, was said to have responded:[28]

> I have spent a lifetime reading polls, and concern for Aboriginal health and Aboriginal issues was not in the top million things of concern to voters.

For as long as issues such as interest rates and the tax cuts centrally occupy the minds and priorities of mainstream Australia the issues around which indigenous health and welfare sit will not be addressed with the urgency that they warrant.

But, there are broader questions than this: we must recognise that issues such as dispossession of land and destruction of culture are things which are widely recognised by the indigenous communities as issues that are central to indigenous health status. More particularly, the history of dispossession has long been said to powerfully and adversely shape the health and life chances of indigenous communities throughout the world. This view is held with great strength and indigenous voices speak powerfully of the link between land and their health and well-being:

> Next to shooting indigenous people, the surest way to kill us is to separate us from our part of the Earth. Once separated we will either perish in our body or our minds and spirits will be altered so that we end up mimicking foreign ways, adopt foreign languages, accept foreign thoughts ... Over time, we lose our identity and ... eventually die as we are crippled or stuffed under the name of 'assimilation' into another society.[29]

> The land is my mother. Like a human mother, the land gives us protection, enjoyment and provides for our needs – economic, social and religious. We have human relationships with the land: mother – daughter, son. When the land is taken from us or destroyed, we feel hurt because we belong to the land and we are part of it.[30]

These views should be reflected against the World Health Organisation definition of health as 'a state of complete physical, mental and physical well being'. Seen in this light, the history of dispossession was a long-standing and fatal cause of ill-health for so many

27 'Black housing plight bigger than *Mabo*', *Weekend Australian*, 11–12 February 1995, p 6.

28 Nelson, B, 'Once, too, were warriors', *Weekend Australian*, 11–12 February 1995, p 25.

29 Burgess, H, 'World Council of Indigenous Peoples', cited in Burger, J, *The Gaia Atlas of First Peoples*, 1990, Ringwood: Penguin, p 122.

30 Reverend Djiniyini Gondarra cited in Stockton, E, *The Aboriginal Gift: Spirituality for a Nation*, 1995, Sydney: Millennium Books, p 81.

indigenous Australians, expressing itself repeatedly in the mortality data we have been considering. There is therefore every hope that indigenous health will improve when these issues are resolved. Their resolution is in part a legal question, prompted most obviously by the *Mabo* decision, which obliged Australians to take indigenous Australian rights seriously. The case led to the Native Title Act 1993 (Cth) and the creation of the indigenous land corporation and land fund (established as a new Part 4A Aboriginal and Torres Strait Islander Commission Act (Cth)) which will administer a land acquisition fund of some estimated $45 million per annum. These amendments promise substantial changes in indigenous land ownership opportunities.[31]

Land rights and ownership can provide the evidence of a meaningful and genuine reconciliation between indigenous Australians and the Australian community more generally; yet it is one element of a broader coming together of the many communities which comprise the continent and with it an appreciation and genuine valuing of the antiquity of the land and the people who inhabit it. In short, land rights legislation, even if it proves to be relatively unimportant, in terms of the hectares given over or the numbers who benefit, will be extremely important as a powerful gesture in helping to visibly right the wrongs of our colonial past.

The public recognition of past wrongs has been expressed prominently since 1991 with the Council for Aboriginal Reconciliation Act 1991 (Cth) which recognises in its preamble both that Australia was occupied by Aborigines and Torres Strait Islanders who had settled for thousands of years, before British settlement at Sydney Cove on 26 January 1788 and also the subsequent history of dispossession and dispersal. The Act claims that:

> ... as a part of the reconciliation process, the Commonwealth will seek an ongoing national commitment from governments at all levels to co-operate and to ... address progressively Aboriginal disadvantage and aspirations in relation to land, housing, law and justice, cultural heritage, education, employment, health, infrastructure, economic development and any other relevant matters in the decade leading to the centenary of Federation, 2001.

Here is a recognition that land, health, housing, legal status and poverty are related to the process of reconciling past deeds with future hopes. The long-term improvement to all these issues and the issue of indigenous health in particular depends upon the process of reconciliation.

In the short term, the deplorable conditions in which so many indigenous Australians live can be improved. Local communities can take charge of their health, while health promotion campaigns can be tailored and then targeted to an indigenous audience. The urgently needed public health and other infrastructure can be put in place with the investment of many resources and a recognition that these communities also have a right to the things that other Australians take for granted. Mick Dodson, the Aboriginal and Torres Strait Islander Social Justice Commissioner, put the point

31 See Stephenson, MA, *Mabo: The Native Title Legislation*, 1995, St Lucia: University of Queensland Press, p 1.

succinctly when he implied that in one sense, the issues of indigenous health were conceptually simple:

> Either indigenous peoples of this country are entitled to a water supply or they are not. Either indigenous peoples of this country are entitled to housing or they are not. Either indigenous peoples of this country are entitled to determine their own future or they are not.[32]

An indigenous health system

There is also a need, which has been recognised by policymakers, to design a health system that is responsive to indigenous Australians.[33] The first contact many indigenous Australians had with our health system was through the government medical officer, a symbol of the benign face of the colonial administration. His or her presence was taken as evidence of the 'civilising mission' which underpinned the rhetoric of colonisation, and they were often empowered to regulate the lives of indigenous communities in more general ways as the officially appointed 'protectors' of Aborigines.[34] Also, such random and limited interventions into the lives of indigenous Australians, even if they were well motivated, needed to be seen against the repressive measures (also part of the broader picture of colonialism) taken against them by police and squatters, when pastoral expansion became necessary or European property perceived to be under threat. In extreme cases, these measures included massacres, that appear to have occurred in rural communities well into the present century.[35] Even assuming a benign and well-meaning application of 'European medicine' to indigenous Australians, we should understand that our way of approaching questions of health and disease is one of many competing models. The Western system of health care has many flaws, including a focus on high technology interventions (often exploited by those who have a financial or professional stake in the technology) and an emphasis on curing illness as opposed to preventing it. Western medicine generates high costs, brings with it its own range of health problems (not the least of them being the unintended side affects and sickness arising out of these highly complex interventions). Medical anthropologists such as Janice Reid and Robyn Mobbs have written about the type of health-care system that is culturally appropriate for indigenous Australians and the question of placing those services into the broader 'world views' that many of their recipients have. One obvious way of achieving this is to accept that indigenous Australians should be in control of

32 Forbes, F, 'Live Black Die Hard', *Australian*, 31 March 1995, p 13.

33 See the discussion in Reid, J, and Dhamarrandji, B, 'Curing not Caring: Why Aboriginal Patients "Abscond"' (1978) 8 *New Doctor*, pp 27–32.

34 See Mobbs, R, in Reid, J, and Trompf, P, *op cit*, 1991, p 315. Also see Marcus, A, *Governing Savages*, 1990, Sydney: Allen and Unwin, esp Chapter 6: an account of the work of Dr Cecil Cook, the chief protector of Aboriginals and chief medical officer for the Northern Territory earlier this century.

35 See, for example, Green, N, *The Forest River Massacres*, 1995, Fremantle: Fremantle Arts Press. This describes a mass killing in 1926 of a large number (perhaps hundreds) of local Aborigines by police and stockmen in the Kimberly region of North West Australia.

their own health services, while ensuring that those services are sufficiently well funded to be effective.[36] Yet, the crisis in indigenous health has prompted bureaucratic crises about this issue and in 1995, the Federal Cabinet was divided over whether programmes should continue to be managed through ATSIC or through the Commonwealth Department of Health. It may be that a technically more efficient delivery of services can be achieved through the latter but this risks being at the expense of self-determination and the 'ownership' of the problem by indigenous communities. Most significantly though, in the absence of adequate funding, the debate about who delivers the services will appear to be rather pointless.

CONCLUSION

The tragedy of indigenous health is to be found easily enough in the statistics; the greater tragedy is that we have become so accepting of them. Intervention *at all levels* is required: at the level of infrastructure and at the level of more available health services. This costs money and the Australian community must recognise its obligation to fund these programmes. This takes us to the last and the most important, also the most fundamental, level; strategies for indigenous health must proceed with the willingness of the community and the acceptance that it must be sustained by a meaningful process of reconciliation. With that acceptance comes an understanding of the wrongs of the past, the willingness to put more of our limited resources into a range of issues such as health (with the trade-offs and anxieties that this will provoke) and the willingness to address the wider questions that so much indigenous ill-health is prompted by. This is where the other issues addressed in this book and the more focused question of indigenous health sit together. The bleak over-representation of indigenous Australians in our criminal justice and custodial systems and their equally bleak over-representation in the ill-health data have the same antecedents, and it is these that must be addressed if real progress is to be made in either direction.

36 See Mobbs, R, 'In sickness and health: the socio-cultural context of Aboriginal well-being, illness and healing', in Reid, J, and Trompf, P, 1991, *op cit*, Chapter 7.

CHAPTER FIVE

INTELLECTUAL PROPERTY AND THE DREAMING

Jill McKeough and Andrew Stewart

In recent years considerable attention has been focused on the significance of land to indigenous communities, and on their claims to assert some form of title or control over areas with which they have (or once had before forcible dispossession) a particular attachment. Wide publicity has also been given to attempts by such groups to reclaim relics or other sacred artefacts from museums and private collectors. It is easy, however, to overlook the fact that much of the most important and enduring Aboriginal heritage is intangible.[1] This cultural heritage takes many different forms. It includes images or 'dreamings' which depict events from an ancestral past or Dreamtime, preserved in tribal lore and periodically recreated in artwork of various kinds (cave paintings, bark paintings, sand sculptures, facial and body painting etc). It also includes each community's oral history, the details of certain rituals and ceremonies, the music and dance sequences used at gatherings, and even knowledge of the natural environment inhabited by the community.

This heritage or 'folklore' is an integral and enduring part of Aboriginal society, as Puri notes:[2]

> For Aboriginal people, folklore performs several important social functions. It helps them to release cultural tensions and ambivalences, and it provides amusement and education. It is a sort of 'social cement' that exists outside the formal or official structures. It strengthens social cohesiveness, raises the quality of life and assists in the development and articulation of cultural identity. Aboriginal people use folklore to reflect the past and make improvements for their future. Folklore gives them a chance for creative self-expression through music, song, dance, speech, and many other avenues. Such cultural manifestations create an invisible bond among individuals and groups and forge social and spiritual contact.

The significance of this intangible heritage is further reflected in its treatment under Aboriginal customary laws. In most communities there are strict controls on the use of certain images or on the revelation of particular information.[3] The nature of such controls is explained in this extract from the judgment of von Doussa J in *Milpurrurru v Indofurn Pty Ltd*,[4] a case discussed in some detail later on in the chapter:

> The evidence led at trial, including the evidence of an Aboriginal artist, Mr Bruce Wangurra, called by the respondents, explained the importance of the creation stories

1 Note that for convenience the term 'Aboriginal' is generally used in this chapter to refer both to Aboriginal peoples and to Torres Strait Islanders.

2 Puri, K, 'Cultural Ownership and Intellectual Property Rights Post *Mabo*: Putting Ideas into Action' (1995) 9 *Intellectual Property Journal* 295 at 300.

3 This is not at all unusual in indigenous cultures: see Suchman, MC, 'Invention and Ritual: Notes on the Interrelation of Magic and Intellectual Property in Preliterate Societies' (1989) 89 *Columbia Law Review* 1264.

4 (1994) 30 IPR 209 at 214–15.

> and dreamings in the cultures of the clans to which they relate. Those stories are represented in ceremonies of deep significance, and are often secret or sacred, known only to a few senior members of the clan chosen according to age, descendence, sex, initiation, experience in the learning of the dreamings and ceremonies, and the attainment of skills which permit the faithful reproduction of the stories in accordance with Aboriginal law and custom. Painting techniques and the use of totemic and other images and symbols are in many instances, and almost invariably in the case of important creation stories, strictly controlled by Aboriginal law and custom. Artworks are an important means of recording these stories, and for teaching future generations. Accuracy in the portrayal of the story is of great importance. Inaccuracy, or error in the faithful reproduction of an artwork, can cause deep offence to those familiar with the Dreaming.
>
> The right to create paintings and other artworks depicting creation and Dreaming stories, and to use pre-existing designs and well-recognised totems of the clan, resides in the traditional owners (or custodians) of the stories or images. Usually that right will not be with only one person, but with a group of people who together have the authority to determine whether the story and images may be used in an artwork, by whom the artwork may be created, to whom it may be published, and the terms, if any, on which the artwork may be reproduced.
>
> ... If unauthorised reproduction of a story or imagery occurs, under Aboriginal law it is the responsibility of the traditional owners to take action to preserve the dreaming, and to punish those considered responsible for the breach. Notions of responsibility under Aboriginal law differ from those of the English common law. If permission has been given by the traditional owners to a particular artist to create a picture of the dreaming, and that artwork is later inappropriately used or reproduced by a third party, the artist is held responsible for the breach which has occurred, even if the artist had no control over, or knowledge of, what occurred.
>
> ... In times past the 'offender' could be put to death. Now other forms of punishment are more likely such as preclusion from the right to participate in ceremonies, removal of the right to reproduce paintings of that or any other story of the clan, being outcast from the community, or being required to make a payment of money; but the possibility of spearing was mentioned by Mr Wangurra as a continuing sanction in serious cases.

While the primary interest of Aboriginal communities in the preservation and control of their cultural heritage has always been grounded in deeply rooted spiritual considerations that are inextricably linked to the very fabric of their society there is today an economic dimension to this issue that cannot be ignored. Over the past few decades there has been an explosion of interest in Aboriginal art on the part of non-indigenous Australians, tourists and international art collectors.[5] This has created incentives for increased production and dissemination of Aboriginal art, and has thereby offered significant benefits to the artists and their communities:[6]

5 In 1993, for instance, a survey of international visitors to Australia indicated that 48% were interested in Aboriginal art and culture, and that these visitors spent an estimated $46 million a year on Aboriginal arts and souvenirs: see Robb, J, 'International Visitors and Aboriginal Art' [1993] 6 *Arts and Entertainment Law Review* 18.

6 Department of Aboriginal Affairs, *The Aboriginal Arts and Craft Industry*, 1989, Canberra: AGPS, pp 286–87.

> The development of informed market interest in Aboriginal art has been, and continues to be, to the advantage of Aboriginal people. There is clear evidence in remote communities that only where there is access to adequate markets will significant production of art and craft be maintained. In these areas, market participation assists in the reproduction of culture. These are also the regions, of course, where distinctly Aboriginal religious systems are maintained. Art also provides an important source of cash income that is independent of the public sector and a vehicle for the expression of Aboriginal cultural values to the wider community.

At the same time, however, the growth of the market for Aboriginal art has created problems as well as opportunities. Unauthorised imitation of such art has become a major issue, with concern emerging not only in relation to the amount of direct copying of works, but also the 'borrowing' of Aboriginal themes, images or styles. Sometimes this imitation can be traced to urban or rural Aboriginal artists working outside the framework of the community to whom the images in question 'belong' and who do not regard themselves as bound by that community's restrictions (if they are aware of them); sometimes to artists (indigenous or non-indigenous) who incorporate traditional motifs into their work in the classic Western art tradition of 'informed quotation';[7] but more often, simply to businesses who see a way of making a buck out of the appetite for indigenous art. In other instances, the problem may not be one of imitation as such, but of culturally insensitive use of work otherwise acquired with the consent of the relevant community, or of use without proper acknowledgment.

In seeking to prevent such abuses, indigenous people may be motivated by one or both of two distinct concerns. The first is purely financial: to secure fair payment for the use of work emanating from within the community. The second is much broader and reflects the desire to preserve spiritual and cultural integrity, especially where sacred images are involved. This concern also underlies more long-standing complaints as to the recording and publication by anthropologists or other researchers of tribal lore whose circulation is meant to be strictly limited. It has been said by indigenous people that the spiritual dimension is more important than the economic:[8]

> We Aboriginals are a religious people. We did not have many material goods. We were rich in spiritual goods. We were rich in ceremony, in law, in legend.

According to Article 29 of the Draft Declaration on the Rights of Indigenous People, prepared by the United Nations Working Group on Indigenous Populations, 'indigenous peoples are entitled to the full ownership control and protection of their cultural and intellectual property'. Article 12 adds that:

> Indigenous peoples have the right to practise and revitalise their cultural traditions and customs. This includes the right to maintain, protect and develop the past, present and future manifestations of their cultures, such as archaeological and historical sites, artefacts, designs, ceremonies, technologies and visual and performing arts and literature, as well as

7 *Ibid* at 293–94.

8 Select Committee of the Legislative Assembly, Parliament of NSW, *Aboriginal Land Rights and Sacred and Significant Sites* (1980), p 55.

> the right to restitution of cultural, intellectual, religious and spiritual property taken without their free and informed consent or in violation of their laws, traditions and customs.

The purpose of this chapter is to consider whether the regimes that presently exist under non-indigenous Australian law to protect such property meet these objectives, and if they do not, what might be done to remedy any deficiencies in those regimes.

INTELLECTUAL PROPERTY UNDER AUSTRALIAN LAW

'Intellectual property' is a generic term. It describes the different kinds of property rights which may be accorded to the fruits of 'intellectual activity in the industrial, scientific, literary or artistic fields'.[9] Just as it is possible to own land or furniture or clothes or any other tangible item, so it is also possible to 'own' an idea or a literary or artistic creation. In such cases, ownership means being able to prevent others from using or copying the idea or creation without permission. By conferring property rights the law encourages creativity and innovation or at least investment in the commercial exploitation of creativity and innovation. Even without intellectual property laws, it is likely that individuals would still write or invent. But who would publish writings (and even pay writers for the privilege), if competitors could simply wait for the published version to appear and distribute their own copies? Who would invest in the development of an invention, if competitors were free to 'reverse engineer' products to figure out how they were made and make their own use of that knowledge without incurring all the research and development costs?

The case for intellectual property laws is essentially therefore based on economic considerations, rather than more idealistic notions of creators having a natural entitlement to the fruits of their labours.[10] At the international level, this is reinforced by the recent moves to encourage all countries, but especially the 'developing' nations, to adopt laws which provide 'appropriate' levels of protection for intellectual property. These moves have culminated in the Trade-Related Aspects of Intellectual Property Rights (TRIPS) Agreement, adopted as part of the Uruguay Round of the General Agreement on Tariffs and Trade (GATT).[11] The agenda underlying this agreement is to 'free up' world trade by encouraging companies (especially American firms) to feel that they can market their products in developing countries without the fear that local 'pirates' will compete by marketing illicit copies.

9 Convention Establishing the World Intellectual Property Organisation (1967), Art 2(viii). The World Intellectual Property Organisation (WIPO) is a United Nations agency whose functions include the promotion of international co-operation in the administration and indeed harmonisation of intellectual property laws.

10 See McKeough, J, and Stewart, A, 1991, Sydney: Butterworths, *Intellectual Property in Australia*, pp 12–17.

11 See Arup, CJ, 'The Prospective GATT Agreement for Intellectual Property Protection' (1993) 3 *Australian Intellectual Property Journal* 181; Polson, G, *Uruguay Round Outcomes,* 1994, Canberra: Services and Intellectual Property Branch, Trade Negotiations and Organisations Division, Department of Foreign Affairs and Trade. For a critical look at the impact of TRIPS on indigenous peoples and developing countries, see Gana, RL, 'Has Creativity Died in the Third World? Some Implications of the Internationalisation of Intellectual Property' (1995) 24 *Denver Journal of International Law and Policy* 109.

In Australia, protection for intellectual property is provided by a series of discrete legal regimes, each with their own history and peculiarities. There is no general principle which prevents 'unfair copying' or 'unfair competition', as in some other countries.[12] Most of the current Australian regimes are to be found in federal legislation, enacted by the Commonwealth using its constitutional powers over 'copyrights, patents of inventions and designs, and trademarks' (s 51(xviii) constitution) and 'external affairs' (s 51(xxix), which permits the implementation of treaty obligations). The main regimes are as follows.[13]

Copyright

The Copyright Act 1968 (63) (Cth) protects the expression in material form of ideas or information – though it does not protect ideas or information as such.[14] Copyright automatically arises when a person exercises originality in creating a literary, dramatic, musical or artistic work. The work need not possess aesthetic qualities, therefore everything from accounting forms to frisbees are protected. This includes computer software, designated as 'literary works' as a result of 1984 amendments. Similarly, the author need only have exercised a slight degree of skill and effort in creating the work for it to be original. Besides the category of 'works', copyright also subsists in four forms in which works are commonly exploited: sound recordings, films, television and sound broadcasts, and published editions.

Copyright is infringed whenever the work or subject matter is reproduced, published, broadcast, sold, imported, etc without the copyright owner's consent. However, an independent creation of the same work or matter will not infringe. As with other forms of intellectual property, the remedies available in the case of infringement may include an injunction to restrain the offending conduct, and/or damages to compensate for any loss suffered. Criminal penalties may also apply. As far as works are concerned, copyright generally subsists until the expiration of 50 years after the author's death (or after first publication, if this occurs posthumously).

Patents

A patent provides the exclusive right to exploit an invention for a limited period, in return for which the patentee must publish details of the invention. To obtain a patent under the Patents Act 1990 (83) (Cth) an application must be made to the Patent Office which fully describes the invention. A standard patent subsists for 20 years. A petty patent, which is cheaper and quicker to obtain and which is designed for gadgets and

12 *Victoria Park Racing and Recreation Grounds Co Ltd v Taylor* (1937) 58 CLR 479; *Moorgate Tobacco Co Ltd v Philip Morris Ltd (No 2)* (1984) 156 CLR 414. *Cf* Ricketson, S, '"Reaping Without Sowing": Unfair Competition and Intellectual Property Rights in Anglo-Australian Law' (1984) 7 *University of New South Wales Law Journal* 1.

13 The summaries of the statutory regimes are adapted from McKeough and Stewart, *op cit*, at footnote 10, pp 6–7.

14 So if you were to photocopy this chapter without permission, you might be infringing copyright; whereas if you read it and took notes, extracting the ideas and information from it and using your own words to express them, there would be no infringement.

appliances with a relatively short life in terms of commercial exploitation, may subsist for up to six years. In order to be patentable, an invention must be a useful product or process which is both 'novel', in the sense that its creation has not been anticipated by others, and 'inventive', in the sense that it is not merely an obvious advance in light of existing knowledge.[15]

Designs

The Designs Act 1906 (4) (Cth) establishes a system for the registration of new or original designs for the visual presentation of commercial products. The design monopoly may last for up to 16 years. Since designs are typically derived from artistic works, important issues arise as to the interrelationship of design and copyright protection, as discussed later on.[16]

Trade marks

Trade marks are marks (including logos, labels, names etc) which indicate that goods or services originate from a particular trader. When registered under the Trade Marks Act 1995 (119) (Cth),[17] the proprietor is entitled to restrain the use of unregistered marks which are substantially identical or deceptively similar. However, in order to obtain and maintain registration, the mark must normally be used in such a way that it becomes and remains distinctive of the proprietor's business.

Performers' rights

Performers' rights, although contained in Part XIA of the Copyright Act 1968, were in fact introduced in 1989 because live dramatic and musical performances do not attract copyright, not being fixed in a material form. The rights involved are more limited than copyright, merely allowing performers to restrain or take action against any unauthorised broadcast or recording of their performance.

Breach of confidence

Apart from these statutory systems, two common law doctrines also play an important role in protecting intellectual property. The first of these is the action for breach of confidence, which permits knowledge to be safeguarded solely on the basis that it has not yet moved into the public domain. Where X possesses information which is at least relatively secret (in the sense that it is known to only a limited number of people and is not readily accessible to the public), and communicates it on a confidential basis to Y, X

15 Note that new plant varieties, which for one reason or another may not be patentable, are the subject of a separate regime established by the Plant Breeder's Rights Act 1994 (110) (Cth). On registration, breeders obtain exclusive rights over their varieties for a period of 20 years (25 in the case of trees and vines).

16 *Op cit*, text preceding footnote 64.

17 This Act took effect on 1 January 1996, replacing the Trade Marks Act 1955 (20) (Cth).

may sue if Y uses or discloses the information without X's consent. The same kind of action may also be brought if Y simply steals X's information without there being any confidential communication between them. Furthermore, in both instances X may take action not only against Y, but against any third party into whose possession the information comes as a result of Y's conduct. The action for breach of confidence is available in relation to any kind of information, whether commercial, governmental or purely personal in nature.

Passing off and misleading or deceptive conduct

A second common law action that is relevant in this context is the tort of passing off. This allows the integrity of the connection between a business and its customers to be protected in a way that backs up and even extends the statutory protection given to trade marks. Passing off occurs when Y deceives a section of the public into believing that there is some sort of business connection between Y and X, thereby damaging the goodwill or business reputation built up by X. For example, consumers may be misled into acquiring Y's goods or services, thinking they are X's, or that they share some essential characteristics with X's goods or services. Or the passing off may consist in a misrepresentation that X (who might for instance be a celebrity) has endorsed Y's product.

Most conduct that amounts to passing off also constitutes misleading or deceptive conduct in trade or commerce. Such conduct is prohibited by s 52 of the Trade Practices Act 1974 (51) (Cth) and also by the various State and Territory fair trading statutes, which cover those situations in which the Federal Act is inapplicable for constitutional reasons.[18] It is increasingly common for plaintiffs to sue under the trade practices or fair trading legislation instead of (or as well as) in passing off, given the greater range of remedies provided by the statutes.

INDIGENOUS CULTURE AND INTELLECTUAL PROPERTY

The remainder of this chapter is concerned with the potential for these intellectual property laws to be used to protect indigenous art and cultural heritage. The principal focus is on the law of copyright, which has been invoked in a number of recent court actions. However something will also be said about the use of other intellectual property regimes.

COPYRIGHT IN INDIGENOUS ART AND FOLKLORE

Copyright law can be and has been used by Aboriginal artists to take legal action against those who misappropriate their work. A good example is provided by the well-publicised action brought by John Bulun Bulun, one of the best known of all Aboriginal artists, in relation to the unauthorised reproduction of two of his paintings on

18 See Fair Trading Act 1992 (ACT), s 12; Fair Trading Act 1987 (NSW), s 42; Consumer Affairs and Fair Trading Act 1990 (NT), s 42; Fair Trading Act 1989 (Qld), s 38; Fair Trading Act 1987 (SA), s 56; Fair Trading Act 1990 (Tas), s 14; Fair Trading Act 1985 (Vic), s 11; Fair Trading Act 1987 (WA), s 10.

commercially manufactured T-shirts.[19] When he sued the manufacturers and two Darwin retailers for infringement of copyright and breach of the Trade Practices Act 1974, the defendants were forced to give undertakings to the court agreeing to cease making and selling the shirts. A further 14 artists then brought similar actions against the manufacturers and other retailers. All these actions were settled out of court, with the defendants agreeing to deliver up the offending garments and to pay compensation totalling around $150,000.

However copyright is far from an ideal vehicle for the legal protection of Aboriginal art and folklore. There are a number of reasons for this, as discussed in the sections which follow:

- copyright may not subsist at all in certain forms of indigenous culture;
- where it does subsist, it may vest (arguably inappropriately) in non-indigenous collators;
- even if copyright vests in indigenous creators, this may be contrary to (or at least not entirely consonant with) the law of the relevant community;
- there may be practical problems in exploiting the economic rights conferred by copyright law; and
- copyright may help to generate or protect income, but it may not suffice to protect the integrity of indigenous artwork.

Subsistence of copyright

It is clear that not all forms of Aboriginal art and folklore attract copyright under the Copyright Act 1968. Four main problems, or at least potential problems, can be identified.

The first is the requirement in s 32 that a work be 'original'. It has sometimes been suggested that where an artist has reproduced a traditional (or 'pre-existing') design or story, this requirement may be lacking.[20] On the other hand, it has also been said of the transmission of themes through artwork that:[21]

> Transmission requires creative reinterpretation of themes by individual artists. Evidently, nowhere is an Aboriginal artist merely an automaton. Nor are new themes completely ruled out. Inevitably, changes occur in depicting the same stories in various artistic forms. These changes often are imbued by each artist's individuality, hence giving the work its 'originality' in the copyright sense.

This view is born out by recent cases in which copyright has been successfully invoked by artists who have reproduced traditional designs. In *Yumbulul v Reserve Bank of*

19 For a detailed description of the litigation, see Golvan, C, 'Aboriginal Art and Copyright: The Case for Johnny Bulun Bulun' [1989] 10 *European Intellectual Property Review* 346.

20 See eg *Report of the Working Party on the Protection of Aboriginal Folklore*, 1981, Canberra: Department of Home Affairs and the Environment, para 1402.

21 Puri, *op cit*, at 314, citing *Report of the Working Party on the Protection of Aboriginal Folklore, ibid*, para 505.

Australia Ltd,[22] a case discussed later in the chapter, it appears that the originality of the work in question was in effect presumed from the artist's standing and the critical acclaim of his work, while in *Milpurrurru v Indofurn Pty Ltd*,[23] also discussed later on, the point was ultimately conceded by the defendants.[24]

The second problem relates to the duration of copyright. The 50-year period of protection for works (dated from the death of the creator or from first publication, whichever comes later) may be inappropriate when applied to indigenous culture. Material that remains unpublished may retain indefinite copyright protection, but the performance of dances in public or the dissemination of Aboriginal culture in the form of music, books, films or broadcasts means that attempts to promote greater understanding to a wider Australian or world community will 'start the clock ticking' to loss of protection. Limited periods of protection are of little use where cultural information, particularly of a sacred nature, is concerned, as the significance of such works will presumably be just as great at the end of the copyright period as at the beginning.[25]

Thirdly, it may be very difficult in some cases to identify the 'author' of a work created within an indigenous community. This is most obviously a problem where the work is very old (such as a cave painting) and no records survive of the original creator. But it may also arise with more modern works which are collaborative in nature, especially if the person whom the community would identify as the 'author' (if anyone) has played little role in the physical creation of the work but merely supplied the ideas, inspiration or instruction.[26] The concept of 'authorship' is crucial to the operation of the Copyright Act in a number of ways. For example, an unpublished work only attracts copyright under s 32 if the author is a 'qualified person' (this includes Australian citizens and residents). More importantly, the principles in s 35 determining ownership of copyright (and therefore the right to sue for infringement or to license others to use the relevant work) all depend on there being an ascertainable author, who is taken to be the first owner unless there is agreement to the contrary or the work is created in the course of employment. If there is no author, there can be no copyright. (Of course even if the 'author' of a work of indigenous art can be identified, this may not at all be consonant with the Aboriginal tradition of collective 'ownership', a point taken up further below.)

Fourthly, it is settled that copyright only attaches to the expression of ideas, not to the ideas themselves.[27] This expression must be fixed in writing or in some other

22 (1991) 21 IPR 481 at 484.

23 (1994) 30 IPR 209 at 216.

24 See also the evidence as to originality presented in the *Bulun Bulun* case: see Golvan, *op cit*, footnote 19 at 349–51.

25 See Weiner, JG, 'Protection of Folklore: A Political and Legal Challenge' (1987) 18 *International Review of Intellectual Property and Copyright Law* 90.

26 As to the difficulties posed by this practice for art dealers in the commercial market, steeped as they are in Western traditions of 'authenticity', see McCulloch, S, 'Authentic Forgery: The Faking of Aboriginal Art', *Weekend Australian*, 7–8 October 1995, 'Review', p 1.

27 *Autodesk Inc v Dyason* (1992) 173 CLR 330 at 344–45.

'material form'.[28] Many forms of indigenous culture do not satisfy that requirement. For example, stories which are never reduced to writing or kept in any tangible record, music and dance which are similarly preserved only by oral tradition, and ephemeral forms of art such as sand sculptures and facial or body paintings.[29]

Collation of works not previously fixed in material form

The requirement of 'material form' may cause difficulties even where it is satisfied. Suppose, for example, that a person collates the oral histories of a community by interviewing some of its members. If the information is written down, both the collator's notes and any subsequent compilation will attract copyright as literary works. If the interview is recorded on cassette or videotape that too will be subject to copyright as a sound-recording or a film. The problem is that unless the collator has been acting solely at the direction of the persons being interviewed or of the community, it is the collator who will own the copyright as the 'author' or 'maker' (ie the one responsible for putting the work into material form).[30] If the collator is an anthropologist, or some other kind of researcher, or indeed anyone who is not a member of the community, the result is that the right to publish or control the dissemination of the work (at least as expressed in that particular way) will have passed outside the control of the community. The same problem may obviously occur where musical or dance performances are recorded. Again, unless this is done at the behest of the community, any copyright will go to the person or organisation responsible for the recording. However, if the recording is unauthorised it may also breach the performers' rights provisions in Part XIA of the Copyright Act.

Customary law and community rights

The copyright system, like almost every other kind of property law brought to Australia by white colonists, is premised on individual ownership and individual rights. As such it sits uneasily with the treatment of artwork and other forms of cultural heritage by the laws of indigenous communities themselves. For many Aborigines, property rights are essentially collective and managed on a custodial basis according to tradition. Under customary law, as we have already seen in the earlier extract from the *Milpurrurru* case,[31] in a community only certain individuals are permitted to depict certain designs. The fact that an artist has been permitted to depict a design does not mean that what is produced is 'owned' by that person. Unfortunately, copyright law does not easily recognise a

28 This is certainly so where unpublished works are concerned (s 22), and for published works is implicit in the way the concept of 'publication' is fleshed out in s 29: see McKeough and Stewart, *op cit*, pp 103–04.

29 *Cf Merchandising Corp of America Inc v Harpbond Ltd* [1983] FSR 32, where pop singer Adam Ant's distinctive (if highly derivative) facial makeup was held not to constitute an artistic work.

30 *Cf Donoghue v Allied Newspapers Ltd* [1938] Ch 106.

31 *Op cit.*

division of rights in this way. As already explained, the owner of copyright under the Copyright Act 1968 is usually the 'author' of the work, or someone to whom the author has agreed to transfer their rights. That owner is assumed to have absolute rights over the work, except to the extent that they fetter themselves by contract (for instance by granting someone else a licence to reproduce or publish the work).

The tension between the copyright system and customary law on this point is perfectly illustrated by *Yumbulul v Reserve Bank of Australia Ltd.*[32] The case revolved around a 'morning star pole' made by Terry Yumbulul, an artist from north-east Arnhem Land. Morning star poles are decorated wooden poles which play an important role in various Aboriginal ceremonies and differ from group to group. They are made in secret and their 'identifying attributes' are jealously guarded. This does not necessarily prevent them being displayed in a public museum and, indeed, some are specifically made for this purpose, as French J explained:[33]

> Aboriginal people often believe that it does not matter if some such designs or objects are revealed to non-Aboriginal people because they will not know their meanings ... It is regarded as important that white people learn to respect the Aboriginal people and their land.

On the other hand, any publication must be handled with care, and is in all cases subject to the approval of those in the relevant clan charged with the responsibility of managing the rights to the pole. The judge heard evidence that:

> the subject of mass production of paintings and important objects is very sensitive because it takes the ability and right to produce and supervise the production of these objects out of the hands of the Aboriginal people.[34]

The case arose when the Reserve Bank reproduced on the 1988 plastic commemorative $10 note (commemorating 200 years of white settlement in Australia) the design of Yumbulul's morning star pole. Yumbulul sued, among other things, for infringement of copyright. French J accepted without question that the pole was an original artistic work within the meaning of the Copyright Act and that Yumbulul was its author. The bank had, however, obtained a licence from Yumbulul to reproduce the design. The licence had been secured through the medium of the Aboriginal Arts Agency Ltd, a company originally established under the auspices of what is now the Australia Council to market Aboriginal artworks. French J rejected the plaintiff's argument that the licence had been procured by misleading or deceptive conduct on the part of a director of the agency. Accordingly the plaintiff's case against the agency failed, his action against the bank having already been settled. The key point about this case is that it was treated as irrelevant that the plaintiff might not have been acting in accordance with customary law. As the judge put it:[35]

32 (1991) 21 IPR 481.

33 *Ibid* at 483. See also *Milpurrurru v Indofurn Pty Ltd* (1994) 30 IPR 209 at 213.

34 (1991) 21 IPR 481 at 483, referring to evidence given by Roy Marika, the senior male member of the Rirratjingu clan.

35 *Ibid* at 490.

> There was evidence that Mr Yumbulul came under considerable criticism from within the Aboriginal community for permitting the reproduction of the pole by the bank. It may well be that when he executed the agreement he did not fully appreciate the implications of what he was doing in terms of his own cultural obligations ... And it may also be that Australia's copyright law does not provide adequate recognition of Aboriginal community claims to regulate the reproduction and use of works which are essentially communal in origin. But to say this is not to say that there has been established in the case any cause of action.

In other words, the position under customary law simply did not matter: Yumbulul had given his permission, as the individual copyright owner, and that was all that counted.

This point was reiterated by von Doussa J in a more recent decision, *Milpurrurru v Indofurn Pty Ltd*:[36]

> In the event of an established infringement, the Copyright Act relevantly provides remedies to the copyright owner. The statutory remedies do not recognise the infringement of ownership rights which reside under Aboriginal law in the traditional owners of the Dreaming stories and the imagery such as that used in the artworks of the present applicants.

Nevertheless, the judge was prepared in this case to adopt a flexible approach which sought to interpret and apply copyright law in a way culturally sensitive to customary law, if not to give effect to that law as such. In particular, he sanctioned a global award of damages for breach of copyright which permitted the various applicants to determine the distribution of the money, thus providing scope for accommodating recognition of communal rights. The damages also included an element of compensation for cultural harm resulting from copyright infringement.

The case involved the work of eight Aboriginal artists whose work had been exhibited in state and national collections of Australian art and who possessed widespread reputations as exceptional artists. Five of the artists were deceased and were represented in these proceedings by the public trustee of the Northern Territory. In accordance with Aboriginal custom their names were not spoken during the trial. Of all the artists involved, George Milpurrurru was perhaps the most famous as his work was the subject of the Australian National Gallery's first solo exhibition of an Aboriginal artist. The works in question were bark paintings, a lino cut and 'Papunya' style paintings in acrylic on canvas. The works had been used in various ways with the approval of the artists and others in their communities whose permission was required. One of Milpurrurru's paintings, 'Goose Egg Hunt', was adopted as a stamp design in 1993, the International Year of the World's Indigenous People. The Australian National Gallery and the Australian Information Service had produced calendars and portfolios including the various artworks. These had been on sale through museum shops and other selected venues.

As explained earlier, the creation stories and dreamings represented by the works were important to the clans to which they related. Under customary law, the right to

36 (1994) 30 IPR 209 at 239.

create and use such paintings and artworks resides in the traditional owners or custodians of the stories or images, and has serious consequences for the particular artist if a third party uses or reproduces work without permission. As one of the applicants, Banduk Marika, explained:[37]

> As an artist, while I may own the copyright in a particular artwork under Western law, under Aboriginal law I must not use an image or story in such a way as to undermine the rights of all the other Yolngu (her clan) who have an interest whether direct or indirect in it. In this way I hold the image on trust for all the other Yolngu with an interest in the story.

As in *Yumbulul,* the work of this artist had been reproduced by permission of the community for educational purposes and display in art galleries to foster a greater awareness of Aboriginal culture.

Against this background the respondents, a Mr Bethune, his company Beechrow (now known as Indofurn) and two of its directors, did something which any artist would regard as being in appalling taste. They arranged to have the artworks reproduced as designs on carpets. Worse still, some of the artworks were regarded by Bethune as 'too busy' and he requested modified versions of them to be woven into carpets and wall hangings. The carpets were commissioned in Vietnam from a carpet factory owned by business associates of his. The factory was already producing some Aboriginal artworks on carpets and, impressed with these, Bethune decided to order some samples to bring back to Australia to test the local market. He became aware through comments from friends that there were copyright issues to be addressed and began to investigate means of obtaining permission to reproduce the artworks and import the carpets into Australia. A letter was sent with an advance on royalties to the Aboriginal Arts Management Association (AAMA), another body established by the Australia Council to provide advice to Aboriginal artists on copyright matters. The letter was incorrectly addressed and did not arrive. Ownership and other intellectual property matters were overlooked under the business pressure experienced by Bethune and his wife in organising to import the carpets, and eventually when they went on sale in New South Wales the artists became aware of their existence. Despite being informed that the artists did not approve of the sale and promotion of the Aboriginal design carpets, Bethune continued to import and offer them for sale.

The elements of copyright infringement were easily established. The circumstances of the creation of the works made it clear that copyright subsisted in them. The respondents imported the carpets containing the protected works in breach of s 37 of the Copyright Act 1968 which prohibits importing or selling material known to be likely to infringe copyright.[38] Although some of the works had been altered, it was held that a substantial part of them had been reproduced in the carpets and therefore that copyright

37 *Ibid* at 215.

38 As to the liability of the other directors of Beechrow, see *ibid* at 232–36. Those directors successfully appealed against the finding that they were responsible for the infringement: *King v Milpurrurru* (1996) 34 IPR 11. However, the appeal did not involve any challenge to the aspects of the first instance decision discussed below.

was still being infringed. In awarding damages von Doussa J accepted that it would be inappropriate to apply the well-established principle in copyright law of awarding separate judgment in favour of each applicant, assessed as to individual loss and damage, where Aboriginal law and custom would treat each of the applicants in the case equally. He agreed that the respondents' liability, although assessed according to the usual rules, should be aggregated and judgment would be awarded to the applicants as a group. This would permit any damages to be distributed not only to the applicants, but to 'those traditional owners who have legitimate entitlements according to Aboriginal law'.[39]

Remedies under the Copyright Act are in any event fairly flexible. On this occasion the judge awarded damages under three categories. Section 116 of the Copyright Act allows for conversion damages, ie the infringer must pay the copyright owner an amount representing the value of the infringing copy (or copies) as if the copyright owner had actually owned the items themselves and they had been stolen by the infringer. The conversion damages were assessed at an average cost, as if the carpets were worth $190.00 per square metre. This came to $90,981.50. This was in addition to damages under s 115(2), which permits compensation for loss of value of the copyright, in this case assessed with reference to the loss of value resulting from the degradation of the artwork and the resulting commercial use to which it had been put by Bethune and Beechrow. These damages were assessed at $1,500.00 in respect of each artwork.

Damages awarded under s 115(2) are usually assessed with reference to monetary loss, but may include compensation for anger, distress or personal suffering caused by the copyright infringement, not just on the part of the copyright owner but of 'those around' them.[40] Importantly, von Doussa J accepted that the 'personal and cultural hurt' suffered by the artists and their communities should be compensated. However, he decided not to compensate for this 'pirating of cultural heritage' under s 115(2). Such damages could not be quantified by reference to the liability of the defendants (as had been requested by the applicants), but only by reference to the individual circumstances of the applicants. Assessment along those lines, artist by artist, would not have been in accordance with the principle of equality which the judge had agreed to follow. However, the Copyright Act does allow for additional damages for flagrant infringement under s 115(4) and in this instance the copyright infringement was found to be deliberate and calculated. Accordingly the element of 'cultural harm' was reflected in an award under that provision. These additional damages were assessed at $70,000 and would have been higher but for the other damages already granted.

The case also involved false representations made under ss 52, 53(c) and 53(d) of the Trade Practices Act 1974, since there were tags on the carpets indicating that the Aboriginal artists had designed the carpets and wall hangings, were paid royalties on every item sold, and would have woven the carpets themselves if it were a tradition of Aboriginal people to do so. No further damages were awarded for these breaches, although the applicants did obtain injunctions to prevent the behaviour of the respondents continuing.

39 (1994) 30 IPR 209 at 240.

40 *Ibid* at 244, citing *Williams v Settle* [1960] 1 WLR 1072 at 1086–87.

While the *Milpurrurru* judgment does at least strive to find ways of moulding the remedies available under the Act to the cultural context in which the works were created, it obviously falls far short of recognising the concept of communal ownership as such. This is not to say, however, that it is impossible to find ways of accommodating such a concept within the current legal framework. For example, Golvan has suggested that Aboriginal communities might be regarded as the 'beneficial' or equitable owners of copyright in works created under the laws of those communities,[41] presumably on the theory that (in the words of Banduk Marika) the works are held by the artists 'on trust' for the communities.[42] This would at least permit a community or its elders to seek an interlocutory or temporary injunction to restrain any breach of copyright, though no permanent relief would be available unless the copyright owner were joined in the proceedings.[43] In order to become the legal owners, a community would need to institute a practice of having all its members sign documents assigning to the community or its elders any copyright they might create.[44]

Exploitation of copyright: enforcement, agreements and remuneration

Establishing that copyright subsists in Aboriginal art or cultural heritage and identifying a suitable owner of that copyright does not necessarily mean that the copyright system will function effectively to protect the creator's interests. Litigation to enforce copyright against infringers necessarily entails the commitment of significant sums of money for uncertain returns. Even where litigation is successful there is no guarantee of being able to enforce the judgment, as the successful claimants in the *Milpurrurru* case have discovered to date in attempting to recover the damages they were awarded.[45] There are also practical difficulties with the more mundane business of using copyright as a basis for commercialisation or educational dissemination. In theory, copyright owners may exploit their property rights by licensing others to use the copyright material on whatever conditions the owners see fit, including of course the payment of remuneration where the owners wish to generate income. In practice, however, as many artists and creative people find, the negotiation of agreements dealing with copyright works is fraught with difficulties for non-lawyers and others unused to striking commercial bargains. The National Indigenous Arts Advocacy Association (NIAAA), the support organisation for Aboriginal artists which has now replaced the Aboriginal Arts Management Association, advises indigenous artists on contracts, in particular copyright licensing deals. 'Unfortunately, a good majority of these agreements are either poorly drafted, so as to create uncertainty for both parties as to their rights and responsibilities, or simply unfair.'[46]

41 See Golvan, C, 'Aboriginal Art and the Protection of Indigenous Cultural Rights' [1992] 7 *European Intellectual Property Review* 227 at 230.

42 *Op cit,* at footnote 37.

43 See authorities cited in Golvan, *op cit,* at 230.

44 Under ss 196 and 197 of the Copyright Act 1968, writing is required in relation to all assignments of present or future works.

45 See Marr, D, 'The Carpetbagger', *Sydney Morning Herald,* 17 August 1996, Spectrum, p 6, where it is reported that the principal defendant Bethune has been declared bankrupt and his company wound up.

46 *Art Law* (Newsletter of the Arts Law Centre of Australia), No 9 (June 1995), p 3.

However, the NIAAA (and its predecessor the AAMA) have had some notable successes in protecting and pursuing artists' rights, the *Milpurrurru* case being the outstanding example.[47]

It is also the case that artists generally, in the absence of a centralised collecting society to administer their rights, have not been able to monitor all uses of their work and ask for appropriate remuneration. However, a copyright collecting society for visual artists and craftspersons in Australia has now been established under the name VI$COPY. At the time of writing this had not yet become fully operational.[48] When it does, it will hopefully provide a further means for indigenous artists at least to protect the economic value of their work.[49]

Integrity and moral rights

A further issue for indigenous people is their capacity to commercialise or disseminate artwork or other manifestations of Aboriginal identity without threatening the cultural and sacred aspects of their heritage. Where copyright material is licensed, it is usually possible to impose contractual restrictions over the use to which the material may be put by the licensee. Frequently, however, artists are put in a position where they have little choice other than to assign or sell the copyright in their work if they wish that work to reach a wider audience. Even if a satisfactory contract is successfully negotiated, the selling of copyright to another person removes control over the material from the hands of the creator. In Australia, copyright law has been overwhelmingly concerned with the exercise of economic interests arising from the creation of material protected by the regime. Once copyright has been assigned away (typically, sold to a publisher), the creator is no longer free to exercise any control over the use of the work, unless provision for this is made in the contract between the parties. In reality, if the publisher (or other assignee) has sufficient bargaining power to insist on an assignment rather than a licence, they will probably be able to resist any attempt to impose significant controls on their use of the material. This raises the issue of whether indigenous artists, and indeed creators of copyright material generally, should have rights over their creations which apply regardless of whether the copyright has been transferred to someone else.

In Europe, and indeed in many other countries around the world, the personal rights of authors or creators of material in which copyright subsists may comprehend 'moral rights' centred around the person of the author. These rights are completely independent of the author's economic rights and continue to exist even after the transfer of those economic rights. The components of moral rights include the right of paternity, the right of the author to be made known to the public as the creator of the work; the

47 *Cf* Golvan, *op cit*, at 228–29, questioning whether what was then the AAMA had sufficient resources for copyright litigation and bemoaning the inability or unwillingness of Aboriginal legal aid services to provide support in such cases.

48 For a discussion of the history and expected scope of operation of this new body, see Simpson, S, *Review of Australian Copyright Collecting Societies*, 1995, Canberra: AGPS, pp 271–78.

49 It is worth noting that the Department of Aboriginal Affairs, in their review of the Aboriginal arts and craft industry, specifically recommended against the creation of a specialised collecting agency for Aboriginal artists: *op cit*, at footnote 6, pp 317–18.

right of integrity, which prevents distortion of the work; and others such as the right to choose whether to publish, to restrain excessive criticism of the work, and, more generally, to prevent violations of the author's personality. An important policy issue is whether the author is allowed to contract away these rights. Unlike many European systems the moral rights provisions in Canada and Britain allow for this to happen. This has been rightly criticised on the ground that the superior bargaining power of most publishers and their control over the content of publishing contracts have the potential to render those rights meaningless in many situations.[50]

In July 1988 the majority of the Copyright Law Review Committee (CLRC) recommended against the introduction of moral rights into Australian copyright law, with one limited exception: that a right of attribution exist in cases where works are subject to use under a compulsory licence. This would have complemented the existing provisions (ss 189–95) in the Copyright Act which prohibit false attribution of authorship. Despite this recommendation, however, the pressure for reform did not die away and, as part of the 'assiduous cultivation of arts industries' by the Keating Labour government,[51] moral rights remained on the agenda, leading to the release of a Discussion Paper in June 1994 prepared jointly by the Attorney General's Department and the Department of Communications and the Arts.[52] The Discussion Paper considered the CLRC's 1988 Report, but unlike the majority on that occasion, went on to propose amendments to the Copyright Act to recognise the rights of attribution and integrity for authors of literary, dramatic or artistic works, composers of musical works and directors and producers of films. In February 1996 the government released an exposure draft of a Copyright Amendment Bill containing the necessary amendments, among other changes to copyright law. The Liberal/National Coalition which took office after the federal election that was held soon afterwards has also expressed its support for these proposals and accordingly the Bill (perhaps with some modifications) is expected to be introduced into Parliament in the near future.

The 'right of attribution' proposed in the Discussion Paper would consist of the rights to be made known to the public as the creator of the work, to prevent others from claiming authorship, to prevent wrongful attribution to an author of works they did not produce, and to prevent unauthorised altered versions of material being attributed to the original author. The 'right of integrity', on the other hand, would consist of the right to object to distortions or mutilations, other modifications, or other derogatory action in relation to an author's work that would harm the honour or reputation of the author.

While the creation of these rights would be a welcome step forward, there are nevertheless aspects of the proposals in the Discussion Paper which are less than satisfactory, especially where indigenous culture is concerned. Inherent in the proposed right of integrity, for example, is the fact that the work has to be 'distorted, mutilated or

50 See, eg Vaver, D, 'Author's Moral Rights–Reform Proposals in Canada: Charter or Barter for Rights of Creators?' (1987) 25 *Osgoode Hall Law Journal* 749.

51 Cooper, M, 'The Politics of Culture' (1995) 14 *Communications Law Bulletin* 1 at 1.

52 *Proposed Moral Rights Legislation for Copyright Creators*, 1994, Canberra: Attorney-General's Department.

altered' in some way and this may not address the issue of using material in an inappropriate context. For example, the depiction of a painting on the $10 note as in the *Yumbulul* case, the use of artistic works on T-shirts as in the *Bulun Bulun* case, and the use of art works as designs for carpets made overseas as in the *Milpurrurru* case, might each be considered highly derogatory even where the whole work was appropriated unchanged. It is also proposed that the new rights may only be enforced by the 'author' (or by their legal representative if the author is dead or mentally ill), and cannot be assigned. Thus even if an indigenous community were recognised as the owner of any copyright in work created under the law of the community, it would be left to the individual creators (at least while still alive) to pursue any infringements of the right of integrity.

More disturbingly, the Discussion Paper envisages that moral rights would be capable of being waived. This is hardly compatible with one of the stated functions of moral rights, which is to shore up the economic potential of protected material by increasing the bargaining power of the creator in negotiating with publishers or employers:[53]

> In theory we should have a neat separation of powers in the arts, in which the managers (producers, publishers etc) retain control of copyright and the artists retain creative control through protection under moral rights. Unfortunately what we are increasingly seeing are deals in which artists lose ownership or control of copyright *and* are asked to waive their moral rights in both existing and future works.

Even in situations where a creator had not waived their moral rights, the Discussion Paper proposes a legislative scheme in which the rights of attribution could only be asserted if it were 'reasonable in all the circumstances', and the right of integrity would only be protected where the treatment of the work was derogatory. The flexible, if somewhat imprecise tests of 'reasonableness' and 'derogatory' would include 'any industry practice relevant to the work' – so presumably if it happens now it can continue to occur. The onus would be on the claimant to establish reasonableness. The efficacy of the scheme proposed by the Discussion Paper has been seriously questioned by those working with authors, musicians and film-makers, and the blanket waiver has been described as 'antithetical to the spirit of the [previous] Federal government's cultural policy statement'.[54]

OTHER FORMS OF INTELLECTUAL PROPERTY

Breach of confidence and community secrets

The action for breach of confidence potentially offers a useful remedy for protecting the secrets of an indigenous community against unauthorised disclosure, as is apparent from

53 Collie, I, 'Multimedia and Moral Rights' [1994] *Arts and Entertainment Law Review* 94 at 98 (emphasis in original).

54 Collie, *ibid* at 101.

the well-known case of *Foster v Mountford*.[55] An action was brought by the Pitjantjatjara Council to prevent the publication of a book entitled *Nomads of the Australian Desert* written by one of the defendants, the anthropologist Charles Mountford. Some of the information in this book was gathered by Mountford on a 1940 field trip into outback areas of the Northern Territory, during which he spoke to a number of the Aboriginal inhabitants of the region. As Muirhead J put it:[56]

> The people were then far less sophisticated than they are, as a group, today as they had not been subjected for so long, or to such an extent, to white man influences. In other words, it is inevitable that they took Dr Mountford into their confidence, they showed him and explained to him sacred sites and objects, paintings and rock engravings, and he recorded their myths and totemic geography by aboriginal drawings, the camera, and notebook.

The judge found that this information was given and received in confidence and that there was a strong *prima facie* case for saying that its publication would breach Mountford's obligation not to use or disclose the information without consent. He accepted the plaintiffs' contention that 'revelation of the secrets to their women, children and uninitiated men may undermine the social and religious stability of their hard-pressed community',[57] a serious loss which would not be reparable by any subsequent award of damages. Accordingly he issued an interlocutory injunction to restrain publication of the book, pending final determination of the issues. As is often the way in such cases, the matter did not proceed to trial but was settled by the grant of 'interim' relief.

What is notable about this decision is not so much the conclusion that the information was given in confidence, nor even that such information falls within the doctrine of breach of confidence, but rather the identity of the plaintiffs. No attempt was made to suggest that the members of the Pitjantjatjara Council who brought the action were the same people who revealed their secrets to Mountford, nor even that they were the direct descendants or personal representatives of those people. Instead, Muirhead J accepted that the action could be brought on behalf of:[58]

> … all those aboriginal people who inhabit what may loosely be described as those lands where aboriginal people … traditionally lived and roamed, and who are now identifiable as a people who use the Pitjantjara [*sic*] tongue, although, as a matter of history, more than one tribal group may be involved.

The plaintiffs also suggested that they were entitled to sue on their own behalf, as persons threatened with damage as a result of the breach of confidence. Strictly speaking, the decision on this point appears to conflict with the accepted principle that an action for breach of confidence may only be brought by the person who disclosed the

55 (1976) 29 FLR 233.

56 *Ibid* at 235.

57 *Ibid* at 236.

58 *Ibid* at 234. Note that throughout the report of this case, the plaintiff is referred to as the 'Pitjantjara' Council. The text of the article uses the more commonly accepted spelling Pitjantjatjara.

information or from whom the information was appropriated.[59] It should also be noted that no argument was addressed to Muirhead J on this point and the decision was one given on an interlocutory application where no final decision was required. Nevertheless, the decision has been followed in at least one subsequent case,[60] and appears to be an entirely sensible and appropriate recognition of the collective interest of such communities in the preservation of their sacred heritage.[61]

The drawback of the action for breach of confidence is of course that it only protects information that has not reached the public domain. Accordingly where members of a community have not taken sufficient care in the past to restrict access to certain knowledge, an attempt to enforce obligations of confidentiality may be met with the defence that the information is no longer secret.[62] No matter how damaging it may be to the community for outsiders (or even uninitiated insiders) to learn of or be free to discuss matters that under customary law should be restricted to certain members or certain occasions, non-Aboriginal law will not intervene if confidentiality has been lost. In *Foster v Mountford* the plaintiffs' case might well have been vulnerable on this score, had it not been for the fact that Mountford's subsequent conduct made it clear that he believed the information to be confidential. Of course it is important not to jump too hastily to a conclusion that information has passed into the public domain. We have seen that in some cases indigenous artists and their communities are prepared to put work on public display, trusting to the fact that most of those who see it will not appreciate its full significance. As von Doussa J explained in the *Milpurrurru* case:[63]

> It is a feature of the style of the artworks in question that the artist will encode into the artwork secret parts of the Dreaming that will be recognised and understood only by those who are initiated into the relevant ceremonies, or at least have a close knowledge of the cultural significance of the story.

In such a case the secret part of the artwork should not be regarded as having reached the public domain, even though the work is readily accessible. It should still therefore be possible to bring an action for breach of confidence against anyone who proposed to reveal information which would allow others to 'decode' the secret details.

Registration of designs

The Designs Act 1906 protects artistic works which are commercialised by being applied to three-dimensional articles. Thus where an indigenous artist or group is prepared to allow their work to be added to T-shirts, mugs and other items, the Designs

59 See eg *Fraser v Evans* [1969] 1 QB 349; *Finnane v Australian Consolidated Press* [1978] 2 NSWLR 435.

60 *Pitjantjatjara Council Inc v Lowe* (unrep, Vic Sup Ct, 26 March 1982), noted in (1982) 4 *Aboriginal Law Bulletin* 11. See further Hennessey, P, 'Common Law Protection of Private or Secret Matters' (1985) 17 *Aboriginal Law Bulletin* 20.

61 *Cf Onus v Alcoa of Australia Ltd* (1981) 149 CLR 27.

62 As to the complicated principles which apply in this regard, especially where it is the defendant or some other third party who has been responsible for the loss of secrecy, see McKeough and Stewart, *op cit*, pp 60–63, 77–78.

63 *Milpurrurru v Indofurn Pty Ltd* (1994) 30 IPR 209 at 215.

Act offers the right to prevent other businesses from copying the design and using it on the same kind of articles. However protection is only available if the design is registered. Worse still, the use of such a design on mass-produced items may result in the loss of copyright protection for the artistic work under ss 74–77 of the Copyright Act, whether or not the design is registered under the Designs Act. In any event the duration of protection under designs law is much shorter than in copyright law (at the moment, up to a maximum of 16 years) and again this has limitations in terms of protecting cultural heritage.

The loss of all protection for artistic works used on articles (ie other than in books, calendars, wrapping paper etc) has long bedevilled artists, who have found the designs legislation difficult to understand and have not always realised the necessity for going through the registration process. In 1989 amendments to the Copyright Act excluded 'flat designs' from loss of copyright protection even if used in a commercial way on a T-shirt or other item. Before that time, the law operated to deprive artists of control over their work as, for example, may have occurred to Darwin artist Harold Thomas, who claims to be the creator of the Aboriginal flag design. Thomas, whose claim to authorship has been disputed by two others, is at the time of writing seeking a declaration that he owns copyright in the flag design. A finding in his favour would allow him to negotiate with the federal government to receive compensation for the Commonwealth's use of the copyright, the Aboriginal flag having been proclaimed in 1995 as a flag of Australia under the Flags Act 1953 (1 of 1954) (Cth). If there were no agreement as to compensation, Thomas would then be able to ask the Copyright Tribunal to fix appropriate terms under s 183(5) of the Copyright Act. However, it is quite possible that Thomas will be held to have lost his copyright through the operation of the pre-1989 law, though he is arguing that any 'industrial application' of the design did not occur with his authority. He is also arguing that even if his copyright was lost prior to the 1989 amendments, it 'revived' when they took effect in 1990.[64] Under the current provisions even an industrial application of the design would mean no loss of copyright protection, since the design is 'flat' or two-dimensional in nature. This is indeed the case with most artwork, though by no means all. If, for example, a design for burial poles or other three-dimensional works were to be mass-produced with the authority of the artist, copyright protection would be lost.

In September 1995 the Australian Law Reform Commission (ALRC) produced its final report on designs law, following an investigation into the registered designs system and its adequacy and appropriateness, in terms of providing protection and remedies for users of the system.[65] The ALRC was also asked to modernise and simplify the Designs Act and remove difficulties that have arisen in the operation of the 1906 legislation. The ALRC has suggested that the Copyright Act have introduced into it an 'adaptation right' for artistic works, giving the copyright owner the right to industrialise a version of

64 Different views have been expressed on whether the amendments can have this effect, though the weight of authority seems to suggest that they can: see *Ametex Fabrics Inc v C & F Fabrics Pty Ltd* (1992) 111 ALR 565; *Interlego AG v Croner Trading Pty Ltd* (1992) 25 IPR 65: *Shacklady v Atkins* (1994) 30 IPR 387; but *cf Roland Corp v Lorenzo & Sons Pty Ltd* (1991) 22 IPR 245.

65 *Designs,* ALRC Report No 74, 1995, Sydney: ALRC.

an artistic work that is itself an artistic work in three dimensions. The adaptation right would apply to two-dimensional versions of three-dimensional artistic works. The effect would be to reserve copyright for artistic works, while more functional products would receive only designs protection. The trouble with designs law is that its primary aim is to do with protecting the shape of manufactured articles ranging from computer keyboards to car exhaust systems. The inclusion of artistic material in the present regime is, perhaps, unfortunate. In essence, therefore, the ALRC's suggested adaptation right would remove artistic works from a scheme designed to protect designers who make our life easier at a practical level.

The ALRC Report specifically recognises that protection of traditional Aboriginal designs is important. However it goes on to state that 'they raise special issues that cannot be adequately addressed through general designs law and that should not be considered in isolation from other issues arising out of Aboriginal art, culture and heritage'.[66] The report accordingly makes no recommendations which are specific to Aboriginal designs.

Misleading and deceptive conduct

In certain circumstances the statutory provisions relating to misleading or deceptive conduct in trade or commerce may be used to pursue those who misappropriate cultural heritage. The most obvious situation is where consumers purchasing or paying to view items of Aboriginal art or culture are deceived into thinking that the original creators have authorised the particular commercial use of the material, when in fact they have not. As we have seen, a misrepresentation of this sort was successfully pursued under the Trade Practices Act in the *Milpurrurru* case. There the defendants had falsely claimed that permission had been granted. However there seems no reason why such an action for misleading or deceptive conduct could not succeed even in the absence of any express claim of authorisation. A useful analogy is provided by *Pacific Dunlop Ltd v Hogan*,[67] where Paul Hogan took action against the makers of a television advertisement which parodied the famous 'knife scene' from his film *Crocodile Dundee*. Hogan successfully argued that a significant number of those watching the advertisement would have erroneously concluded that he had approved it, given the clear connection to his film. So similarly it can be argued that if consumers acquire an item of Aboriginal art, they would naturally assume that the artist has consented to its distribution; if no permission had been given, they would accordingly have been deceived.[68]

Another possibility is for the laws relating to misleading or deceptive conduct to be used against those who borrow from Aboriginal themes and styles and market items

66 *Ibid*, para 1.17.

67 (1989) 14 IPR 398.

68 Note that while Hogan was also able to sue in the tort of passing off, this will rarely be available to Aboriginal artists. Passing off requires the plaintiff to be able to establish that they have built up a distinctive reputation, and that the defendant's conduct has falsely suggested some connection between the defendant and the plaintiff. It is unlikely that there are many Aboriginal artists whose individual styles are so well-known to at least a section of the public that these requirements could be satisfied. The statutory provisions, by contrast, are not limited in this way: deception is all that need be established.

which look like Aboriginal art, but are in fact not the work of indigenous artists. Here there is no individual artist who has been wronged. Nevertheless, it may be argued that consumers are being deceived into thinking that the art they are purchasing or viewing is 'genuine'. It is worth pointing out that under s 80 of the Trade Practices Act any person can seek an injunction to restrain a contravention of the consumer protection provisions, so that there would be nothing to stop an entire community or even a body such as the NIAAA from bringing such a claim; though in the event that they wished to claim damages under s 82, they would need to show that they had personally suffered some kind of loss as a result of the contravention.

A further development in this regard is the proposal for an 'authentication' trade mark, currently being formulated by the NIAAA in consultation with Aboriginal organisations and business organisations.[69] This would be attached to goods to help consumers distinguish authentic indigenous art from fakes or unauthorised copies.

Environmental knowledge and the patent system

Most of this chapter has been concerned with indigenous art. However it is worth commenting briefly on the protection of a rather different aspect of the cultural heritage of indigenous communities. Over recent years there has been considerable debate in international circles as to whether indigenous peoples, and indeed 'developing countries' as a whole, should in effect be permitted to lay claim to the bio-diversity of the environments they inhabit and to the special knowledge they have accumulated as to those environments.[70] In the Australian context, for example, an important aspect of Aboriginal heritage is knowledge of harvesting techniques and uses for traditional foods: for example, abalone, now a keenly sought food among the wider community.

The desire to assert some form of 'ownership' over such knowledge has arisen in reaction to the 'raids' increasingly being made by scientific researchers on the natural resources of undeveloped environments. It is becoming common, for instance, for companies to obtain genetic material from animals and plants and then to seek to use the patent system to acquire monopoly rights over the organisms, or some genetically altered version thereof, or some product derived from them. Naturally, this has caused great concern. A good example is provided by a US patent on a pesticide derived from the seeds of the neem tree (*Azadirachta indica,* a native of India). The patent is being opposed by a coalition of pressure groups, as the tree's pesticidal properties have been used for centuries by the people living where it grows. 'The patent, owned by the giant seed company WR Grace, has become a cause celebre in the fight to prevent rich

69 See *Stopping the Rip-Offs: Intellectual Property Protection for Aboriginal and Torres Strait Islander Peoples*, 1994, Canberra: Attorney-General's Department, pp 8–9.

70 See, for example, Da Casta e Silva, E, 'The Protection of Intellectual Property for Local and Indigenous Communities' [1995] 11 *European Intellectual Property Review* 546; Doucas, M, 'Intellectual Property Law – Indigenous People's Concerns' (1995) 12 *Canadian Intellectual Property Review* 1; Huft, MJ, 'Indigenous Peoples and Drug Discovery Research: A Question of Intellectual Property Rights' (1995) 89 *Northwestern University Law Review* 1678; Fournile, H, 'Protecting Indigenous Property Rights in Biodiversity' (1996) 72(5) *Current Affairs Bulletin* 36.

nations from plundering the biological resources and traditional knowledge of developing countries.'[71]

A more remarkable (some would say sinister) example is provided by the recent report that the US patent office has issued a patent over the genetic material of a foreign citizen, an indigenous man of the Hagahai people of Papua New Guinea. The patent claims a cell line containing unmodified Hagahai DNA and several methods for its use in detecting certain retro-viruses.[72] This patenting activity is being seriously opposed on a number of grounds. For reasons that will be explained shortly, the legality of patenting 'naturally occurring' information such as a stretch of DNA is greatly in doubt, without even considering the serious ethical and moral aspects of allowing third party (and foreign) ownership of someone's very genes. The issues raised concern the fundamental question of to what extent 'bio-colonialism' and commodification of human life should be allowed, and at the other end of the spectrum the usual commercial issues as to what compensation, royalties or other remuneration may be allowed to the originators of the raw material, since there is 'no concrete provision for the Hagahai to receive any compensation for becoming the property of the US government'.[73]

As a general rule, something which is merely 'discovered in nature' is not regarded as an 'invention', and therefore cannot be patented.[74] Where a person uses inventiveness to put the known characteristics of a naturally occurring organism or substance to some new use, the resulting product or process may constitute an invention.[75] However, if a group of indigenous people have made use of the same knowledge for any length of time, this should suffice to rob the invention of any novelty and therefore render it unpatentable. While this means the indigenous people themselves cannot benefit from their knowledge by securing a legal monopoly under the patent system, neither, more importantly, should anyone else be able to. The problem in practice is that patent offices, especially in the US, seem all too willing to grant patents on the basis that their validity will ultimately be challenged and settled in the courts. Indigenous groups and even smaller developing countries may often lack the considerable resources necessary to have a patent overturned through litigation, raising the spectre that multi-national companies will eventually acquire extensive monopoly rights over large tracts of the biosphere. Against that background, it can be expected that indigenous groups and their supporters will continue to press for special measures to be introduced to affirm what Article 26 of the Draft Declaration on the Rights of Indigenous People describes as:[76]

71 Kleiner, K, 'Pesticide Tree Ends Up in Court' *New Scientist*, 16 September 1995, p 7.

72 See Mooney, P, 'Indigenous Person from Papua New Guinea Claimed in US Government Patent', Press Release by Rural Advancement Foundation International, 30 November 1995.

73 *Ibid*, p 1.

74 *Lane Fox v Kensington and Knightsbridge Electric Lighting Co* (1892) 9 RPC 413 at 416; *National Research Development Corp v Commissioner of Patents* (1959) 102 CLR 252 at 264.

75 *National Research Development Corp v Commissioner of Patents* (1959) 102 CLR 252.

76 See also Article 29, which specifically refers to 'the right to special measures to control, develop and protect ... human and other genetic resources, seeds, medicines [and] knowledge of the properties of flora and fauna'.

> … the right to own, develop, control and use the lands and territories, including the total environment of the lands, air, waters, coastal seas, sea-ice, flora and fauna and other resources which they have traditionally owned otherwise occupied or used.

PROPOSALS FOR REFORM

There have been a number of different suggestions over recent years as to how to improve the legal position of indigenous people and their communities in relation to the intangible aspects of their cultural property. The most comprehensive set of proposals can still be found in the Report of the Working Party on the Protection of Aboriginal Folklore.[77] This was the product of an interdepartmental working party, originally set up by the Federal government in 1975, which completed its work in 1981, although the Report was not publicly released until 1983. It proposed an Aboriginal Folklore Act which would, among other things, prohibit any non-traditional use of sacred-secret folklore, or the debasement, mutilation or destruction of folklore. There would also be a Commissioner for Aboriginal Folklore to issue clearances and negotiate payment for approved use of folklore. As yet these recommendations have not been implemented.

In the meantime, other proposals have surfaced. Golvan, for example, has suggested that the Aboriginal and Torres Strait Islander Heritage Act 1984 (79) (Cth) be amended to allow Aboriginal communities to pursue unauthorised use of Aboriginal artwork. At present the Act applies to areas and relics of cultural significance. Under Golvan's proposals, it would be expanded to recognise 'civil rights of action akin to copyright rights available to 'local Aboriginal communities' to prevent the unauthorised reproduction or adaptation of artistic works or designs of traditional Aboriginal significance'.[78] An alternative possibility is to amend the Copyright Act 1968 itself to incorporate such a right. However there are a number of practical difficulties with the notion of vesting what might be regarded as competing rights in the original creator (as the 'author') on the one hand, and an Aboriginal community on the other, especially where the creator is not prepared to recognise the community's authority.[79]

A more radical suggestion is that reform might be achieved through the common law 'recognising' or giving effect to Aboriginal customary law on matters of cultural property. The basis for this suggestion is of course the *Mabo* decision on native title.[80] According to Puri:[81]

> Although the High Court was careful to point out that the *Mabo* decision applied only to the Murray Islands under certain conditions, the case has far wider ramifications and raises

77 *Op cit.* For a detailed account of the Report and its background, see Bell, R, 'Protection of Folklore: The Australian Experience' (1985) 19 *Copyright Bulletin* 4.

78 *Op cit*, at footnote 41 at 231.

79 For a thoughtful discussion of some of the issues and problems involved, see Ellinson, D, 'Unauthorised Reproduction of Traditional Aboriginal Art' (1994) 17 *University of New South Wales Law Journal* 327 at 334–43.

80 *Mabo v Queensland (No 2)* (1992) 175 CLR 1.

81 *Op cit*, at 323. The quotation in the extract is from Gray, S, 'Wheeling, Dealing and Deconstruction: Aboriginal Art and the Land Post-*Mabo*' (1993) 63 *Aboriginal Law Bulletin* 10 at 11.

> a wide range of legal issues. It is submitted that the recognition of Aboriginal customary laws with respect to land extends to the recognition of customary laws with respect to Aboriginal folklore, including ancestral designs. This is supported by the fact that through Aboriginal eyes, ancestral designs themselves represent a proprietary interest in the sense that they represent the 'title deeds' of Aboriginal land ownership. The connection between 'real' property and 'intellectual' property under Aboriginal law is a relationship so close that 'the two in fact are quite inseparable if not actually the same'.

Puri even goes so far as to suggest that 'an action to protect proprietary rights in folklore could probably be brought under the Native Title Act 1993', on the basis that s 223(1) of that Act defines 'native title' to mean 'the communal, group or individual rights of Aboriginal peoples or Torres Strait Islanders in relation to land'.[82] However apart from the fact that on this approach only those communities which had maintained unbroken connections with their traditional lands would be entitled to recognition of their customary laws, it is hard to see how far that 'recognition' could be taken in the face of statutory provisions (especially those in the Copyright Act) which plainly disregard those customary laws in allocating property rights.[83]

If reform is to come, therefore, it would seem advisable that it be in the form of some kind of special legislation. In 1994 the Federal government released an issues paper which canvassed some of the suggestions just discussed, and foreshadowed widespread consultation with indigenous groups and other interested parties as the basis for the development of further policy options.[84] It is to be hoped, especially with the recent election of a coalition government, that any concrete proposals that emerge from this process do not go the way of the 1981 Report's recommendations.

CONCLUSION

The main purpose of (non-indigenous) intellectual property laws in Australia is to remove disincentives for investment in the exploitation of intellectual or creative effort. As such, these laws may sometimes be useful to individual indigenous persons, especially artists whose work has been flagrantly misappropriated. They can even be useful to communities seeking to protect their traditions, either directly as in *Foster v Mountford*, or indirectly (through flexible and culturally-sensitive interpretation) as in *Milpurrurru*.

However it is unlikely that Australia's intellectual property laws will ever be able to attain the objectives set by the Draft Declaration on the Rights of Indigenous People, at least not in their current form. As far as purely economic interests are concerned, these can be protected tolerably well – or at least as well as those of non-indigenous people.

82 *Op cit*, at footnote 2 at 324.

83 The same point can be made in relation to the intriguing suggestion, also inspired by *Mabo*, that the common law of blasphemy, traditionally restricted to protecting the Christian faiths, might be capable of being extended to cover any use of sacred material which would be offensive to Aboriginal beliefs: see Miller, D, 'Collective Ownership of Copyright in Spiritually-Sensitive Works: *Milpurrurru v Indofurn Pty Ltd*' (1995) 6 *Australian Intellectual Property Journal* 185 at 202–05.

84 *Op cit*, at footnote 69.

However spiritual or cultural interests are another matter altogether. If these are to be appropriately accommodated, a different legislative framework altogether would seem to be needed. Apart from the long overdue enactment of a moral rights regime (hopefully in a form which goes beyond the present, slightly disappointing proposals), there appears to be a strong case either for implementing the key recommendations of the 1981 Working Party Report, or for adopting Golvan's suggestion of an extension to existing laws relating to sacred sites and objects.

CHAPTER SIX

ABORIGINAL CUSTOMARY LAW AND THE COMMON LAW

Bruce Debelle

WHAT IS ABORIGINAL CUSTOMARY LAW?

A long-existing culture

When the First Fleet arrived in Sydney Harbour in January 1788 the Aborigines had been living in Australia for more than 40,000 years. To the new settlers, the Aboriginal inhabitants of Australia appeared primitive. They had few possessions, no pottery, iron or bronze, no large houses and no tall monuments. But the Aborigines had a society and culture of considerable complexity and diversity. The long cultural heritage of the Aborigines included means by which order was maintained and disputes resolved.

In 1788 there was no single Aboriginal nation and no shared language. It has been estimated that there were as many as 500 tribes or nations, all varying in size and each speaking a different dialect.[1] They each occupied more or less discrete areas and there was considerable diversity of language and culture. This diversity was in part the product of different degrees of contact with non-Aborigines and part the product of differences in the environment in which different groups lived. Aborigines of the north coastal regions had had contact with Macassan and Indonesian traders or fishermen while others, for example, central desert Aborigines, had had little contact with others. The food gathering practices and customs of coastal Aborigines differed from those of desert Aborigines. This diversity resulted in differences in some aspects of the law applying in each tribe or nation. Yet, despite these differences, an 'Aboriginal commonality' has been perceived and some basic generalisations can be made.

Recognise the differences

When examining Aboriginal customary law, the white Australian inquirer must look out for and recognise the differences in customary law in different parts of Australia. It is also essential to recognise differences between the Aboriginal legal system and the British legal system introduced to Australia. Care must be taken to avoid preconceptions. The law and legal systems would, for many Australians, be defined as a system of rules enforced by a hierarchy of courts, from the magistrates' courts, through to the district or county courts, Supreme Courts, Federal Courts and up to the High Court. It would also recognise the role of the police force and other law enforcement agencies. Rules of law are identified as consisting of the common law expressed in judicial decisions, statutes made by Parliament, and the plethora of regulations and byelaws made by executive agencies and local authorities. A distinction is made between

1 Berndt, RM, and CH, *The World of the First Australians*, 2nd edn, 1977, Sydney: Ure Smith, pp xi–xii and 364 (hereafter cited as 'Berndt').

those rules of law and norms of social behaviour such as rules of etiquette and standards dictated by good manners or ethical and moral values rather than by legal obligation.

In Aboriginal society there was no system of government in any institutionalised sense. There was no body which made any laws and no hierarchy of courts or other enforcing authorities. There were tribal elders but no chieftains nor any ruling class.[2] There was no hierarchical system of government within a tribe or group of tribes. Nevertheless, mechanisms for the maintenance of order and the resolution of disputes existed. When they spoke of law, Aborigines did not distinguish in the way white Australians do between norms of social behaviour and mandatory rules, a breach of which might result in severe consequences. All of this would be understood as law. The law had no separate identity so that a system of legal rules cannot be easily identified. Yet, as Blackburn J observed of the Aborigines at Yirrkala, an Aboriginal community near Gove in the Northern Territory:[3]

> The evidence shows a subtle and elaborate system highly adapted to the country in which the people led their lives, which provided a stable order of society and was remarkably free from the vagaries of personal whim or influence. If ever a system could be called 'a government of laws, and not of men', it is that shown in the evidence before me ... Great as they are, the differences between that system and our system are, for the purposes in hand, differences of degree. I hold that I must recognise the system revealed by the evidence as a system of law.

White Australian preconceptions or values must, therefore, be avoided. When examining Aboriginal customary law, it is better to ask 'how is order maintained?' or 'by what means are quarrels or disputes resolved?' than by asking 'do Aborigines have a legal system?'

The importance of religion and land

To all Aborigines in Australia religion was the mainstay of social existence. There was no systematic belief in gods nor any institutions of priesthood, prayer and sacrifice.[4] The mythical characters of the Dream Time provided their source of religion which focused on every aspect of life. They laid down precepts or made suggestions of which people were expected to take notice.[5] They defined the broad rules to be played by both men and women in such matters as sacred ritual, economic affairs, marriage, child-bearing and the conduct upon the death of relatives. They were the source of Aboriginal life and

2 There is a debate among anthropologists whether political authority was vested in elders or in a council of elders. The former view is held by Berndt, RM, 'Law and Order in Aboriginal Australia', 1965, pp 167 and 177 and Elkin, AP, *The Australian Aborigines*, 1976, Angus & Robertson, p 114 (hereafter cited as 'Elkin'). The latter view is held by Hiatt, LR, *Kinship and Conflict*, 1965, ANUP, pp 141–47; Meggitt, MJ, *Desert People*, 1976, Angus & Robertson, pp 248–50 (hereafter cited as 'Meggitt'); and Wilson, J (1961) *Authority and Leadership in a 'New Style' Australian Aboriginal Community*, unpublished MA thesis, University of Western Australia Pindan, WA, MA Thesis, University of WA.

3 *Milirrpum v Nabalco Pty Ltd and The Commonwealth* (1971) 17 FLR 141 at 267–68.

4 Stanner, WEH, *Religion, Totemism and Symbolism*, in Berndt, RM and CH (eds), 1965, pp 207 *et seq* (see above).

5 Berndt, *op cit*, p 337.

law. Knowledge and control of certain religious rites, mythology and songs, and possession of sacred objects was vested in a few men of each local group. The authority was not inherited but rather passed on to men chosen from initiated men.[6] Their special knowledge was kept secret from all uninitiated persons, be they other men, women or children. Women had their own secret-sacred religion and knowledge. Today, the white inquirer will still find a curtain being drawn once questions touch on some of these secret-sacred matters.

The relationship of Aborigines with land was both spiritual and physical. Certain sites or areas of land were of special or sacred importance, some falling within the secret-sacred category. Land was also important as a source of food.

Social organisation

The social organisation of Aborigines was complex. The basic social unit was the family and a group of families made up a band. A group of bands made up a tribe. In Aboriginal belief, all things in the physical and spiritual universes belonged to one or the other of two classes of moieties. Different social units, therefore, belonged to one moiety or the other. Another important social unit was the clan, which is a descent group. Every human being had his clan membership determined at birth. Sections and subsections added to an already complex social organisation.

One of the most important characteristics of Aboriginal society was the concept of kin relationship, which transcended both band and tribe. It is not to be identified with the family system of kinship which many white Australians might understand. Although the nuclear family was the basic kinship and social unit for Aborigines, there was also a classificatory system of kin relationship which operated throughout Aboriginal society.[7] The system still operates among traditional Aborigines and in modified forms among many non-traditional Aborigines. The details can be quite complex. It is sufficient for present purposes to know that kin relationships extend well beyond familial blood ties and are the basis of all social relationships, indicating the range of behaviour expected. 'It is the anatomy and physiology of Aboriginal society and must be understood if the behaviour of Aborigines as social beings is to be understood.'[8] Thus, everyone in traditional Aboriginal society must be identified as part of a kin relationship so that the two persons concerned will know what their behaviour to one another should be. A person coming into a strange group for trading or ceremonial purposes is always allocated a kinship position, if one is not already held.

Kin relationship resulted in obligations. Rules of kinship regulated such matters as marriage and private arrangements, food gathering, distribution and sharing; sharing of other goods, certain trading relationships, and educational roles. Other aspects of kinship obligations were rules by which certain relatives must be avoided.[9] Serious breaches of

6 Maddock, K, *The Australian Aborigines*, 1975, Ringwood: Penguin, p 43.

7 Elkin, AP, *op cit*, p 84.

8 Elkin, AP, *op cit*, p 85.

9 *Ibid*, pp 148–49.

the rules would usually be punished but failure to meet minor kinship obligations need not attract more than expressions of disapproval.

SOME ASPECTS OF CUSTOMARY LAW

Except for a few specific areas our knowledge about traditional Aboriginal life and its laws is sketchy. The task of identifying legal rules is made more difficult by regional variations. Some rules of fairly common application have been identified.

Women, children and uninitiated persons who saw things forbidden to them such as certain *Tjuringa* (sacred objects), a sacred place or sacred ceremony, committed an offence against sacred laws. If a person privy to knowledge or custody of sacred matters were to disclose them to a person not entitled to that information he too might be guilty of a breach of a breach of law. The penalty was often death. In other cases the offender might be speared. Rules permitted or encouraged marriage with certain relatives and prohibited marriage with others. Marriages were normally arranged, usually between a young girl and a man many years older. The girl was sometimes promised before she was born. In the context of incest, according to customary law, a man must not co-habit with his sister, mother or wife's mother. The punishment was death but if the degree of relationship was not close, banishment from the corporate life of the tribe or some other punishment might suffice.

Adultery and elopement were serious offences and might attract spearing as a penalty. The inflicting of serious physical injury must also be punished by spearing. Murder could be dealt with in a number of ways. Firstly, there might be open physical retaliation usually by a member of the family under a kinship obligation to the deceased, what has often been called 'payback'. The kinship obligation would require a certain relative to avenge the death notwithstanding his own personal views. It could not be relied on to put an end to disputes. Blood feuds extending over many years and breaking out into open violence were not unknown.[10] Secondly, compensation in the form of goods may be offered, or demanded, for a death but acceptance was no guarantee that revenge would not be attempted. Thirdly, where physical vengeance was not practicable the murderer would be identified to the satisfaction of the victim's relatives. One of them would perform sorcery, or threaten to do so, or claim to have done so if that particular person became ill or died. The fourth method still used throughout northern Arnhem Land was the *magarada,* a form of settlement by combat involving a ceremonial running of a gauntlet of spears, usually blunted.

A convenient summary of the rules of customary law as practised by one tribe of Aboriginal people is contained in a study of the Walbiri tribe by Meggitt in 1962 which has categorised a number of offences which are commonly recognised by the Walbiri as unlawful forms of behaviour.[11] The totality of the rules expresses the law, *djugaruru,* a term he translated as 'the line' or 'the straight or true way'. He continued:

10 Berndt, *op cit*, p 346.

11 Meggitt, *op cit*, pp 251–63.

> The law not only embraces ritual, economic, residential and kinship rules and conventions but also what we would call natural laws and technological rules. The care of sacred objects by the men of one patrimoiety, the sexual division of labour, the avoidance of mothers-in-law, the mating of bandicoots, the rising of the sun, and the use of fire-ploughs are all forms of behaviour that is lawful and proper – they are all *djugaruru*.

Meggitt goes on to point out that, although in precontact times Aborigines were probably rarely required to distinguish between rules of law and norms of polite behaviour, contact has sharpened the distinction. Today, differences can be seen between an offence and poor taste. He is thus able to identify a set of legal rules:[12]

A. Offences of commission:

1. Unauthorised homicide (that is, not decreed as a punishment for another offence).
2. Sacrilege (that is, the unauthorised possession of sacred knowledge and objects and the unauthorised observation of sacred rituals).
3. Unauthorised sorcery (1 and 3 are not easily distinguished).
4. Incest (copulation with actual kin of certain categories).
5. Cohabitation with certain kin (usually classificatory relatives in the categories associate with 4).
6. Abduction or enticement of women.
7. Adultery with certain kin (usually classificatory relatives in the categories associated with 5).
8. Adultery with potential spouses (7 and 8 in effect cover all cases of fornication).
9. Unauthorised physical assault, not intended to be fatal.
10. Usurpation of ritual privileges or duties.
11. Theft and intentional destruction of another's property (exclusive of 2).
12. Insult (including swearing, exposure of the genitals).

B. Offences of omission:

1. Physical neglect of certain relatives.
2. Refusal to make gifts to certain relatives.
3. Refusal to educate certain relatives.

Meggitt has identified the following punishments for these offences:

Punishments

1. Death:
   a. caused by a non-human agency (A2)
   b. caused by human sorcery (A1, possibly A3)
   c. caused by physical attack (A1, possibly A3).
2. Insanity caused – by a non-human agency (A2).

12 *Ibid*, pp 256–57.

3. Illness – caused by human sorcery (A1, A2, A3, A5, A6, A7, A8; B1, B2).
4. Wounding – attack with a spear or knife, intending to draw blood (A5, A6, A7, A8, A9, A10, A11).
5. Battery – attack with a club or boomerang (A6, A7, A8, A9, A10, A11, A12; B1, B2, B3).
6. Oral abuse – this accompanies all human punishments.
7. Ridicule – this is directed mainly at offences of omission.

The range of penalties is as limited as the range of offences. There is some debate whether ostracism and exile were ever traditional punishment.[13] The state of penalties were in fact the maximum but it was possible for those sympathetic to the offender or his kin to plead for a lesser punishment. Partly because most social behaviour conforms to a regular pattern, partly because of the limited number of possible offences, and partly because of the relative inability to offend without others knowing, it was rare that public opinion was divided on the question whether a person had broken the law. Such popular consensus of course does not always mean that he is guilty but it appears that miscarriages of justice were uncommon. Punishment was usually meted out in the public gaze. There was almost no privacy in any camp. The publicity may have been a significant factor determining the general conformity of the people to the more important rules.

Who is subject to Aboriginal customary law?

The change in traditional Aboriginal society as a result of British settlement has altered the extent to which Aboriginal customary law governs the lives of many Aborigines. Policies of settlement and dispossession have displaced some Aborigines from traditional lands and thus affected traditional authority. Other Aborigines have come to reside in cities and rural centres thus increasing contact with European culture. Although many Aborigines may originally have had no intention of giving up traditional ways they nevertheless became less inclined to return to them. The availability of medical skills, education and modern technology have all increased the degree of contact with Europeans and European ways. Modern telecommunications and means of travel add further pressures. Aircraft, motor cars, telephones, radio and television provided in remote areas by satellite and other means may lead to a conflict between the desire to take advantage of what western civilisation has to offer and a retention of traditional lifestyle. Western society has introduced foreign problems to traditional Aboriginal law. Alcohol has had a devastating effect, removing the restraints and social inhibitions which regulated Aboriginal society. The capacity to buy food at a store has altered obligations concerning hunting and food gathering. Payments of social service benefits often cut across traditional family structures and kinship rules. Aborigines seek education for their children. On the other hand, that very education can undermine traditional authority and lead to questioning of traditional rules and punishments.

13 Meggitt says that neither ostracism nor exile was practised by the Walbiri, *op cit*, p 258.

Encouragement now given to the establishment of Aboriginal organisations and the granting of land rights may assist in some kind of revival of Aboriginal law and culture. But the influences which might displace Aboriginal customary law continue to exist. In addition, the establishment of Aboriginal organisations with office-bearers often being younger Aborigines educated in Australian schools and universities and more experienced in the ways and concepts of the wider Australian community sometimes cut across traditional lines of authority. The granting of land, the impact of mining and the payment of mining royalties, will also have their effect upon traditional life and culture.

Aborigines today live in a wide variety of communities varying from cities to remote communities. Aborigines represent a little over 1% of the Australian population and about 80% of Aborigines live outside major urban centres.[14] Non-urban Aborigines live in communities which vary enormously in size, character and location. They include small, remote communities, outstations, missions, groups on pastoral properties, pastoral properties owned by Aborigines, and those residing in or on the fringe of country towns. For many urban Aborigines living in cities and large towns, traditional rules no longer have the force they once did.[15] This is not to say that aspects of kinship and other rules have no place in their lives. More traditionally oriented Aborigines reside in the more remote areas of Australia, some living in small communities and others in large communities numbering over 1,000. Between these two groups of Aborigines is a large number of Aborigines for whom traditional Aboriginal law, culture and ways of life have been extensively modified by residence close to towns in more remote areas. They are sometimes referred to as fringe dwellers.[16]

There is, therefore, an enormous variation in the extent to which Aborigines are governed by Aboriginal customary law. Although these three groups have been identified, generalisations must be avoided. There will be differences in the composition and nature of these groups in different parts of Australia. Nor should it be assumed that in any one area there is any inevitable or regular movement away from more traditional to less traditional ways of life. The extent to which there is any movement from traditional ways of life is influenced by factors such as economic development, the level of Aboriginal and non-Aboriginal population, the degree of government intervention and non-intervention, land rights, the impact of pensions and other inroads on kinship and other traditional obligations and the internal dynamics of the community. The extent to which Aboriginal customary law will continue to exist will vary from community to community and, as a general rule, will be stronger in more remote communities.

14 A convenient demographic survey based on 1981 census is found in ALRC 31, paras 29–36.

15 See Gale, F, *Urban Aborigines*, 1972, Canberra: ANU Press; Rowley, CD, *Outcasts in White Australia*, 1972, Ringwood: Penguin.

16 House of Representatives Standing Committee on Aboriginal Affairs, *Strategies to Help Overcome the Problems of Aboriginal Town Camps*, 1982, Canberra: Australian Government Publishing Service, para 31 and generally paras 15–33.

The application of English law

Initially, English law was applied to colonists who had committed offences against Aborigines and to Aborigines who had committed offences against colonists. But the application of English law to Aborigines who had committed offences against one another was less certain and the wisdom of doing so was questioned. Although some, including judges, took the view that, in respect of purely Aboriginal matters, Aborigines should be governed by 'their own ancient usages', the Supreme Court of New South Wales in 1836 in *R v Jack Congo Murrell*[17] decided that English law should apply to offences committed by one Aborigine upon another. The Supreme Court had to deal with two distinct cases where one Aborigine had been charged with the murder of another. In *Murrell* the defendant alleged that he was so drunk he could not help the killing. In the other, the defendant relied on Aboriginal customary law. His victim was, apparently, a member of the group which had killed his brother and it was a case of obedience to the aboriginal custom of revenge killing. The court held that there was no distinction between offences committed by white people upon one another and by Aborigines upon one another:[18]

> Serious cases might arise if these people were allowed to murder one another with impunity, our laws would be no sanctuary to them. For these reasons, the court has jurisdiction.

Although the decision was ultimately regarded as settling the issue, judges in other jurisdictions questioned whether Aborigines should be subject to English law.

In South Australia, Cooper J held the view that it was:[19]

> ... impossible to try according to the forms of English law, people of a wild and savage tribe whose country although within the limits of the province of South Australia, has not been occupied by usurpers, who have never submitted themselves to our dominion and between whom and the Colonists there has been no social intercourse.

Similar views were expressed by Willis J in 1841 in the Supreme Court of Victoria when he said that 'there is no express law which makes the Aborigines subject to our Colonial Code'.[20] Cooper J in South Australia remained unwilling to concede that Aborigines should always be tried for offences under British law. In 1846 an Aborigine was brought before the court for killing another. Cooper J argued that he required a legislative direction if such cases were to be justiciable and the accused was discharged because no competent interpreter was available.[21] In 1848 the judge accepted jurisdiction when an Aborigine was tried for an offence against another but indicated

17 (1836) 1 Legge (NSW) 72.

18 *Ibid* at 73.

19 CSO 511/1840, Advice from Cooper J to the government of South Australia.

20 *R v Bon Jon, Port Phillip Gazette*, 18 September 1841. The case did not proceed and Bon Jon was handed over to the Protectorate to be educated. He escaped and was later murdered in a payback killing.

21 *Larry v R* (1846) Register, 14, 25, 28 November, Cooper J referred the matter to the Governor; CSO 1564/1851.

before the trial commenced that 'in the case of a conviction he would stay any execution required by law and specifically refer the case to the governor'.[22] In Western Australia, views differed as to whether Aborigines should be subject to European law.[23]

The rule in *Murrell* was tempered by a practice of non-involvement of law enforcement agencies in disputes between Aborigines and by decisions not to prosecute for that offence or by mitigating sentences for offences between Aborigines. But the basic rule remained and Aborigines were subject to English law. In the case of criminal law, in practice, both before and after 1836, the law was applied differentially and, especially in remote areas, haphazardly, so that few killings (whether an Aborigine was an offender or victim) were prosecuted.[24]

The rule that Aborigines are subject to the same criminal law as non-Aboriginal Australians was reaffirmed by Mason CJ in the High Court in 1994 in *Walker v State of New South Wales*.[25] Walker, an Aborigine, was charged with an offence against the law of New South Wales. He claimed that the Parliament of New South Wales lacked the power to legislate in the manner affecting Aboriginal people or, alternatively, that State legislation affecting Aboriginal people had no operation until it was adopted by them. Mason CJ rejected the claim holding that Australian criminal law does not accommodate a body of law operating alongside it and that there is nothing in *Mabo v Queensland (No 2)* to provide any support at all for the proposition that criminal laws of general application do not apply to Aboriginal people.[26]

Notwithstanding that Aborigines and non-Aborigines are all subject to the same law, courts in Australia have from time to time recognised certain aspects of Aboriginal customary law. Most of the recognition has occurred in relation to the criminal law but there has been very significant in aspects of the civil law. Some of those aspects of Aboriginal customary law which have been recognised will now be examined. What follows is not a complete examination and reference should be made to more detailed studies. Reference should also be made elsewhere to those aspects which have received legislative recognition.[27] The issues involves in recognition have been examined by the Australian Law Reform Commission. A few of its recommendations are noted below but reference should be made to its report.[28]

22 Castles, AC, *An Australian Legal History*, citing (1848) Register, 14, 17 June; *Robe to Grey* (1848) 10 July, GRG 2/6/4.

23 Hasluck, P, *Black Australians*, 1942, Melbourne: Melbourne University Press, p 129.

24 Reece, RHW, *Aborigines and Colonists*, 1974, Sydney: Sydney University Press, pp 194–95, 225–27.

25 (1994) 126 ALR 321. See also *Coe v The Commonwealth* (1993) 118 ALR 193. The issues involved in the application of one law to all Australians are also noted in *Ngatayi v The Queen* (1980) 147 CLR 1 at 10–11.

26 126 ALR 321 at 323–24.

27 Some examples of legislative recognition are noted in ALRC 31, Chapter 35.

28 ALRC 31.

THE CRIMINAL LAW AND ABORIGINAL CUSTOMARY LAW

Courts in Australia have for a long time taken Aboriginal customary laws into account when determining what is an appropriate penalty for an Aborigine convicted of an offence. The sentencing of convicted Aborigines is dealt with elsewhere in this work and will not now be examined. Courts have also from time to time had regard to customary law when determining the responsibility of an Aborigine for an offence.

Recognition of Aboriginal customary law and of the special problems Aborigines have when they come into conflict with the criminal justice system occur at each levels of the process of investigation, prosecution and trial of an alleged offender. It is convenient to examine them in turn.

Interrogation

Procedural rules and rules of evidence have been modified to have regard for relevant aspects of customary law and the special problems of Aborigines. Those special problems are not limited to language barriers and a lack of understanding of the criminal justice system.[29] They also include concepts of time and distance which often differ from those of white Australians. It is well recognised also that Aborigines have a deference to authority which can lead to a propensity to give answers thought to be expected rather than to state what actually occurred. In addition, rules of customary law may lead to inhibitions in answering questions. The suspect may be unwilling to mention the name of a dead person or to disclose secret matters or matters that are someone else's business. The suspect may lack authority to speak on an issue.[30] There may be an avoidance relationship with a translator or someone else involved in the interrogation. Differences in language are not confined merely to the need for translation but also include the difficulties in explaining legal concepts and the different meaning of some words.

In an attempt to overcome these difficulties, Forster J, then a Justice of the Supreme Court of the Northern Territory, formulated a series of guidelines which have become known as the *Anunga Rules*.[31] They are a modification of the Judges Rules which since the early 20th century have regulated the interrogation of suspects. The guidelines were in 1979 incorporated in a police circular issued by the Northern Territory Police Commissioner.[32] The guidelines require:

- an interpreter to be present if the suspect is not fluent in English;
- the presence of a 'prisoner's friend' (someone in whom the Aborigine has apparent confidence);
- great care in administering the caution (the right to silence) and ensuring it is understood;
- the provision of basic refreshments and substitute clothing if needed;

29 The problems are examined in ALRC 31, para 546.

30 See ALRC 31, paras 644 and 645.

31 *R v Anunga* (1976) 11 ALR 412.

32 Police Circular – Memorandum No 13 of 1979.

- no questioning while the person is ill, drunk or tired; and
- reasonable steps to obtain legal assistance if requested.

Recommendations for such guidelines have also been made by judges in South Australia, Western Australia and New South Wales.[33] They have not been implemented in all States. Police departments in Victoria, the Northern Territory, South Australia and the Australian Capital Territory have some system for notifying the local Aboriginal Legal Service after an Aborigine has been arrested.[34] In Queensland, South Australia, the Northern Territory and the Australian Capital Territory there are guidelines for police when questioning Aboriginal suspects.[35] A departure from the guidelines without sufficient reason may result in a judge ruling that the statement obtained from a suspect is inadmissible in the exercise of the judicial discretion to exclude such evidence. Thus, a confession may be excluded if there has been a failure to comply with the guidelines.[36]

In order to achieve uniformity throughout Australia, the Australian Law Reform Commission has made recommendations as to rules relating to the interrogation of Aboriginal suspects. In broad terms they follow the *Anunga Rules*. The Commission has recommended that the guidelines should be enacted in legislation to make it clear both to the police and to the courts that the interrogation rules are to be taken seriously.[37]

Prosecutorial discretion

Although not strictly an aspect of the common law, it is convenient to refer to the discretion invested in both the police and the Crown whether to charge an accused person with an offence and the nature of the offence with which the accused will be charged. Although the discretion is not unlimited,[38] it does enable prosecuting authorities to consider whether a prosecution will be in the public interest and thus determine whether it is appropriate not to prosecute because of the operation of customary law in a particular case. The discretion may be exercised in a number of ways. They include:

- non-prosecution for certain offences (for example, in cases regarded as strictly 'traditional' or 'tribal');
- prosecution for a lesser offence, such as reducing murder to manslaughter. In the case of less serious offences, the prosecution of the lesser of two alternative offences

33 See *R v Gibson*, 12 November 1973, Supreme Court of SA (unreported), *R v Williams* (1976) 14 SASR 1 at 6, *Grantham v Thomas* Supreme Court of SA, No 2808 of 1980 (unreported); *Abdullah v O'Meara*, Supreme Court of WA, Appeal No 44 of 1979 (unreported); *McKellar v South* [1982] 2 NSWLR 950 at 962.

34 Section 1.3.7 Victoria Police Manual; NT Police, General Orders A12 and Q2; s 79A Summary Offences Act 1953 (SA) combined with General Order 3015, Aboriginals; Australian Federal Police, General Instruction 1 (27 February 1984).

35 For details see ALRC 31, paras 554–560.

36 For example, *R v Ajax* (1977) 17 SASR 88; *R v Williams* (1976) 14 SASR 1; and see generally *R v McKenzie* (1977) 17 SASR 304.

37 ALRC 31, para 573.

38 *Cf R v Metropolitan Police Commissioner, ex p Blackburn* [1968] 2 QB 118 and *R v Metropolitan Police Commissioner, ex p Blackburn (No 3)* [1973] QB 241.

may allow a matter to be dealt with locally by a magistrate rather than in a distant centre by the Supreme Court or District Court; and

- entering of a *nolle prosequi* by the Crown.

The prosecutorial discretion may be relevant in those cases where Aboriginal customary law, without necessarily justifying or excusing criminal conduct, is a significant mitigating factor, and where the Aboriginal community in question has through its own processes resolved the matter and reconciled those involved. Factors relevant in such cases would include the following:[39]

- that an offence has been committed against the general law in circumstances where there is no doubt that the offence had a customary law basis;
- whether the offender was aware he was breaking the law;
- that the matter has been resolved locally in a satisfactory way in accordance with customary law processes;
- that the victim of the offence does not wish the matter to proceed;
- that the relevant Aboriginal community's expectations (or the expectations of each community, if there is more than one) is that the matter has been resolved and should not be pursued further;
- that alternatives to prosecution are available, for example, a diversion procedure; and
- that the broader public interest would not be served by engaging in legal proceedings for little or no purpose.

An example of how the prosecutorial discretion can have regard to Aboriginal customary law in both charging the accused person and in sentencing him is provided in a recent case in the Supreme Court of South Australia.[40] Fighting had broken out in the course of a dispute at Amata in the Pitjantjatjara lands in north-west South Australia. The accused, Burton, had stabbed another Aborigine in the leg, severing the femoral artery causing a massive blood loss. The other Aborigine died soon after. It appeared that, in the course of the fighting, the deceased had speared Burton in the back of his thigh. After being speared, Burton went to the house and quickly returned carrying a large knife. In accordance with what was said to be the Anungu way of not hitting and running but exchanging one stab for another, the deceased presented his leg to Burton to be stabbed. Burton failed to execute the stabbing in a way to cause minimal injury. After the incident, Burton himself was punished by spearing in accordance with traditional custom. Burton was committed for trial on a charge of murder. The Director of Public Prosecutions had regard to the customary law aspects and charged Burton not with murder but with manslaughter. When sentencing, Duggan J had regard to the punishment already meted out by the Aboriginal community.

39 See ALRC 31, para 478.

40 *R v Burton* (1994) 18 July, No 81 of 1994, (unreported).

Provocation

The killing of one person by another with an intention to kill or do serious bodily harm is murder. At common law or under the codes, the crime of murder will be reduced to manslaughter if the killing resulted from a sudden and temporary loss of self-control on the part of the killer which is brought about by acts or words of the deceased amounting in law to provocation. Thus, provocation is a defence to murder in the sense that it reduces the charge from murder to manslaughter. To amount in law to provocation, the acts or words must satisfy the following tests:[41]

1. they must be done or said by the deceased to or in the presence of the killer; or
2. they must have caused in the killer a sudden and temporary loss of self-control rendering the killer so subject to passion as to make him for the moment not master of his mind; or
3. they must be of such a character as might cause an ordinary person to lose his self-control to such an extent as to act as the killer has acted.

Common sense and justice dictate that this concession to human frailty should be limited by the requirement that the provocation would cause an ordinary person to lose self-control lest an exceptionally pugnacious person or a bad-tempered or over-sensitive person be liable only for manslaughter but a sober and even-tempered person would be guilty of murder.[42]

Until the late 1970s, the test of what constituted provocation at law was strictly applied and the concept of what would provoke an ordinary person resulted in an objective test of how a reasonable English man or woman would respond. Except in cases of a most extreme or exceptional character, mere words were not capable of constituting provocation.[43] Thus, a sudden confession of adultery by a wife could not amount to provocation.[44] This was an inappropriate test as it made no allowance for persons from cultural or ethnic backgrounds quite different from those of the ordinary English man or woman. In 1977 the High Court recognised it was proper to have regard to the ethnic background of the accused.[45] An Italian migrant had killed his wife after she had rejected his continual advances and contemptuously stated her pleasure in promiscuity with neighbouring men. It was held that the issue of provocation had been correctly left to the jury. In 1978 the *House of Lords in Camplin v DPP*[46] reviewed earlier decisions concerning the law of provocation and held that the defendant's age and characteristics were relevant in assessing whether a reasonable man would have been provoked. As Lord Morris said:[47]

41 *The Queen v R* (1981) 28 SASR 321 at 321–22.

42 *DPP v Camplin* [1978] AC 705 at 725.

43 *Holmes v DPP* [1946] AC 588.

44 *Bedder v DPP* [1954] 2 All ER 801.

45 *Moffa v The Queen* (1977) 138 CLR 601.

46 [1978] AC 705.

47 *Ibid* at 721.

> If the accused is of particular colour or particular ethnic origin and things are said which to him are grossly insulting it would be unreal if the jury had to consider whether the words would have provoked a man of different colour or ethnic origin – or to consider how such a man would have acted or reacted.

Thus a greater degree of subjectivity was introduced into the test. Since then Australian courts have held that when determining provocation regard should be had to the ethnic or cultural background of the accused. As Cox J of the Supreme Court of South Australia noted:[48]

> The ordinary man against whom the actions of the accused are to be judged is one possessing all the characteristics and idiosyncrasies of the accused himself – age, sex, race, colour, physical defects and so on – that would have affected his conduct in the circumstances in which the accused found himself, with the exception of any extraordinary excitability or pugnacity that the accused happened to possess.

Thus, when determining whether the words or conduct of the deceased provoked an accused Aborigine, regard would be had to whether those words or conduct would provoke an Aborigine who has a like background and cultural beliefs and influences of the accused.

These developments had been anticipated in the Northern Territory in relation to Aborigines. The Privy Council had in 1946 recognised the inappropriateness of an objective test of how an ordinary person would react when considering an appeal concerning a West African villager.[49] In the 1950s Kriewaldt J in the Supreme Court of the Northern Territory recognised that regard should be had to the cultural factors which cause an Aborigine to lose self-control. In *R v Patipatu*[50] in 1951 the accused had put his young son in the charge of the deceased woman but she had left the child by the side of a track and abandoned him there. Patipatu was so enraged by this conduct that he threw a spear at the woman which killed her. The judge directed the jury as follows:

> If you think that in the circumstances prevailing in that particular locality the abandonment of a young child ... by the person appointed to look after it ... would cause an ordinary reasonable person in that vicinity and of that description, so to lose control of his emotions as to retaliate with a spear then you would be entitled in this case to find a verdict of manslaughter.

In another case he declined to apply the English rule that mere words could not constitute provocation. In *R v Muddarubba*[51] in 1956, the defendant had speared the deceased woman after she had used an Aboriginal term which constituted an extreme insult. He explained:

48 *R v Dutton* (1979) 21 SASR 356.

49 *Kwaku Mensah v The King* [1946] AC 83.

50 [1951] NTJ 18 at 20. This and the following two decisions are noted in Morris, N, and Howard, C, *Studies in Criminal Law*, 1964, Oxford: Clarendon Press, pp 93–97.

51 [1956] NTJ 317 at 322.

> In my opinion, in any discussion of provocation, the general principle of law is to create a standard which would be observed by the average person in the community in which the accused person lives. It is clear from the cases decided by courts whose decisions bind me that in white communities matters regarded as sufficient provocation a century ago would not be regarded as sufficient today. This suggests that the standard is not a fixed and unchanging standard; it leaves it open, and I think properly so, to regard the Pitjantjatjara tribe as a separate community for the purpose of considering the reaction of the average man. I tell you that if you think the average member of the Pitjintjara tribe ... would have retaliated to the words and actions of the woman by spearing her, then the act of spearing is not murder but manslaughter.

Again, in *R v Nelson*[52] Kriewaldt J directed a jury that it could have regard to customary law when determining whether there had been sufficient time for passions to cool. The deceased had attacked and injured the defendant who then went off and fetched two boomerangs with which he later killed the deceased. At the time of the killing, the defendant was under the impression that the deceased had harmed his wife:

> If the accused in this case were a white person I should have to tell you as a matter of law that the defence of provocation would not be open because on Nelson's story a sufficient time had elapsed between the time he was wounded and the time he struck Dann for passions to have died down. But the accused is not a white man ... In the case of a native you may think it right to say that the effect of provocation lasts longer than in the case of a white person.

However, this approach was not always followed in other jurisdictions and it was not until authoritative decisions such as *Moffa* and *Camplin* that Australian courts were free, when determining the standard of an ordinary person in the defendant's situation, to have regard to how those of his cultural and ethnic background would act rather than some abstract disembodied standards of reasonableness.

An Aboriginal customary law defence?

There are other areas where it appears to be appropriate to take Aboriginal customary law into account when assessing responsibility for a criminal act. An Aborigine may believe that he is required by Aboriginal customary law to act in a particular way and the resulting conduct may be an offence against the criminal law. In *R v Isobel Phillips*[53] the defendant, a woman from the Warumungu tribe, was required by Warumungu customary law to fight in public any woman involved with her husband. Warumungu law also set limits to the fight, which were not exceeded in this case. Anthropological evidence showed that the defendant was under a threat of death or serious injury if she did not respond but the magistrate held that:

> A Warumungu woman of ordinary firmness would have carried out the instructions she was given ... as the defendant did ... The threats ... are backed up by the sanctions of the

52 21 March 1956 (unreported).

53 Northern Territory Court of Summary Jurisdiction (Mr JM Murphy SM), 19 September 1983, (unreported).

> Warumungu law and, she cannot, as she remains in the Warumungu environment, evade these consequences.

The charges were dismissed on the ground that the defence of duress applied. A defence of duress will not be available if the accused is charged as a principal with murder. Further, Aborigines might have voluntarily acted in accordance with external pressure. In *R v Old Barney Jungala*[54] Muirhead J commented:

> There is no suggestion that (the defendant) intended to cause the death of this young woman and, I accept the fact that he acted as he believed the law which he respected compelled him to do.

The defendant was convicted of manslaughter on the grounds of lack of intent to kill, not duress.

The Australian Law Reform Commission considered whether a customary law defence exonerating the defendant from liability in such cases should be created.[55] As Commissioner Crawford has reported,[56] a customary law defence would involve endorsing tribal killings, and would deprive persons, including Aboriginal victims of offences, of legal protection. The defence, therefore, raises serious problems of equal protection under the law. The Commissioner concluded that evidence of Aboriginal customary law can be taken into account sufficiently in the general criminal law through the exercise of sentencing and other procedural discretions, and that the customary law defence was neither necessary nor desirable. The Commissioner did, however, recommend the creation of a partial defence, similar to a defence of diminished responsibility, which would operate to reduce the level of liability in particular cases from murder to manslaughter. The advances of this defence were that it would not involve condoning or endorsing payback killings or woundings, nor would it deprive victims of legal protection or the right of redress. Nevertheless, it represented direct acknowledgment of conflicts that can occur between a general legal system and Aboriginal customary laws and would operate as adjunct to the sentencing discretion.

THE CIVIL LAW AND ABORIGINAL CUSTOMARY LAW

Recognition of Aboriginal customary law is not confined to the criminal law. Of paramount importance is the recognition of land rights. As land rights is the subject of detailed examination elsewhere in another of the chapters in this work, it will not be examined here other than to note the highly significant decision of the High Court in *Mabo v Queensland (No 2)*.[57]

54 Supreme Court of NT, 8 February 1978 (unreported).

55 ALRC 31, paras 442–453.

56 Crawford, J, *The Recognition of Aboriginal Customary Laws: An Overview, in Aboriginal Perspectives on Criminal Justice*, 1992, Canberra: Australian Institute of Criminology, pp 65–66.

57 (1994) 175 CLR 1.

Confidential information

The common law has also recognised the confidential nature of Aboriginal customary law. In *Foster v Mountford*[58] common law recognised the secret-sacred aspects of Aboriginal customary law. Mountford was a highly distinguished anthropologist. For more than 35 years he had worked with Pitjantjatjara Aborigines. He wrote a substantial work concerning his research which included photographs, drawings and descriptions of persons, places and ceremonies with deep religious and cultural significance to the Aboriginal plaintiffs. It included matters which were hitherto secret. Muirhead J accepted that the publication of the work had caused dismay, concern and anger and might further disrupt the social system of Pitjantjatjara Aborigines. He issued an interlocutory injunction restraining the publication of the work on the ground that some of the information in the book could only have been supplied and exposed in confidence, a confidence which he found had been recognised by the author in a preface to the work.[59] Thus, the rules in equity as to disclosure confidential information were applied. The defendants did not seek to set aside the injunction.

Different issues concerning confidential information were examined by the Full Court of the Supreme Court of South Australia in *Coulthard v South Australia*.[60] The issues involved the unauthorised publication of an anthropologist's report concerning a meeting between Aborigines and officers of state and Federal governments. In 1987 a dispute broke out between two Aboriginal communities, the Kuyani and Kokotha people, who had competing claims to traditional rights in respect of Coorlay Lagoon near Roxby Downs in South Australia. The Kuyani asked the Aboriginal and Torres Strait Islanders Commission (ATSIC) to intervene. ATSIC arranged meetings with both the Kuyani and Kokotha in August 1990. ATSIC also asked officers of the Aboriginal Heritage Branch of the South Australian government to attend the meeting. The meeting was held first with the Kokotha on 22 August and with the Kuyani on 23 August. The issues at the trial concerned the second meeting. Four representatives of government, two from ATSIC and two from the Aboriginal Heritage Branch, were present at the meeting. One of the representatives of the Branch was an anthropologist. He prepared a report of the meeting. At the meeting, three Aborigines made statements which were not only inflammatory in European terms but were severe breaches of Aboriginal customary law. Each of the three Aboriginal speakers had transgressed, one in uttering a curse and the other two in expressing views on matters about which by customary law they had no authority to speak. The anthropologist's report was stolen by an unknown person from the docket in the Branch and copies were circulated in Port Augusta, causing considerable embarrassment to the three Aboriginal speakers. They each brought an action against the government of South Australia claiming, among other things, a breach of confidence.

The plaintiffs' claims were dismissed at first instance and an appeal from the decision was dismissed by the Full Court of the Supreme Court. The court held that the state of

58 (1976) 14 ALR 71.

59 *Ibid* at 72–73.

60 (1995) 180 LSJS 1.

South Australia was not liable as the state could not, in the circumstances, be vicariously liable for the act of an unknown employee who had wrongfully removed the report from the docket which was held in a reasonably secure place. However, the Full Court held that the information imparted at the meeting was of a confidential nature and was imparted to officers of government on an occasion which imported an obligation of confidence. Although there had been no resolution or statement that anything said at the meeting was confidential, the court had regard to the serious nature of the dispute, the sensitive nature of the matters discussed at the meeting and in particular matters related to sacred sites, the fact that it was a private not a public meeting, the fact that the press were expressly excluded from the meeting, and the fact that it was explicit from the nature of the meeting that whatever was said would be regarded as confidential and used only for the purpose of enabling the respective governments to seek to resolve the dispute concerning Coorlay Lagoon. The court held that disclosure of what was said at the meeting would be limited to those officers of government involved in seeking to resolve the dispute. This decision also represents the application of well-established principles in equity concerning the duty of confidence to an aspect of customary law.

Copyright

It might be possible for the customary law to be used to protect intellectual property in Aboriginal society. For example, there might be a material which is suitable for copyright protection. Copyright might exist in designs or the words or music of a song. Some of the difficulties are examined by Professor Ken Maddock[61] and in another chapter in this work.

Hunting, fishing and gathering

Allied to land rights are traditional rights to hunt, fish and gather food. Aborigines have had to adapt and change to outside influences. Hunting and gathering in traditional societies have been substantially affected by the payment of welfare benefits and the introduction of rations and food bought at community or other stores. Nevertheless, particularly in more remote areas, hunting, fishing and food gathering continued to be of economic and ritual importance. Modern technology is frequently used and has replaced many traditional weapons or instruments. Guns may replace spears, vehicles enable large distances to be quickly traversed, aluminium boats replace dugouts, fishing nets are made of nylon fibre, and fishing gear will bear little resemblance to traditional fishing spears. The decision in *Mabo v Queensland (No 2)*[62] may influence the capacity of the common law to recognise customary rights concerning hunting, fishing and food gathering. The present position is that the common law has not recognised such rights and there is a body of legislation which may have cancelled or overridden many customary rights.

61 Maddock, K, 'Copyright and Traditional Designs' (1988), 2 *Aboriginal Law Bulletin* 34.

62 (1994) 175 CLR 1.

The decision in *Mason v Tritton*[63] illustrates the difficulties facing a person seeking to advance a claim for traditional fishing rights. An Aborigine had been charged with having more than the permitted quantity of abalone in his possession contrary to Fisheries and Oyster Farms (General) Regulations 1989 of New South Wales. He had dived for abalone and had brought 92 to shore. He claimed a traditional right to fish coastal waters near Dalmeny on the South Coast of New South Wales. It was held that he had failed to prove that, in diving for abalone on this occasion, he had exercised a traditional and customary right to fish. It was held that the defendant had failed to prove any recognised system of rules or the content of the rules – for example, did they permit the taking of commercial quantities of abalone – and whether the defendant was bound by them.

The need for evidence to establish claims was also examined in the Supreme Court of Western Australia in *Taylor v Webb* and *McGinty v Webb*.[64] The appellants had been charged with remaining on premises without lawful authority after being warned by police officers to leave them. The charge related to the occupation by a number of Aborigines of an old brewery site on the Swan River at Perth. The appellants claimed that they were custodians of the land pursuant to Aboriginal law and tradition and, in that capacity, had a right to be on the premises and to invite others to join them. No evidence was led to establish the claim. They were convicted. The court held that it was necessary for the appellants to lead evidence to establish the asserted right and that they were custodians of the land. Appeals against their convictions were, therefore, dismissed.

Suppression of names

It is contrary to Aboriginal customary law and extremely offensive to many Aborigines to speak of a dead person by name. A number of Australian courts and particularly those in the Northern Territory have recognised this and do not refer to a deceased Aborigine by name. In *R v Bara Bara*[65] Mildren J of the Supreme Court of the Northern Territory took judicial notice of this aspect of customary law and, when dealing with an Aborigine who had pleaded guilty to manslaughter of another Aborigine, made an order suppressing from publication the name of the deceased. The judge was also influenced to make the order because it was likely to reduce the danger of a 'payback' killing. Thus, the name was suppressed not only in the conduct of the proceedings but also from publication in the media.

Assessment of damages

Aborigines who have suffered injuries in motor vehicle accidents have sometimes been prevented by their injuries from continuing to participate or engage in traditional practices or undertake traditional responsibilities. Regard has been had to these

63 (1994) 34 NSWLR 572.

64 Both decisions were delivered by the Full Court of the Supreme Court of WA on 27 November 1990 and were unreported.

65 (1992) 87 NTR 1.

disabilities when the assessing the damages to be awarded for the injuries they have suffered. In *Napaluma v Baker*[66] the plaintiff had begun to undertake traditional ceremonies of the Pitjantjatjara people and had been initiated. When assessing damages for a loss of amenities resulting from his injuries, Zelling J had regard to the fact that, because of his injuries, further secrets could not be entrusted to him and he would not, in our parlance, rise to higher degrees in Aboriginal society. Accordingly, he was left out of some ceremonies and played a minor passive role in others and was less than a full member of the Aboriginal community. In the Supreme Court of the Northern Territory regard has been had to tribal customs in assessing the effects of an injury sustained in a motor vehicle accident.[67]

Proof of Aboriginal customary law

The question of the proof of the Aboriginal customary law has not been examined in any detail in this paper. The question is examined in the Law Reform Commission's report.[68] There must be evidence to prove that the manner in which an Aborigine has conducted himself is, in truth, in accordance with customary law and not simply an angry reaction, say, to a particular event or events. Proof of customary law is highly important in land rights claims. Methods of proof and determining who are qualified experts are important issues as are the ultimate issue question and the law relating to hearsay. The fact that there are secret aspects of customary law may lead to difficulty particularly if an attempt is made to test the legitimacy of the claim. These issues will have to be addressed by tribunals dealing with land rights claims.

The future

The extent to which the common law has recognised Aboriginal customary law has not been uniform throughout Australia and on occasions it has been haphazard. The Australian Law Reform Commission has concluded that other aspect of Aboriginal customary law in addition to those mentioned here should be recognised. The Commission's recommendations relate to a wide range of matters including evidence and procedures; marriage, children and family property; the substantive criminal law and sentencing of Aboriginal offenders, secrecy and confidentiality; proof of Aboriginal customary law. Little effect has yet been given to its recommendations. Perhaps the decision in *Mabo v Queensland (No 2)* may provide added impetus to the adoption of the Commission's recommendations.

66 (1982) 29 SASR 192.

67 *Weston v Woodroffe* (1985) 36 NTR 34.

68 ALRC 31, Chapter 24.

CHAPTER SEVEN

ABORIGINES AND THE LAW

Elliott Johnston

The subject is extremely wide and invites discussion of topics ranging from Aboriginal customary law to the impact of non-Aboriginal law upon Aboriginal society for more than 200 years. This contribution will concern itself with the question of the relationship between the contemporary Australian law (which of course can only be fully understood against some historical background) and Aboriginal people. I make clear the sense in which I use certain terms.

By 'law' I mean the whole body of law (statute, regulations etc made pursuant to statute and common law) and also the administration of those laws; so that when I refer to the criminal law I intend to refer not only to the law in relation to criminal offences, but also to the activity of police who are charged with the task of detecting and investigating breaches and laying charges, the courts which deal with the charges and the departments (eg Correctional Services) which administer orders made by the courts. The total of these activities are covered by the concept of the Criminal Justice System.

I have used the phrase 'contemporary Australian law' to mean the whole system applied by Australian courts. Quite significant parts of the contemporary law are the result of Aboriginal demand, or have strong Aboriginal support, for example the lands rights legislation in some states, the Commonwealth Northern Territory Land Rights Act and now the native title legislation following the *Mabo* decision; Aboriginal heritage legislation, anti discrimination legislation, the legislation containing grants for Aboriginal purposes etc. Additionally it should be noted that courts in some circumstances have regard to matters of Aboriginal customary law, particularly in relation to sentencing.

I am particularly concerned to discuss Aboriginal relations with the law very generally on the one hand and with the criminal justice system on the other.

Overwhelmingly public discussion about Aboriginal people and the law centres around criminal justice (and this is so whether those involved in the discussion are Aboriginal or non-Aboriginal).

The most immediate reason for this concentration is the enormous publicity properly given to the over representation of Aboriginal people in the criminal justice system as found by the Royal Commission into Aboriginal Deaths in Custody (hereinafter referred to as the 'Royal Commission'). There are certain things about the Commission to be noted in this respect. The establishment of the Commission took place against the background of what was clearly a disproportionately high number of deaths amongst Aboriginal people in custody, plus the occurrence in 1987 of a number of deaths in what appeared to be circumstances that called loudly for inquiry; it was prompted by Aboriginal demand and (as it seems to me) by desire to meet the demand as an indication of goodwill on the eve of the celebration of 200 years of settlement. The terms of reference focused on custodial deaths but allowed for inquiry into 'why' and what came to be called 'underlying issues'.

The question of disproportion was not open to argument on the figures readily available. It appeared that the proportion of known Aboriginal deaths in prison custody exceeded the Aboriginal percentage of the population of the country by 13 or 14 times. But research going a little deeper showed that, in respect of prison custody, (for which substantially accurate figures were available over quite a period of time) the number of Aboriginal deaths was not disproportionate to the Aboriginal prison population. To put it another way; Aboriginal prisoners died at almost exactly the same rate as non-Aboriginal prisoners. The disproportionate number of Aboriginal deaths as against Aboriginal presence in the entire population was found to be an expression of the disproportionate number of Aboriginal people in prison custody. That finding had a profound effect on the work of the Royal Commission. 'The underlying issues' became dramatically important. Why were so many Aboriginal people in the prisons, how to put an end to it?

(I have referred to the numbers of people in prison custody and to deaths in such custody. No statistics were available in relation to custody in police cells. The first ever investigation was carried out in August 1988 in a joint effort by the research unit of the Royal Commission in conjunction with the heads of all police services in the states and the Northern Territory. Agreed particulars of all incidents of police cell custody were recorded for that month. The degree of Aboriginal over-representation was 27 times. There is nothing whatever to suggest that the number of Aboriginal deaths in police custody was or is disproportionate to the number of Aboriginal people in such custody. It was a recommendation of the Royal Commission that the August 1988 audit be repeated at regular intervals. That recommendation was adopted and a similar audit was conducted in 1992. That audit confirmed both the Aboriginal over-representation in the cells and that the number of Aboriginal deaths in such custody was not disproportionate to other deaths.)

The activity of the Royal Commission, the evidence which emerged before it, the publicity given to that evidence and the findings based on that evidence, and particularly the clear proof of the gross over-representation of Aboriginal people in both police and prison custody have led to the concentration in the public mind on the operations of the criminal justice system.

But is of great importance to understand that Aboriginal concerned with the criminal justice system has much deeper roots than current statistics about Aboriginal over-representation in custody.

Historically (meaning 'until 1967', to take a very general time indicator) the criminal courts were the only courts in which Aboriginal people ever appeared (with very few exceptions) and overwhelmingly they appeared as the person charged; generally they had no knowledge of the law itself or of the procedures or of what was going on. Frequently they were not charged with a breach of the criminal law, as the community would understand that term (eg assault, theft etc), but with a breach of law relating to Aboriginal people only (eg they had in their possession liquor, they were not on a reserve where they should be, or were on another reserve without permission). Routinely they pleaded guilty. Routinely they were not represented except no doubt in the serious matters in which (in South Australia at least) the Supreme Court Judge would assign a lawyer. I have a very vague recollection that it was the late 1950s or perhaps the early 1960s when three or four of us, practising lawyers in South Australia, were occasionally asked by the Law Society of South Australia Poor Persons Legal Assistance Scheme (the first generally available scheme in Australia) to appear for Aboriginal defendants before magistrates. I now realise that I did not understand how it came to happen. I suppose that very occasionally an Aboriginal person would make an approach to the Society for assistance; I suspect that a few magistrates, realising that a case was out of the ordinary or otherwise called for special assistance, may have made an approach to the Society.

When the Aboriginal Legal Rights Movement was established in South Australia, its work was 99.9% assistance to people charged with offences. In the early 1970s the Movement decided to send a lawyer, assisted by an articled clerk and field officers, to Ceduna, on the far west coast of South Australia to investigate and to represent a large number of Aboriginal people charged with various offences arising out of an incident at an hotel following a football match. Space prevents detail. Some pleaded guilty as charged, but only after proper investigation and advice; some entered pleas of guilty (which were accepted) to lesser charges; in a substantial number of cases, a plea of not guilty was entered and the charges were subsequently withdrawn. But the really important thing was this; reliable people with long experience of the Ceduna area said that this was the first time in living memory that an Aboriginal person had appeared in a Court of Summary Jurisdiction at Ceduna and pleaded not guilty; a moment in history.

But it goes much deeper even that this. The police historically had to undertake the carrying out of all sorts of tasks associated with white domination which had nothing to do with the criminal law. As evening approached in country towns, the Aboriginal people were expected to make their way back to their side of town, often on 'the other side of the railway line' and police officers saw that they did so; police would often perform the actual task of picking up the young Aboriginal children who were being taken from their parents (usually mothers) to be placed with white families or in white institutions in the cities. And where this was done by other officials, it was the police and if necessary the courts which backed the power and authority of those officials. If a mother refused to hand over a child, claiming a right to refuse, the department did not go to the civil court seeking a declaration that the officer was entitled to take the child. The mother was not offered legal assistance to fight the matter. The child was taken. If necessary the police were called if not actually there. If resistance was offered, it was simply brushed aside by superior force. The criminal justice system was seen as the instrument of tyranny, not because those in the system were more tyrannical than others, but because they were obliged by the law to carry out social policy based on a concept of superiority and imposed assimilation. (This is not to say that some of these people did not enjoy what they were doing nor that some were not more aggressive than others nor that some hated what they were doing; it is merely to say that nothing is gained by picking on individuals for special blame – what was done was the will of the then white society as a whole.)

It is of some value to reduce such generalities to specific examples. I will speak of one such incident which may be thought to be trivial as compared with other events (and so it is), but it exemplifies the mindless tyranny that often prevailed backed up by the power of the system, and in 1996 it has a certain poignancy. David Unaipon (1873–1967) was a Ngarrindjeri man born at the Point McLeay mission in South Australia (now Raukkan). He was the first Aboriginal person to have a book published in Australia, a book about the legends of his people. An unusual man, an inventor interested in perpetual motion, recognised as a scholar by the University of Adelaide and encouraged both to study and to teach. He was permitted to leave the mission and work in Adelaide. In 1926 he visited the mission where he had grown up to contact his relatives and his people about some matters of research for university work. He did not seek the permission of the European superintendent to come upon the land of the mission; the latter was greatly offended. Unaipon explained his purpose; he explained that he was not 'sponging', (he produced from his pocket £3 (roughly about three-quarters of the then weekly basic wage)). It was to no avail. The superintendent called the police. He was arrested, charged and locked up.[1] Trifling, you might say, in the whole scheme of dispossession and destruction. The poignancy is that our 1996 Australian $50 note reproduces on one side a photograph of David Unaipon and alongside it some of the words that he wrote.

For more profound examples I refer to the report of the Laverton Royal Commission, 1975–76 (and in particular to the question of the 'doctored' charge sheets and briefs) and to the report of Commissioner Wootten on his Royal Commission inquiry into the death of Malcolm Smith.

For all these reasons the Aboriginal perception of the operation of the criminal justice system is at the heart of Aboriginal perceptions of and attitudes to the wider society and to the law as a whole.

There have been improvements and some of great moment. I indicate a few, stressing that I am speaking at this point only as to the criminal justice system.

In the first place, considerable funding has been provided for Aboriginal legal services all over the country so that Aboriginal people are now properly advised and represented. Procedures have been put in place for an independent friend of the suspect to be present when police are interviewing suspects who are Aboriginal. It represents an enormous change from the past. In a number of parts of Australia there have been dramatic improvements in the relations between police and Aborigines. In the Northern Territory in some towns there have been formal written agreements arrived at between police and important Aboriginal organisations about policing in the town camps (and this may have happened in other places without my being aware of it). In many places there are regular discussions between police and the appropriate Aboriginal organisations. It is my observation that in South Australia (and I believe that the trend is the same in other parts of the country) there is a much greater willingness on the part of judges and magistrates to take account of the special difficulties encountered by

1 See the *Oxford Companion to Australian Literature*, 1994, Melbourne: Oxford University Press and Mattingley, C, and Hampton, K (eds), *Survival in Our Own Land*, 1988, Adelaide: Wakefield Press.

Aboriginal people. I believe that the attitude of the courts is different to that which existed prior to the 1960s, and is changing further.[2]

There is encouragement for Aboriginal people to join various police forces. In some places there are Aboriginal police aides; there are Aboriginal people working in the correctional services. Aboriginal people are entering the law schools of Australian universities in significant numbers; a few have graduated and been admitted as lawyers, soon the numbers will be quite significant. This will have some profound long-term effects.

However, the fundamental fact is that despite these improvements, the disproportion of Aboriginal people in custody remains, in round figures, as high as it was.

How to reduce the number of Aboriginal prisoners

The view of the Royal Commission was that reduction of the number of Aboriginal people involved in the criminal justice system depends partly on change within that system itself; but primarily and much more importantly in the long run, on the elimination of Aboriginal disadvantage, social, economic and cultural.

As to the criminal justice system:

(i) Undoubtedly, one of the most important issues is the reduction of tension between Aboriginal people and police on the streets. A reduction of tension means fewer arrests, more cautions and fewer people before the courts. The immediate key to lesser tension appears to be consultation between Aboriginal and police organisations.

(ii) Determination by the legislatures to try to devise more sentencing options that do not involve imprisonment and determination by judges and magistrates to apply them and to order imprisonment as a last resort; and generally, a wide discretion in sentencing. In South Australia the youth court, required to order loss of driving licence following a certain conviction, cannot limit the order so as to allow driving for employment. Is this wise? (This, of course, is a general law, nothing special to Aboriginal youth.)

(iii) A vigorous effort to find ways of enforcing non-compliance with non-custodial sentences other than by imprisonment. In this respect non-payment of fines is a particular problem. Can there not be provision for very moderate but compulsory deductions from wages and/or social security payments to meet fines, along with provision for simple reviews of the amount of fines where it can be demonstrated that there has been through no fault of the defendant a substantial change in his/her financial position since the fixing of the fine? Such steps would involve

2 See the recent unreported case of *R v Gooley*, judgment no S5624, published 23 April 1996, Chief Justice of South Australia. The offender had been badly beaten up by friends of the victim (all parties being non-Aboriginal). The Chief Justice wrote: 'The conduct of the victim's friends ... cannot reduce the appropriate sentence ... To allow it to do so would be to allow private revenge ... to replace punishment by the State'. But he adds, '[I]n my opinion tribal punishment by Aborigines is in a different category.'

administrative expense but surely less than imprisonment. Between January 1992 and January 1993 there was on any given day in Australian prisons more than 1,000 people in there for failure to pay fines – more than 7% of the total in custody (another such special problem is the extent of remand in custody).

(iv) It is important that where Aboriginal people are placed in custody there should be an effort to provide training in useful skills, but perhaps more importantly in projects directed to the establishment of self respect and a sense of having a place in the future. Such objectives can also be associated with many of the non-custodial sentences including bonds to be of good behaviour and community service orders. In these matters the development of appropriate working relations between the courts (in the sentencing process) and the correctional services (in the carrying out of the various orders) on the one hand, and the Aboriginal community organisations and the families involved on the other is crucial. This is a commonplace thing in many remote communities where various methods have been devised which allow magistrates to know the views of the communities as to how the problem presented by the particular offence is thought to be best dealt with, and most importantly how the community can help in dealing with the problem, both in general and as far as the particular offender is concerned. It is important that this be extended to country towns and to cities. Reference is made to the report of the Royal Commission, Volume 3, Chapter 21.3, and more particularly to the report of Commissioner JH Wootten, of his inquiry into the death of Harrison Day where the work of the Victorian Justice Panels is discussed. It has since occurred to me that in those places where Community Development Employment Schemes (CDEPs) are in operation, there may be scope for agreement between the Aboriginal communities, scheme managers and the appropriate correctional officers for Aboriginal persons to serve out community service orders in the CDEP. They would have the great advantage of working with other Aboriginal people in schemes directed towards community progress and under the overall control of the community. Many variations on this sort of co-operation are possible. For example, excellent work has been done in Roebourne (WA) in the way offenders going to work on Aboriginal-owned pastoral properties in the region.

In the capital cities and major country towns is there scope for community service orders to be served by assisting in the work of Aboriginal organisations (eg housing health etc) subject of course to the agreement of the organisations concerned?

(v) The recommendations of the Royal Commission that cultural awareness programmes should be provided for people engaged in the criminal justice system have been adopted, but there is need for greater effort to apply the recommendations in practice. If these efforts are to be successful Aboriginal people and organisations must be involved to a very great degree in the actual presentations and in determining their content

But the key to a lasting solution to the over-representation of Aboriginal people in the criminal justice system and the key to changing the general Aboriginal attitude to the law, is the elimination of aboriginal economic, social and cultural disadvantage. There are, I suggest, three essentials to achieving that aim (see final report of Royal Commission, Chapter 1 (Overview)(1.7)):

(i) A strong desire on the part of Aboriginal people to achieve the objective and willingness to work for it. There is no lack of evidence of the existence of both. The evidence is particularly apparent in the existence of Aboriginal organisations in the area of health, legal rights, housing associations, educational bodies, cultural bodies, preserving the languages bodies, community development employment schemes etc etc.

(ii) The willingness of the broad society to assist in the process in a wide variety of ways. Basically this means Government assistance (both Commonwealth and state) in the provision of financial and other resources. But it is much broader and deeper than that. Local government can play a very significant part, employers and trade unions, the offices (particularly the regional offices of various departments), sporting bodies, churches, indeed, all citizens, since it is individuals who influence the attitudes of these organisations.

(iii) A policy, a mode of behaviour, an attitude on the part of the wider society which enables it to render the assistance and enables the Aboriginal society to receive it whilst at the same time maintaining its independence and avoiding a welfare-dependent position being established between the two groups. This policy ((c) above) is referred to as self-determination, it is the direct opposite of the policy of white superiority, of assuming that Europeans knew what was best for Aboriginal people in all situations. Self-determination is a concept which (to quote the final report of the Royal Commission) '... does not have a precise definition; it is a developing concept, one as to the limits of which there can be some disagreement but about which, as I believe is shown in Chapter 20 of this report, there is an enormous common area of agreement quite sufficient to allow progress to go forward with great benefit to the Aboriginal people'. A joint committee of the House of Representatives in 1990 expressed support for the self-determination policy which it defined as meaning 'Aboriginal people having the resources and capacity to control the future of their own communities.' In practice the application of this policy frequently comes down to a question of relations between individuals and groups. However, I express the point of view that the greatest chance of solving problems exists where there are on the one hand:

   (a) Aboriginal communities or organisations having good support among their members; and on the other

   (b) people in positions of authority or influence in the corresponding area of the broad society, who recognise the rights of Aboriginal people, who treat them with respect and as equals.

The importance of such individuals and/or groups cannot be over-estimated. I do not say this on the basis of some preconceived ideas as to how social problems can be solved generally or specifically in this area, but on the basis of scores of perceived examples and an even greater number of examples reliably reported. I referred earlier to improvement in police/Aboriginal relations in the Northern Territory. An examination of how these improvements came about will reveal the co-existence of fine Aboriginal local organisations and fine police leadership prepared to meet with them on the basis of mutual respect and the recognition that each side has an important role and that problems will be solved by grappling with them, not by chatter. I refer to the relations which I have observed between Aboriginal organisations and local government bodies in various country towns. I particularly remember a conference in Alice Springs where the executive officer of the council eloquently and passionately defended the council's policy of contracting Tangentyere (the over-arching organisation of the Aboriginal town camps in Alice Springs) for that body to provide the local government services in the town camp areas. In a totally different area of activity, there is the increasing frequency of agreements being arrived at between mining companies and Aboriginal organisations as to mining on Aboriginal land and or on land which is of particular concern to Aboriginal people. An outstanding example, of the value of working together on the basis of equality and mutual respect is provided by the Reconciliation Council composed as it is of people from all over the country and from a wide variety of backgrounds, Aboriginal and non-Aboriginal.

One might give endless individual examples of such effective co-operation and it is important that there should be greater public awareness of the fact that such examples exist. Outstanding is the recent announcement of agreement reached between Aboriginal, pastoral and Green organisations as to land use in the Cape York area. I have heard that some Queensland government action may be necessary to implement the agreement; but irrespective of whether that is right and intervention is favourable, the fact of the successful negotiations between these parties is a great step forward in the process of learning how to solve problems. In very recent times I have seen something in South Australia of the development (in pursuance of Royal Commission recommendations) of a cultural awareness programme which will involve judges and magistrates in South Australia from all jurisdictions. The way in which this programme has been developed with Aboriginal involvement at every stage of the process, will, I hope, be published and will merit very close study. I have recently attended a ceremony at the Yatala Prison in Adelaide, during which certificates were issued to Aboriginal prisoners who had voluntarily participated in a full-time four week course called 'Reclaiming our Future'. The course was presented jointly by an Aboriginal and a non-Aboriginal person. It was designed specifically to meet the Royal Commission recommendation of making available to Aboriginal prisoners courses which would assist them in the acquisition of self-development skills. It was a moving occasion with families present. Prisoners spoke of their self-evaluation, of reconciliation, of the desire to see further such courses, the desire to see the participation of non-Aboriginal prisoners in the courses and in some cases of staff. The course was conducted with the approval of the Director of the Department and of the superintendent of the prison. Both of these people are known as people with a commitment to a proper Aboriginal and non-Aboriginal relationship. The superintendent was already lending support to the conduct of a further course (which is now in fact in progress). This superintendent is, in fact, a police officer temporarily released to Correctional Services to be the superintendent of the prison. As a police officer placed many years ago in charge of a region, he made contact with Aboriginal groups and arranged for regular discussions with them about problems. On an occasion when the Aboriginal groups were having some disagreement with the local council over an aspect of the celebration of the National Aboriginal and Islander Day Observance Committee (NAIDOC) week, this officer, at the request of the Aboriginal people, intervened (successfully) with the council in support of the Aboriginal position and subsequently participated in the NAIDOC march in police uniform. I mention this because it is practical support for my proposition that success depends very often upon the co-existence of people on both sides who act on the basis of equality and mutual respect. The CDEP schemes operating in South Australia are forming a co-operative to work together with a view to expanding their activity, widening the job training for their members and developing economic initiatives. The idea is just conceived but it can be of great significance.

Such local initiatives are taking place against the broad background of such national trends as the *Mabo* decision, native title legislation, the growth in the recognition of Aboriginal art and culture, the support for Cathy Freeman and the development of an Australian Football League policy against racism. Some readers will think this is a very curious collection of references. Perhaps it is. It just so happens that there is a very broad move in our country against old racist ideas and because of the broadness of the move it is reflected in many different ways.

Of course, there are mountains of difficulties. The retention of old ideas, conscious and particularly unconscious racism, and ingrained attitudes are to be overcome.

I return to the title: of Aboriginal people and the law. As the society as a whole, Aboriginal and non-Aboriginal, succeeds in doing away with social, economic and cultural disadvantage for Aboriginal people, the attitude of Aboriginal people towards the wider society and to the law generally will change. Aboriginal people will no longer be just the objects of the criminal law as they were in the old days; they will be participants in the operation of laws and will use the law as is done by members of the wider community. There are many ways in which progress can be measured. Of course it is a great mistake only to see progress without noticing the problems left unsolved but sometimes it is necessary to step back: and take a broad view. I said earlier that when the Aboriginal Legal Rights Movement Inc started in South Australia some 25 years ago, 99.9% of its work was directed to the assistance of people charged with an offence. I understand that that is still the greater part of its work. But additionally it has a native title section and a civil section. There are, I am told, 20 lawyers employed by the movement – 16 in Adelaide, of whom four work in the civil section, plus a part-timer. Most of their work is plaintiff-based. This is indeed a great change: it is indicative of changes over a broad area: it has promise of greater change.

CHAPTER EIGHT

SENTENCING AND INDIGENOUS AUSTRALIANS – ADDRESSING OVER-REPRESENTATION FROM WITHIN THE CRIMINAL JUSTICE SYSTEM

Martin Hinton

INTRODUCTION

> The indigenous population of imprisonable age (17 and over) is projected to rise by almost a third by the year 2001 and by over two thirds by the year 2011, compared with its 1991 figures ... If it were assumed that imprisonment rates remain at 1992 levels ... the number of indigenous people in prison can be projected to increase by almost 50% by the year 2011 ... Unfortunately, this projection line already appears to be on the conservative side.[1]

When one considers that in 1992 more than 14% of Australia's total prison population were of indigenous descent, and that Aboriginal people were 13 times more likely to be imprisoned than non-Aboriginal people, one cannot help but be moved to a sense of urgency by this bleak prognosis for the future of the indigenous people who come in contact with the criminal justice system. It is tempting to look immediately to the state and Commonwealth governments for new initiatives or renewed vigour in this connection. It is equally tempting to scour the pages of the many reports concerning the implementation of the recommendations of the Royal Commission into Aboriginal Deaths in Custody (RCIADIC),[2] for the slightest hint of a scapegoat or a recalcitrant government body.[3] Without doubt the efforts of governments to address the problems associated with the over-representation of the indigenous people in the prison system should be, and are continuously, reviewed.[4] But the rise of the rate of over-representation despite the reviews, the supposed reforms and the much repeated commitment, to unprecedented highs ensures that the spotlight remains firmly focused upon the criminal justice system.[5] In such circumstances, it would be remiss of the players in that system not to address over-representation from within.

1 'The Over-representation of Indigenous People in Custody in Australia' (1995) 47 *Trends and Issues in Criminal Justice*, Australian Institute of Criminology. See also *Justice Under Scrutiny*, Report of the Inquiry into the Implementation by Governments of the Recommendations of the Royal Commission into Aboriginal Deaths in Custody, 1994, Canberra: AGPS, Chapter 5.

2 Royal Commission into Aboriginal Deaths in Custody, National Report, 1991, Canberra: AGPS.

3 See for example, *Justice Under Scrutiny, op cit*. See also the various reports of the Watch Committees in each state. For example, *Royal Commission into Aboriginal Deaths in Custody 1993: Implementation Report of the South Australian Government*, 1994.

4 See recommendation 1 RCIADIC, National Report, Vol 5, 1991, Canberra: AGPS. *Justice Under Scrutiny, op cit,* esp Chapter 2, which contains a commentary upon the various bodies involved in the continual monitoring and review of the implementation of the recommendations of the RCIADIC. See also the various implementation reports prepared by the federal, state and territory governments referred to therein.

5 In 1994 it was reported that an indigenous person was 19.4 times more likely to be imprisoned than a non-indigenous person. See *Justice Under Scrutiny, op cit*, p 79.

To look solely to government for the answers permits those of us at the coalface to avoid the reality to which we unwittingly contribute and the simple fact that as individuals practising in the law we can effect change.

In this chapter it is my intention to look at sentencing for, as the vast majority of matters instituted in the criminal courts end with a guilty plea,[6] the sentencing hearing is crucial to the attitude adopted by the court toward the indigenous offender in ultimately imposing sentence. Thus, to look at the sentencing process in isolation is a legitimate avenue of addressing over-representation. Obviously this means concentrating in particular on the role of the judiciary and the legal profession in contributing to over-representation. Whilst the former were to some extent scrutinised by the RCIADIC,[7] the latter were not.

Bearing in mind that this book is written for lawyers and judges of the future, it is particularly appropriate that we look at their responsibilities in representing and dealing with indigenous people. That this is so is compelling in light of the fact that the vast majority of lawyers and judges in the future will be people who have had very little, if any, contact with the indigenous people of Australia. They will be people whose insight into the culture of the indigenous people is minimal, to say the least. They will be people vulnerable to the heresies of stereotypes and false characterisations. They will be part of a system that is not necessarily inherently racist but is capable of operating as such more by reason of ignorance than design. To my mind the Chairperson of the Council for Aboriginal Reconciliation is right when he says that the concept of dignity underpins the movement toward reconciliation. 'Dignity' he says, involves the 'recognition of the just and equitable positions that the indigenous people of this country aspire to in the political, economic, cultural and civil domains'.[8] The vesting of dignity in the indigenous offender who becomes embroiled in the criminal justice system demands of the lawyer, of the judge, a true understanding of that offender, their culture, their history. Armed with such an understanding the criminal courts can best fulfil their responsibility to the community and to the offender.[9]

It has been said that it 'is time to move from description to explanation' in our consideration of the causes of over-representation:

> ... to demonstrate the connection between what happens on the one hand on the station, in the street, in the courts and in prisons and on the other hand the political and economic forces in particular historical periods which result in the location of property and power in the hands of a few who then control relations of production as well as cultural beliefs and practices.[10]

6 For example, in 1993 in South Australia only 16.5% of criminal matters proceeded to trial. In most of the remaining matters the case was disposed of after a guilty plea was entered. See South Australian Office of Crime Statistics, *Crime and Justice in South Australia 1993*, No 21.

7 See in particular Recommendations 96, 97 and 98. RCIADIC National Report, Vol 1, 1991, Canberra: AGPS.

8 Dodson, P, *Addressing the Key Issues for Reconciliation*, a publication of the Council for Aboriginal Reconciliation, 1993, AGPS, preface.

9 *Webb v O'Sullivan* [1952] SASR 65 at 66 *per* Napier CJ.

10 Parker, D, 'The Administration of Justice and its Penal Consequences', in Hazelhurst, KM (ed), *Ivory Scales: Black Australia and the Law*, 1987, Sydney: University of New South Wales Press, p 140.

This statement, although aimed at the work of researchers, is just as relevant to the lawyer representing the indigenous client. But to move on, as we are urged, is to assume that the reality of over-representation has filtered down to the rank and file in the legal profession, and that their efforts in representing indigenous people are expended against that background. In light of the fact that the representation of indigenous people in Australian prisons continues to increase without any sign of abatement, this is an assumption that should not lightly be made. That this is so is an indictment upon the legal profession and the players within the criminal justice system. As Lincoln and Wilson have said, over-representation is not an 'Aboriginal problem; instead it is one of professional accountability and of non-Aboriginal criminal justice methods and processes'.[11] Sadly, therefore, it remains important to set out the true extent of the over-representation of indigenous people in the Australian prison system before moving on to consider what we as lawyers can do to address this predicament in the context of the sentencing process.

THE OVER-REPRESENTATION OF INDIGENOUS PEOPLE IN THE PRISON SYSTEM – THE STATISTICS

In 1991 the RCIADIC reported that, as at the 30 June 1989, 'there were 15 times as many Aboriginal people in prison than there were non-Aboriginal people'.[12] That is, for every 100,000 Aboriginal people making up the general adult population of Australia, 1,464.9 were in prison as compared to only 97.2 non-Aboriginals per 100,000 non-Aboriginal persons. On a state-by-state basis the Royal Commission found that this level of disproportion varied. For example, in Tasmania for every 100,000 Aboriginal people 258.2 were in prison, whereas for every 100,000 non-Aboriginal people only 69.3 were in prison, ie per capita there were 3.7 times as many Aboriginal people in prison in Tasmania than there were non-Aboriginal people. In Western Australia the level of over-representation far exceeded that of Tasmania and was, in fact, the worst in the country. There for every 100,000 Aboriginal people 2,665.6 were in prison, whereas for every 100,000 non-Aboriginal people only 101.5 were in prison, ie per capita there were 26.3 times as many Aboriginal people in prison than there were non-Aboriginal people.[13] These figures concern the adult population of the Australian prison system and, therefore, reflect more accurately the level of disproportion as non-adults, people of

11 Lincoln, R, and Wilson, P, 'Aboriginal Offending: Patterns and Causes', in Chappell, D, and Wilson, P (eds), *The Australian Criminal Justice System – the Mid-1990s*, 1994, Sydney: Butterworths, p 62.

12 RCIADIC, National Report, Vol 1, Chapter 9, p 225; for information regarding the methodological approach adopted by the RCIADIC in determining custody rates and a greater discussion thereof, see *Deaths in Custody Australia 1980–1989*, research papers of the RCIADIC as edited by Biles, D, and McDonald, D, 1992, Australian Institute of Criminology. Wherever this chapter speaks of rates of over-representation it relates to people who are serving a period of imprisonment as a consequence of committing a criminal offence. In the majority of cases those people are in prisons, but in some instances they are serving their sentences in institutions controlled by the police. The rate of over-representation as referred to in this chapter does not include remandees.

13 *Ibid*, at p 224, see Table 9.2.

less than 17 years, are less likely to be imprisoned for their offending.[14] When the detention of juveniles is taken into account the level of disproportion was found to be less – nationally 11 times as many Aboriginal people were in prison or detained as non-Aboriginal people.[15]

When these figures were broken down to account for gender, the RCIADIC discovered that Aboriginal males made up 14.1% of the total male prison population, whilst Aboriginal females accounted for 16.4% of the total female prison population of Australia. Overall Aboriginal inmates accounted for 14.1% of the prison population.[16] This is particularly alarming when one considers that at the time the indigenous people, both Aboriginal and Torres Strait Islander, constituted only 1.46% of the total population of the country.[17] It was the fact that so many Aboriginal people were in custody, whether it be in prison or police lock-ups, along with the underlying socio-economic issues that impact upon the Aboriginal people, that, in the opinion of the RCIADIC, explained the large number of Aboriginal deaths in custody.[18]

> If white Australians had died in custody at the same rate as Aboriginals between 1980 and 1988, there would have been some 7,000 deaths in custody, or about two per day, and no doubt a Royal Commission would have been established much sooner.[19]

Satisfied that the unacceptably high number of Aboriginal deaths in custody were not caused by the infliction of intentional violence,[20] but were the consequence of the over-representation of the indigenous people in the criminal justice system, the RCIADIC made numerous recommendations aimed at reducing the number of indigenous people exposed to the criminal justice system and thereby the number imprisoned, at reducing the risks of deaths in custody, and at addressing the underlying socio-economic issues that led to the disproportionate custody rates.

In 1993 Walker and Salloom report some improvement in the disproportionate level of Aboriginal people in prison.[21] In Western Australia an Aboriginal person was now 20.8 times more likely to be in prison than a non-Aboriginal person. The over-representation rate in Tasmania had dropped to 3.3, whilst on the national level there was now 13.2 times as many Aboriginal people in prison as there was non-Aboriginal people. However, it must be born in mind that the prison population as a whole has

14 *Deaths in Custody in Australia 1980–1989, ibid,* Research Paper No 19, *Aboriginal People in Prisons and Non-custodial Corrections* (see p 483).

15 *Ibid,* p 225.

16 *Deaths in Custody in Australia 1980–1989, ibid,* Research Paper No 19, *Aboriginal People in Prisons and Non-custodial Corrections* (see p 481).

17 *Deaths in Custody in Australia 1980–1989, ibid,* Research Paper No 6, Biles, D, *Aboriginal Imprisonment,* p 91.

18 RCIADIC National Report, Vol 1, 1991, Canberra: AGPS.

19 Wootten, H, *Report of the inquiry into the death of Mark Wayne Revell,* Royal Commission into Aboriginal Deaths in Custody, National Report, 1991, Canberra: AGPS, pp 2–3.

20 RCIADIC National Report, Vol 1, 1991, Canberra: AGPS, Chapter 3.

21 Walker, J, and Salloom, S, *Australian Prisoners 1992,* 1993, Canberra: Australian Institute of Criminology.

risen considerably since 1989,[22] thus despite the comparative level of the representation of Aboriginal people in prison having statistically declined, the actual numbers in prison has not declined. Hence Aboriginal people were found by Walker and Salloom to constitute 14.3% of the prison population, and increase of 0.2% since 1989.[23] This is consistent with the findings of Cunneen and Behrendt to the effect that there had been a 36.5% increase in the imprisonment of Aboriginal people between 1987 and 1993.[24] That this occurs despite the recommendations of the RCIADIC and the commitment of the Commonwealth and state governments to using imprisonment as a punishment of last resort, is astounding.

The RCIADIC looked at the data provided by the 1989 National Prison Census. This revealed, contrary to that school of thought, that Aboriginal people primarily committed crimes of a nuisance value such as offensive language and public drunkenness, that the offences giving rise to imprisonment were 'generally of a very serious nature' for both Aboriginal and non-Aboriginal people.[25] Greater than three-quarters of the total prison population had been imprisoned for committing offences falling into only seven offence categories. Those categories were, homicide, assault, sexual offences, robbery, breaking and entering, theft and drug-related offences.[26] Interestingly, the proportion of Aboriginal people incarcerated for sexual offences, assault, and break and enter were considerably higher than for non-Aboriginal people, whereas the opposite was true for robbery and drug-related offences.[27] The RCIADIC observed that this did not mean that Aboriginal people were less likely to be imprisoned for drug-related offences or for robbery. Having regard to a study performed by Walker, the Royal Commission was satisfied that Aboriginal people were still over-represented in every offence category.[28] But most importantly from the RCIADIC's point of view, Aboriginal people were over-represented in the categories of good order offences, traffic offences, property damage and justice procedures.[29]

Some three years later Walker and McDonald report that:

> ... indigenous people are over-represented in virtually every category (of offence), but are most over-represented in offence types involving violence, breaking and entering,

22 In August 1992 the Australian prison population was 14,315, in April 1994 it was 15,345. See Australian Institute of Criminology, Facts and Figures Nos 195 and 215. See Walker, J, and Salloom, S, *Australian Prisoners 1992, op cit*; 'Results of the National Prison Census', 30 June 1992.

23 *Op cit*, at p 3.

24 Cunneen, C, and Behrendt, J, 'Aboriginal and Torres Strait Islander Custodial Deaths between May 1989 and January 1994', 1994, a report to the National Committee to Defend Black Rights, unpublished, as cited in Cunneen, C, and Libesman, T, *Indigenous People and the Law in Australia*, 1995, Sydney: Butterworths, p 59. See also Cunneen, C, 'Aboriginal imprisonment during and since the Royal Commission into Aboriginal Deaths in Custody' (1992) 3 *Current Issues in Criminal Justice* 351.

25 *Deaths in Custody in Australia 1980–1989, op cit*, Research Paper No 6 and 19.

26 *Ibid*. See also RCIADIC National Report, Vol 1, 1991, Canberra: AGPS, Chapter 7.

27 *Ibid*.

28 RCIADIC National Report, Vol 1, 1991, Canberra: AGPS, p 209; see also Walker, J, 'Prison Sentences in Australia' (1989) 20 *Trends and Issues*, Australian Institute of Criminology, Canberra.

29 *Ibid*.

> breaches of justice procedures and driving offences, and are very much less over-represented in fraud and drug offence categories.[30]

Of some consolation for the RCIADIC is the fact that since 1988 the number of indigenous people in prison for offences against good order, and justice procedures have decreased.[31] I say that this is consoling for these categories of offence undoubtedly include such offences as public drunkenness and offensive language, offences which the RCIADIC went to great lengths to ensure did not result in indigenous people being taken into custody.[32] The decline in numbers imprisoned for such offences has continued.[33] Some consolation though when one considers the bigger picture.

The most recent statistics published with respect to the rate of over-representation of Aboriginal and Torres Strait Islander people in Australia's prison system are those contained in the House of Representatives Standing Committee on Aboriginal and Torres Strait Islander Affairs report entitled *Justice Under Scrutiny*. This report states that the rate of over-representation in 1993 had risen to 14.6 before rising again to 19.4 in 1994.[34] The prediction quoted in opening this chapter, and indeed, that made with *reticence* by the RCIADIC itself are, ashamedly, proven true.[35]

It is tempting to conclude that on their face these statistics bespeak a bias when it comes to the use of imprisonment by the criminal justice system exercised in favour of non-Aboriginal offenders, but that would be erroneous. In the absence of statistics recording the degree of over-representation of indigenous offenders before the courts, bias in the sentencing of indigenous offenders to periods of imprisonment cannot be asserted. That is, if the number of indigenous offenders before the criminal courts as a percentage of the total number of offenders before the courts was less than the number of indigenous offenders serving a sentence of imprisonment as a percentage of the total number of offenders serving a sentence of imprisonment, then it could be concluded that there was a greater tendency to use imprisonment as a means of imposing punishment where the offender was indigenous, but such statistics are unavailable.

Nevertheless, the absence of statistical evidence of bias does not detract from the fact that an indigenous person is now 19.4 times more likely to receive a sentence of imprisonment than a non-indigenous person. The question is, why? As the degree of over-representation is prevalent in every offence category, it is no answer to say that indigenous people are more likely to commit crimes of greater gravity than non-indigenous people. There are undoubtedly other factors that work against the indigenous offender receiving a non-custodial penalty – previous convictions, unemployment, racism, negative stereotypes. So too there are valid factors not taken into account such as the impact of colonisation and cultural differences.

---

30 *Op cit.*

31 *Ibid.* The most recent statistics presented by the House of Representatives Standing Committee on Aboriginal and Torres Strait Islander Affairs confirm this trend. See *Justice Under Scrutiny*, *op cit*, Chapter 5, p 81.

32 RCIADIC National Report, Vol 1, 1991, Canberra: AGPS, Chapter 7.

33 *Justice Under Scrutiny*, *op cit*, Chapter 5, p 81.

34 *Ibid* at p 79.

35 RCIADIC National Report, Vol 3, 1991, Canberra: AGPS, pp 63–64.

It is my opinion that too often indigenous people are sentenced on an assimilationist footing. By that I mean, that unless their adherence to their traditional ways is apparent, or their life bears the scars of colonisation for all to see, they are sentenced against a 'white' background, they are sentenced as equals when in reality the indigenous people have been prevented from participating in our society as equals. As Aristotle once said, 'It is as unjust to treat unequals equally as it is to treat equals unequally'.

THE IMPACT OF COLONISATION AND ITS RELEVANCE TO SENTENCING – INDIGENEITY

In the opening chapter to this work Maria Lane has set out the impact upon the indigenous people that the colonisation of Australia has had. Without doubt it has been devastating. Too often nowadays 200 years of oppression and repression and its wider ramifications are collapsed into the concept of dispossession. Whilst the denial of access to traditional lands struck and continues to strike at the very core of indigenous existence, to gloss over the full impact of colonisation permits us all too easily to forget the true cost to the indigenous people that it has meant. In the RCIADIC National Report, Elliott Johnston QC, the National Commissioner, portrays the history of the Aboriginal people since colonisation because 'what is known is known to historians and Aboriginal people; it is little known to non-Aboriginal people and it is a principal thesis of this report that it must become more known'.[36] It must become more known so as, amongst other things, to dispel the fiction perpetrated for 200 years that the indigenous people are inferior. And further, so as to make clear that the consequences of colonisation are ingrained within the very existence of the indigenous community. That is, the problems experienced by indigenous people in Australia as a consequence of colonisation are current. They are real. Whilst perhaps they are not the direct product of the actions and decisions of modern generations, they are inadvertently perpetuated by such generations via avenues that include the criminal justice system. The impact of colonisation must also become more widely known in the interests of advancing the movement toward reconciliation and in preventing the development of complacency or acceptance of the status quo. Unless the general population know why 'White Australia' and 'Black Australia' seek reconciliation, the whole process is easily undermined. There then could arise an environment ripe for the development of attitudes which will only serve to compound the damage that has already been done and its ramifications.

> What troubles me most is an attitude of mind that could come to prevail amongst white Australians: a feeling of irritation apparently based on a conviction that we are saddled with the responsibility for problems not really of our making, and by their nature probably insoluble. The underlying thought is twofold: no one now alive has hurt the Aborigines or their legitimate interests, and no one contemplates deliberately doing so. Whatever wrongs may have been done in the past are surely long ago and far away – the wrongs inflicted by whites long since dead on Aborigines no longer alive. The thought runs on: the worst that white Australians did to black Australians was to come here at all.

36 Volume 1, p 7.

> That is something which now cannot ever be undone. To argue that every new generation of white Australians must accept a liability to compensate every new generation of Aborigines is simply not an argument from a domain of the real world. I have argued of course that it is a question of whose reality is to be consulted. I have identified things being done now by us living to Aborigines which are very 'real' indeed. Once admit this proposition as true, and our 'real' position changes.[37]

A knowledge of the impact of colonisation is crucial to understanding the present plight of the indigenous people and the obstacles to be overcome by all in moving toward reconciliation. In the context of sentencing, a consideration of colonisation and its ramifications for the indigenous people reveals many of the forces that have shaped the lives of the indigenous people and will continue to do so well after any sentence imposed is served. But that is not to portray the indigenous people as helpless victims to be pitied or patronised. The history of colonisation embodies fact without regard to which, in proceeding to sentence an indigenous offender, equality cannot be expected.

In *Neal v The Queen Murphy* J noted:

> Aboriginal sense of grievance has developed over the two hundred years of white settlement in Australia. Early in the 19th century Aborigines were 'being treated with arrogant superiority, often accompanied by considerable brutality' (Teasdale and Whitelaw, *The Early Childhood Education of Aboriginal Australians* (1981)). The plight of the Aborigines was compounded by the introduction of European diseases and alcohol which, in addition to white colonisation, 'contributed to the fragmentation of Aboriginal society and helped to promote the apathetic attitudes erroneously attributed by the Europeans to inferior intellectual capacity' (King-Boyes, M, *Patterns of Aboriginal Culture: Then and Now*, 1977). Aborigines have complained bitterly about white paternalism robbing them of their dignity and right to direct their own lives. In 1938 the New South Wales Aborigines' Progress Association protested:
>
> ... you took our land by force ... you have almost exterminated our people, but there (are) enough of us remaining to expose the humbug of your claim ... We do not wish to be regarded with sentimental sympathy like koala bears as exhibits ... (nor) studied as scientific or anthropological curiosities ... why do you deliberately keep us backward? Is it merely to give yourselves the pleasure of feeling superior? ... that we are naturally a backward and low race is a scientific lie ... At worst we are no more dirty, lazy, stupid, criminal or immoral, than white people. Also your slanders against our race are moral lies, told to throw all the blame for our troubles on to us. (See Watson, L, *The Aboriginal and Islander Child and the Welfare System (An Approach to a Study)*, Vol 1, 1982, Continuum, p 14.)[38]

Although penned in 1938, the comment of the New South Wales Progress Association remains, to a large extent, current. In 1991 Johnston wrote:

> From that history many things flow which are of central importance to the issue of Aboriginal over-representation in custody.

37 Stanner, WH, *White Man Got No Dreaming*, 1979, Canberra: ANU Press.

38 (1982) 149 CLR 305 at 317–18.

> The first is the deliberate and systematic disempowerment of Aboriginal people starting with dispossession from their land and proceeding to almost every aspect of their life. They were made dependent upon government or non-Aboriginal pastoralists or other employers for rations, clothing, blankets, education, living place and living conditions. Decisions were made about them and for them and imposed upon them ... Aboriginal people were made dependent upon non-Aboriginal people. Gradually many of them lost their capacity for independent action, and their communities likewise. With loss of independence goes a loss of self-esteem.
>
> Of course, I speak in general terms; in the most remote communities society went as before and in all areas there were and are strong people, many of them, men and women, who kept alive the culture and pride in the Aboriginal society. Some of them strove to organise a better deal, to call for rights but the battle was uphill and while some slight gains were made it was a slow and painful progress. People were still not counted in the population, they were not entitled to and did not get social security benefits, mothers still gathered their children about them and ran into the bush when they heard 'the welfare' was about. The damage to Aboriginal society was devastating. In some places, it totally destroyed the population. In others, dependency, despair, alcohol, total loss of heart wrought decimation of culture. So it was on the Aboriginal side.
>
> There is the other side of the coin, the effects of history upon the non-Aboriginal people. Every turn in the policy of government and the practice of the non-Aboriginal community was postulated on the inferiority of the Aboriginal people; the original expropriation of their land was based on the idea that the land was not occupied and the people uncivilised; the protection policy was based on the view that Aboriginal people could not achieve a place in the non-Aboriginal society and that they must be protected against themselves while the race died out; the assimilationist policy assumed that their culture and way of life is without value and that we confer a favour on them by assimilating them into our ways; even to the point of taking their children and removing them from family.
>
> Every step of the way is based upon an assumption of superiority and every new step is a further entrenchment of that assumption.[39]

This is in part what it means to be an indigenous Australian. Colonisation has resulted in their being marginalised. This, as the RCIADIC sought to point out, and Elliott Johnston QC has elucidated upon earlier in this book, explains to a large extent why indigenous people regularly find themselves embroiled in the legal system and the criminal justice system in particular.

It is important that judges be aware that the devastation brought upon the indigenous people by virtue of colonisation has rendered them dependent, generally speaking, upon the welfare system. The forced collapse of many cultural strictures has resulted in the institutionalisation of many indigenous people. Rowley has said that this in turn results in many indigenous people becoming 'inmates' of the system. Further, '[t]he controlled institution, by conditioning inmates, constitutes the hindrance to enterprise, mobility, and experiment'.[40] It is self-perpetuating in that dependence upon

39 RCIADIC National Report, Vol 1, 1991, Canberra: AGPS, pp 8–9.

40 Rowley, CD, *The Remote Aborigines*, 1972, Ringwood: Penguin, p 117.

the welfare system becomes all the people know and something that they hand on to their children. In the recent case of *Aubrey* institutionalisation loomed large in the determination of penalty.[41] In that case a Supreme Court judge refused to imprison an Aboriginal youth found guilty of the manslaughter of the local publican, Mr Tiernan. The incident occurred in the Queensland country town of Murgon. On the evening of show-day a fight broke out in front of Mr Tiernan's pub involving, amongst others, a number of Aboriginal youths from the Cherbourg community which was not far from Murgon. Mr Tiernan stepped into the fray in an effort to restore order. The defendant punched him once to the head causing him to fall over backwards striking his head on the road surface. He later died. In sentencing the defendant White J of the Queensland Supreme Court said:

> The system operating in Cherbourg and Murgon communities shaped the criminal behaviour you have espoused. ... You, like so many young men and women, seem to be trapped in the tragedy that is Cherbourg. It cannot be regarded as a place which encourages lawful conduct or hopefulness for the future.[42]

In the Court of Appeal Fitzgerald P said this of Cherbourg:

> The appellant's all too-common life experience had left him poorly educated, unemployed, angry, aggressive and sometimes violent, especially when intoxicated. Cherbourg is an unattractive town, and young people living there have virtually no cultural, recreational or employment opportunities; many are bored, and gravitate to Murgon, which is about five kilometres away, where they drink in the hotel and, often, fight; fighting between young Aborigines and white persons is common, frequently leads to the police charging the youthful offenders, who quickly build up a criminal record, and thus are initiated into a lifestyle which often ends in tragedy ...[43]

Often the indigenous people that become embroiled in the criminal justice system are welfare dependent and have become institutionalised. What is most disturbing for judges and lawyers alike is that the institutionalisation of the indigenous people is inadvertently contributed to by the adherence of the law to customs and practices that do not adequately account for the cultural background of the indigenous people and the consequences that colonisation has brought to it. The RCIADIC makes it clear that the problems confronted by the indigenous people – economic depravity, poor health, over-representation in the criminal justice system, lack of education and training, dispossession – may best be overcome by empowering the indigenous people. Obviously, many forms of punishment are specifically designed to disempower the offender punished, but they need not be comprehensive nor demoralising. Even imprisonment can be constructive. A primary example of empowerment in this regard is the experience at Yatala Labour Prison written about by Elliott Johnston QC in this book above. Those responsible for the determination of the appropriate penalty to be imposed must, therefore, be imaginative in prescribing such penalty particularly where it

41 (1995) 79 A Crim R 100. See also the stories contained in the *Australian* on 19 and 20 July 1994.

42 *Australian*, 19 July 1994.

43 *Ibid.*

is one served in the community if the perpetuation of institutionalisation is to be thwarted. But of course it does not stop there. Those responsible for the implementation of the penalty must also do what they can to minimise institutionalisation. So too policymakers should turn their efforts to consider and develop new penal options, options that are forward looking, options designed to be constructive and instructive.

Lastly, the rapid social change that has been foistered upon the indigenous people as a consequence of colonisation has rendered redundant many traditional means of maintaining social control. The classic example is the want of an answer to the issue of how to deal with alcoholism and petrol sniffing amongst some rural communities in particular. Those responsible for ensuring the maintenance of order have been disempowered by the presentation of social problems to which their traditional responses have proven ineffective.[44]

> Social disorganisation ... originates from one of Durkheim's arguments that rapid social change is associated with increases in crime due to the breakdown of social controls ... the term is generally used to describe conditions that undermine the ability of the traditional institutions to govern social behaviour.[45]

The point to be had is that the very fabric of indigenous society has been in part eroded by colonisation. Structures within the society designed to ensure order and maintain control have been damaged. In these circumstances it is all the more difficult for the indigenous person to cope with the challenges that colonisation has presented, particularly against a background of economic depravity. This must be accounted for in fashioning an appropriate sentence for an indigenous offender. If possible, social control mechanisms within communities must be supported by the courts. By way of example, in *Robertson v Flood*, the appellant, an initiated Aboriginal man who lived in a rural community called Ali Curung, appealed against his sentence of four months imprisonment for assaulting two police officers and a police aide.[46] The appellant was grossly intoxicated when he committed the offences despite the fact that Ali Curung was a 'dry community'. When invited to make certain assumptions about the role of the appellant in his community and the character of that community, Mildren J refused preferring to hear evidence. In fact he adjourned the appeal to enable him and counsel to visit the community of Ali Curung. He took evidence from the police based at Ali Curung and prominent members of the community regarding the problem that alcohol posed and the steps that they had taken together to overcome it. Of course, he learnt much about the community, its make-up and history as well. He also listened to the community's attitude regarding the appropriate punishment to be imposed. With his first hand knowledge he was able to determine how the court could contribute to and support the efforts of the community and the police in dealing with its alcohol problem.

44 For an example of a community successfully developing methods of dealing with alcoholism see the judgment of Mildren J in *Robertson v Flood* (1992) 111 FLR 177.

45 Hagan, J, (1989) 'An Analysis of American Indian Homicide: A Test of Social Disorganisation and Economic Deprivation at the Reservation County Level', unpublished paper, Rutgers University, Newark, as quoted in Chappell, D, and Wilson, P (eds), *The Australian Criminal Justice System – The Mid-1990s*, 1994, Sydney: Butterworths, Chapter 3, p 79.

46 (1992) 111 FLR 177.

It is interesting to note that the possibility of leaving the appellant's punishment to tribal custom was mooted, but the community felt it better for the courts to deal with the matter. So too the appellant's immediate family, who would normally have a significant part to play in his punishment, felt it better that he go to gaol. In the end a period of imprisonment was deemed the best means of addressing the interests of all concerned.

By contrast the response of the Cherbourg community in Aubrey discussed above is interesting.[47] The Cherbourg Aboriginal Council responded to the fight outside the pub in Murgon and to Mr Tiernan's death by banishing those youths involved from the community for life.[48] This was done in the absence of the youths who at the time were remanded in custody. No one appeared on their behalf before the council. The council ordered the banishment in its capacity as a court legally constituted under the Community Services (Aborigines) Act 1984 (Qld).[49] Whilst the Act does not provide the council with any explicit power regarding banishment, by virtue of its dominant position as landowner and law giver in the community, the council was in a relatively strong position to enforce the penalty. The council resorted to banishment, a traditional method of punishment, due to its lack of faith in the mainstream justice system.[50] Fighting and alcohol abuse had been problems that had plagued the community for a long time and a severe deterrent penalty was, in the opinion of the council, warranted. A co-ordinated response between the magistrates' court at Murgon or the superior courts in Toowoomba or Brisbane and the community had never occurred. This is unfortunate for close co-operation is essential particularly if those measures implemented by the Council within its jurisdiction are to be supported outside that jurisdiction, and, more importantly, if the move toward self-determination that the Community Services (Aborigines) Act 1984 (Qld) embodies is to be successful in a pluralist society. That is not to be taken as indicating that the courts should condone banishment, but that the despair felt by the council and, indeed, by White J sitting in the Supreme Court, when confronted by the Murgon incident could well have been avoided if in the past the mainstream courts, the police and the Murgon and Cherbourg communities had all worked together to support the Cherbourg community in its efforts to deal with alcohol abuse.

47 (1995) 79 A Crim R 101.

48 Council for Aboriginal Reconciliation Key Issues Paper No 7, *Agreeing a Document*, 1994, Canberra: AGPS, p 32.

49 'This court is constituted by two Justices of the Peace who are indigenous Australian residents. If there are no resident justices available, the court can be constituted by members of the Aboriginal Council. The council can confer jurisdiction and powers on the court by by-laws which have to be authorised by the Queensland Governor-in-Council. As well as dealing with breaches of by-laws, the Aboriginal Court has jurisdiction to hear and determine matters accepted by the community as being rightly governed by the usages and customs of the community'. *Ibid*, p 33.

50 *Ibid*, p 33.

ACKNOWLEDGING INDIGENEITY IN SENTENCING

Indigeneity is a factor to be taken into account in mitigation of penalty.[51] The handicap that colonisation has been to the prosperity of the indigenous people must be acknowledged for if it is not then the sentencer begins their consideration of penalty upon the footing that all people are equal, when in fact colonisation has served to deny equality to the indigenous people of Australia. By acknowledgment I mean that the sentencer must gain a full appreciation of what the indigenous people were subjected to, the cost it has had, and the painfully slow progress toward recovery that is being made. But so too it means acknowledging the false sense of superiority with which non-indigenous people have approached all things indigenous and all indigenous people. It means ensuring that whatever decision is made is an informed one, made against the background of obtaining a full understanding of what it is to be indigenous generally, and what it has and does mean specifically for the individual indigenous offender. There are to be no assumptions or stereotypes. To borrow in part from the constitution, full faith and credit must be accorded indigeneity. Dignity is then restored to the indigenous offender. Granted it may be fleeting, as once the indigenous offender leaves the courtroom he becomes exposed to others, but the passing of sentence being an act of public condemnation, the importance of the vesting of dignity by the judge cannot be underestimated.

If what I have written appears to be a plea for differential treatment, it is not. I seek to point out no more than that history has denied the indigenous people those opportunities that are readily available to non-indigenous people. Thus that basic tenet marking the starting point of the consideration of penalty – equality – must be adjusted in the case of the indigenous offender. For example, employment, familial support networks, and education are all factors referred to time and again in sentencing individuals. They are indicative of character assessed from a white Anglo-Saxon point of view. But indigenous people are still reeling from the days when their children were removed from their parents 'for their own good', remain bereft of educational opportunities and, lacking in skills for want of training, are more often than not unemployable. In short they have been denied the means to fully participate in society and yet are subject to character assessments conducted on the basis of criteria that assume an ability to do so. Furthermore, they are adjudged against that considered valuable by a culture totally divers from their own. Undoubtedly in modern Australia education and employment are valued by the indigenous people, but it is only now that opportunities are being made available. If the difference between non-indigenous people and the indigenous people in terms of opportunity to participate in society is not recognised,

51 In *Iginiwuni,* 12 March 1975 (unreported), Supreme Court NT, Muirhead J said:

> 'Both Aboriginal and white people are generally speaking subject to the same laws. For years, however, the judges of this court in dealing with Aborigines have endeavoured to make allowance for ethnic, environmental and cultural matters ...'.

The application of this approach in sentencing Aboriginal people was accepted in *Juli* (1990) 50 A Crim R 31 at 37 as being the position in Western Australia *per* Wallace J. In *Jabaltjari v Hammersley* (1977) 15 ALR 94 at 98 Muirhead J held that in sentencing Aboriginal children regard must be had to the 'tremendous social problems that they face'.

insupportable value judgments are made and equality before the law is sacrificed.[52] The High Court itself has acknowledged that cultural difference is a factor to be accounted for in sentencing:

> The same sentencing principles are to be applied, of course, in every case, irrespective of the identity of a particular offender or his membership of an ethnic or other group. But in imposing sentences courts are bound to take into account, in accordance with those principles, all material facts including those facts which exist only by reason of the offender's membership of an ethnic or other group. So much is essential to the even administration of criminal justice. That done, however, the weight to be attributed to the factors material in a particular case, whether of aggravation or mitigation, is ordinarily a matter for the court exercising the sentencing discretion at first instance or for the Court of Criminal Appeal.[53]

It should not be expected that each time counsel makes submissions in mitigation on behalf of an indigenous person that they will lead the court through the history of colonisation and its impact upon the indigenous people. Judges should become familiar with this history and its impact. This was the intention of Recommendations 96 and 97 of the RCIADIC:

> *Recommendation 96*
>
> That judicial officers and persons who work in the court service and in the probation and parole services and whose duties bring them into contact with Aboriginal people be encouraged to participate in an appropriate training and development programme, designed to explain contemporary Aboriginal society, customs and traditions. Such programs should emphasise the historical and social factors which contribute to the disadvantaged position of many Aboriginal people today and to the nature of relations between Aboriginal and non-Aboriginal communities today. The Commission further recommends that such persons should wherever possible participate in discussion with members of the Aboriginal community in an informal way in order to improve cross-cultural understanding.
>
> *Recommendation 97*
>
> That in devising and implementing courses referred to in Recommendation 96 the responsible authorities should ensure that consultation takes place with appropriate Aboriginal organisations, including, but not limited to, Aboriginal Legal Services.

Unfortunately, amongst the judiciary there have been mixed feelings regarding the establishment of judicial studies boards or programmes. This has frustrated the implementation of Recommendations 96 and 97. Nevertheless, the individual judge is duty bound to ensure that in sentencing an individual he or she is in possession of all

52 See Detmold, MJ, 'Law and Difference: Reflections on *Mabo's* Case', in *Essays on the Mabo Decision*, 1993, Sydney: Law Book Company, for a jurisprudential discussion of the necessity to recognise difference.

53 *Per* Brennan J in *R v Neal* (1982) 149 CLR 305 at 326. See also E (a child) (1993) 66 A Crim R 14 at 19 *per* Franklyn J; see also *Clinch* (1994) 72 A Crim R 301, *Juli (op cit)*, *Jabaltjari v Hammersley (op cit)*, *Neal (op cit)*, *Rogers and Murray* (1989) 44 A Crim R 301, and *Yougie* (1987) A Crim R 471.

information readily available that may assist in fashioning the appropriate penalty for that individual.[54]

In the past the inquiry into the impact of colonisation upon the individual has rarely been adequately conducted.[55] Too often stereotypical assumptions are made. This is born out by Christopher Charles in his article 'Sentencing Aboriginal People in South Australia'.[56] Charles refers to the use by judges of the Supreme Court of South Australia of a classification of Aboriginal people as being either tribal, semi-tribal or urban.[57] Only those Aboriginal people considered 'tribal' were to be accorded mitigation derived from their indigeneity. The fallacious supposition inherent in such categories is that Aboriginal people who have seemingly forgone their traditional ways either in whole or in part by virtue of living in cities, are less Aboriginal than those that do not live in the cities and adhere to tradition. The logic that follows on from this is that the less traditional an indigenous offender was the more blameworthy he or she became, the assumption being that indigenous people who reside in the city have either voluntarily exchanged their culture for that of white Australia, or must make such exchange as they cannot expect special treatment just because they are indigenous.[58] That is, those in the city either are, or must become, assimilated.

> It is appropriate, I think, that I should make one or two comments of a general character with relation to an aboriginal native's duties and responsibilities when he comes into contact with the differently organised life of the white community. A tribal aboriginal native may have to be dealt with in a very special way if he is brought before one of the ordinary courts of the land for an offence allegedly committed by him against the criminal law; but where an aboriginal native has established himself in the more general community and intends to remain there and to work side by side with other members of that community, he must accept the ordinary standards of behaviour expected of his fellow citizens. If he drinks intoxicating liquor, he must expect that all laws that control the orderliness of those who consume liquor, whether in a hotel or outside it, shall be applied to him without any distinction by reason of his race. If he inhabits and uses the cities and towns of our country, then he must expect to abide by the ordinary rules by which law and order are there maintained. He cannot expect that special exceptions will be made for him. No doubt his personal characteristics and background and history will be taken into account by a court in the ordinary way; but he cannot expect special treatment just because he is an aboriginal native, any more than he would expect that he should, on that account, receive any worse treatment if he comes before a court. In such a case, he comes as a citizen of Australia and must be treated just like any other citizen who lives in a town or in a city ...[59]

---

54 *R v Kear* (1977) 75 LSJS 311.

55 See also the protestations of O'Shane, P, 'Aborigines and the Criminal Justice System', in Cunneen, C (ed), *Aboriginal Perspectives on Criminal Justice*, 1992, Sydney: University Institute of Criminology.

56 (1991) 13 Adel LR 90.

57 Charles cites cases such as *Roberts v Young; Lovegrove v Milera; Wanganeen v Smith* (1977) 73 LSJS 139 in support of his assertion.

58 See *Wanganeen v Smith* (1977) 73 LSJS 139 *per* Wells J as quoted in Charles, C, *Sentencing Aboriginal People in South Australia.*

59 *Wanganeen v Smith, ibid.*

The perceived degree of assimilation marked by the categories, traditional, semi-urban and urban, manifests the assumption as to the significance of culture to the individual. The inquiry into what it has meant for the individual to be an indigenous Australian goes no further. A demeaning stereotype is applied. Charles concludes by referring to a more recent South Australian case in which stereotypes and assimilationist perceptions in accounting for indigeneity had been abandoned. In that case, *Leech v Sansbury*, Mullighan J approaches the issue of indigeneity in accordance with the principles enunciated in *Neal v R*.[60] Whilst this change in approach is to be encouraged one wonders whether what has happened is merely the exchange of one set of assumptions for another.[61]

It is also important to point out that it is not the judiciary and the lawyers involved in sentencing alone that must become familiar with the impact of colonisation. Probation officers, sociologists, and psychologists who are regularly called upon to prepare reports on offenders in an effort to assist the court in fashioning an appropriate penalty must also learn what it means to be indigenous. Otherwise, the reports they prepare do not address one of the fundamental forces that have served to shape the offender's life and lifestyle, rendering such reports of questionable utility. Undoubtedly Recommendations 96 and 97 were intended to, and necessarily must, apply to these professionals. One not only hopes that these recommendations will be fully implemented in the future, but that indigenous people currently taking full advantage of educational positions made available to them will soon occupy such positions.

Before leaving this point it is perhaps most important to note that consultation with the indigenous people themselves will be invaluable to the sentencer. Often it is thought that such consultation is only of use where the offender is part of a readily identifiable urban community, or that that community may play some part in the implementation of any penalty, or that its views are integral to the determination of such penalty. And this is true, but the 'community' does not perish in suburban Australia. This is palpably clear from works such as Irene Moore's *Voices of Aboriginal Australia*.[62] When indigenous people come to live in suburbia they, as one would expect, gravitate to those areas and people where they feel most comfortable. Their culture is not abandoned. Their familial ties not cut. Their indigeneity not surrendered. The community may become re-fashioned, but it remains a valuable source of information crucial to understanding the cultural heritage and influences upon an indigenous offender.

It is important, therefore, for those representing the indigenous offender to become familiar with that individual's history. So what, many will say, as it current practice for counsel in making submissions in mitigation as to penalty to put before the court the personal history of the offender highlighting any traumatic experiences that mark a shift

60 Charles, C, *op cit*, at p 95.

61 See also McCorquodale, J, 'Judicial Racism in Australia? Aboriginals in Civil and Criminal Cases', Hazelhurst, KM, (ed), *Ivory Scales: Black Australia and the Law*, 1987, Sydney: University of New South Wales Press, Chapter 2, where he argues that looking across the breadth of the criminal and civil jurisdiction in Australia cultural insensitivity and the use of negative stereotypes on the part of the judiciary is evident.

62 1995, Springwood: New South Wales.

in their behaviour or attitude. To those people I would advise caution, for it is easy to overlook the impact of colonisation for the individual, or to portray the impact of colonisation and its ramifications for the individual through 'white-eyes', or in a manner that invites assumptions or permits categorisation according to perceived stereotypes. For my part the cautionary words of Hal Wootten ring all too true:

> One of the most important and all-pervading issues of which I have become aware is the almost invariable failure of non-Aboriginal people to listen seriously to Aboriginal people who are trying to explain the issues from their own direct and personal experience. Unconsciously or consciously, the assumption is that white experts know best, and certainly better than Aboriginals, not only what the problems are, but what should be done about them. Even those rare white Australians who do not think that they themselves are experts usually give their ear to other whites whom they regard as experts. 'Consultation' there is *ad nauseam*, but it usually means telling Aboriginal people, not seriously treating them as a source of information, ideas, experience and wisdom. To my observation this has been a primary cause of failure on the part of the police of goodwill, as well as other operators in the criminal justice system, to achieve results commensurate with their efforts.[63]

It must be remembered that sentencing involves the making of value judgments by the sentencer.[64] In the case of indigeneity this is so whether it is put forward by way of explanation or mitigation. It is crucial therefore that counsel not only gain a true appreciation of the impact of colonisation, but be able to pilot the sentencer through the history of an indigenous offender and the direct and indirect influence upon it that can be attributed colonisation.

But what weight should be accorded indigeneity? The portrayal of the devastation brought to the indigenous people by colonisation is not, of itself, indicative of the invisible handicap born by the individual offender. Once difference is recognised the sentencer must determine what impact colonisation has had upon the individual. Thus, the weight to be given indigeneity will vary from case to case.

ETHNOCENTRISM AND SENTENCING

The Aboriginal Council for Reconciliation in its fifth Key Issues Paper, *Addressing Disadvantage,* states that despite the removal of most obstacles to the indigenous people participating in the legal system, many remain excluded due to 'ethnocentrism'.[65] Ethnocentrism was defined by the RCIADIC as a 'belief in the inherent superiority of one's own group and culture accompanied by a feeling of contempt for other groups and cultures'.[66] Ethnocentrism impacts adversely upon the indigenous people by fostering the 'continuation of racial stereotypes and discrimination at both individual and

63 Wootten, H, 'Aboriginal People and the Criminal Justice System', in Cunneen, C (ed), *Aboriginal Perspectives on Criminal Justice*, 1992, Sydney University: Institute of Criminology.

64 See Ashworth, A, *Sentencing and Criminal Justice*, 1992, London: Weidenfeld and Nicolson, p 32.

65 1994, Canberra: AGPS.

66 *Ibid*, at p 22.

institutional levels, and, by the 'use of non-indigenous cultural norms to determine rules and practices for key institutions and government services'.[67] Ethnocentrism is akin to what Daryle Rigney has termed racialisation. That is, it concerns the inadvertent perpetuation of racism by the adherence of people, even those who abhor racism and discrimination, to systems and procedures that exclude others of a different cultural background. As such ethnocentrism amounts to indirect racism and indirect discrimination. Immediately one can see the scope for the existence of ethnocentrism within sentencing. In fact, much of what has been written in this chapter has been aimed at encouraging counsel to act to deflate any perception amongst sentencers of a feeling of cultural superiority, against the resort to stereotypes, and against insensitivity to the culture of the indigenous offender and what it means in modern Australia to be an indigenous Australian. But the question remains, does ethnocentrism influence sentencing?

For a long time there was no empirical evidence indicating that racism or discrimination had any part to play in sentencing.[68] Few people were persuaded by such studies however, and their scepticism was fuelled by isolated and yet all to frequent instances of racist remarks made by members of the judiciary or magistracy.[69] In 1976 Eggleston first drew attention to judicial racism, but since then the focus has firmly been upon the police.[70] Numerous studies both in Australia and abroad have shown that racist or discriminatory attitudes held by the police contribute to the over-representation of minority groups in custody. Where the over-policing of a minority group is motivated by racist attitudes and persons are resultantly arrested, the entire criminal justice system becomes tainted by such attitudes. In such circumstances it has been the traditional position of the judiciary that there is little it can do to offset the damage already done. In part this is true. If an indigenous person is brought before the court to be sentenced upon committing a criminal offence, the court is duty bound to deal with the matter. But there is nothing to stop the court from commenting fully upon the context in which the offence occurred and in which it is called to impose sentence, and from making known its views of the police action undertaken. In fact there is a school of thought to the effect that as the court acts in the interests of the community it should make such further comment wherever warranted on behalf of that community.

But what of the judiciary itself, in imposing sentence is it discriminatory or racist, is it ethnocentric? In sentencing the judiciary strives to be impartial, objective, fair and

67 *Op cit*, at footnote 55; see also Cunneen, C, 'Judicial Racism', in McKillop, S (ed), *Aboriginal Justice Issues*, 1992, Australian Institute of Criminology Conference Proceedings.

68 See, for example, Victorian Sentencing Committee Report, Vol 1, 1988, p 380; Australian Law Reform Commission Report No 31, *The Recognition of Aboriginal Customary Laws*, 1986, at para 107; McConville, M, and Baldwin, J, 'The Influence of Race on Sentencing in England' (1982) Crim LR 652; Moxon, D, *Sentencing Practice in the Crown Court*, Home Office Research Study No 103; Crowe, I, and Cove, J, 'Ethnic Minorities and the Courts' (1984) Crim LR 413; Mair, G, 'Ethnic Minorities, Probation and the Magistrates' Courts' (1986) 26 Brit J of Criminol 147; Walker, M, 'The Court Disposal of Young Males by Race in London' (1983) 28 Brit J of Criminol 441.

69 See Cunneen, C, 'Judicial Racism', in McKillop, S (ed), *Aboriginal Justice Issues*, 1992, Australian Institute of Criminology Conference Proceedings; O'Shane, P, 'Aborigines and the Criminal Justice System', in Cunneen, C, *Aboriginal Perspectives on Criminal Justice*, 1992, Sydney: University Institute of Criminology; Eggleston, E, *Fear Favour or Affection*, 1976, Canberra: ANU Press.

70 Eggleston, E, *Fear Favour or Affection*, 1976, Canberra: ANU Press.

merciful, and yet too often the judiciary is perceived as discriminatory.

> Ask an Aboriginal person what he or she regards as the important factors underlying deaths in custody often elicits as a first reply 'Racism'. An increasing number of Aboriginals are seeing racism as a key concept in understanding and explaining their relations with the rest of the community. It is an uncomfortable subject which tends not to be talked about very openly and the existence of which is often vigorously denied by those who are its most obvious practitioners.[71]

In 1987 John Walker conducted a survey of the statistics produced by the 1982 and 1987 National Prison Censuses in an effort to uncover possible reasons for the over-representation of the indigenous people in the prison system.[72] His conclusions were surprising. Rather than discover evidence of racism or discrimination emanating from the judiciary and contributing to over-representation, he discovered that the judiciary was lenient in its treatment of indigenous offenders by comparison to non-indigenous people.[73] What is not scrutinised by Walker, and no doubt was not available to him, were the reasons for imprisonment in the first place. Thus, Walker's results operate upon the assumption that as at the date of the censi, those indigenous persons who had been imprisoned merited imprisonment, and furthermore, that their prior record of imprisonment was also merited. When one considers the gross disparity in prior record between non-indigenous and indigenous offenders – 81.1% of indigenous offenders had been imprisoned previously whereas only 57.5% of non-indigenous offenders had been imprisoned previously[74] – and that indigenous offenders were exposed to imprisonment much earlier in life, not to mention the rate of over-representation, one concludes that there is hardly any cause to celebrate. Furthermore, one wonders whether the leniency extended indigenous offenders amounts to tacit compensation for the fact that imprisonment is ordered where a non-custodial penalty would normally be imposed but the sentencer perceives that the indigenous offender's circumstances render him or her inappropriate for such penalty.[75] If it were to transpire that this was the practice of certain courts then, as LaPrairie points out, significant consequences follow. 'For example, does the combination of incarceration and shorter sentence lengths result in higher recidivism rates and longer prior records? Do longer records make incarceration more likely in the event of subsequent conviction?'[76]

71 Wootten, H, *Report of the Inquiry into the Death of Malcolm Charles Smith*, 1989, Canberra: AGPS, p 87.

72 Walker, J, 'Prison Cells with Revolving Doors', in Hazelhurst, KM (ed), *Ivory Scales: Black Australia and the Law*, 1987, Sydney: University of New South Wales Press.

73 'Even though 81.1% of Aboriginal prisoners have previously been in prison under sentence, compared with only 57.5% of non-Aboriginal prisoners, the average sentence for Aboriginal prisoners is only 42.6 months compared with 74.9 months for non-Aboriginals. This cannot be entirely attributed to the different types of offences committed by Aboriginals since the sentencing disparity is roughly consistent across the whole range of offences.' *Ibid*, at p 111.

74 *Ibid*, at p 111.

75 See Hudson, B, 'Discrimination and Disparity: The Influence of Race on Sentencing' (1989) *New Community* 16.

76 LaPrairie, C, 'The Role of Sentencing in the Over-representation of Aboriginal People in Correctional Institutions' (1990) *Canadian Journal of Criminology* 429 at 435.

In recent years Dr Roger Hood conducted a study of the sentencing decisions of five Crown Courts in the West Midlands, England.[77]

> The 'null hypothesis' tested was that the observed differences in the proportions of blacks, whites and Asians sentenced to custody, both in the sample case as a whole, and between cases dealt with at each of the five Crown Courts in the West Midlands, could be explained by differences in the characteristics of the cases of a kind which could legitimately be taken into account in deciding whether or not to impose a custodial sentence.[78]

Hood identified 15 case characteristics in all. These fell into four main categories:(i) the legal processing of the case prior to sentence; (ii) the offence(s) of which the accused stands convicted; (iii) past convictions; and (iv) personal and social characteristics of relevance. Race, being a characteristic that should not be considered, was excluded. By controlling for these characteristics Hood sought to determine whether or not his null hypothesis could be accepted. Prior to controlling for the case characteristics Hood found there to be a 17% greater probability of a black male offender receiving a custodial sentence than a white male offender. Furthermore, he found there to be an 18% lesser probability that an Asian male offender would receive a custodial sentence than a white male offender. After controlling for the case characteristics Hood found that a male black offender was still 5% more likely to receive a custodial sentence than a white male offender and an Asian male offender was 5% less likely to receive a custodial sentence than a white male offender. The question then confronted by Hood was what to make of the residual 5% difference in treatment.

It is normally the case that an outcome will not be considered conclusive statistically unless there is less than a one in 20 chance that the result could have occurred by chance. Hood's results were significant at a 0.07 level, that is, there was a one in 14 likelihood that they could have occurred by chance. Despite this however, Hood decided that as discrimination was such a threat to the criminal justice system, the 5% discrepancy could not be ignored. Put another way, the fact that differential treatment would occur by chance only once in 14 times 'should not be lightly dismissed'.[79] Accordingly, Hood concluded that it would be wrong to accept the null hypothesis. His study does not go so far as to unequivocally show that the judiciary are discriminatory in sentencing, but it does provide an indication that it may well occur and thereby provides impetus for further research.

Interestingly, Hood did discover that unemployment affected the sentencing of black offenders but not white.[80] In his article in *Criminology Australia*, Walker suggests that there is a correlation between social disadvantage and imprisonment. Indigenous rates of imprisonment are, he suggests, no higher than rates of imprisonment for non-

77 Hood, R (in collaboration with Cordovil, G) *Race and Sentencing; A Study in the Crown Court. A Report for the Commission of Racial Equality*, 1992, Oxford: Oxford University Press.

78 Hood, R, 'Race and Sentencing: A Reply' [1995] Crim LR 272 at 273.

79 *Ibid* at 277.

80 See also Hudson, B, 'Discrimination and Disparity: The Influence of Race on Sentencing' (1989) *New Community* 16.

indigenous offenders of a similarly low economic standard.[81] In applying this theory to employment Walker discovered that:

> On 30 June 1992, 25 out of every 100,000 non-indigenous people who were not 'unemployed' were in prison. (These could have been employed, running a business, in full or part-time education, occupied with 'home duties', or retired prior to their arrest.) However, indigenous people of a similar unemployment status found themselves in prison at roughly 13 times this rate. But the affect of being unemployed is over twice the effect of being indigenous: the chances of an unemployed non-indigenous person being in prison are almost 30 times higher than those who are not classified as unemployed. The chances of a person who is both indigenous and unemployed being in prison are over 250 times the chances of the non-indigenous non-unemployed![82]

Walker concludes that the rate of over-representation is not as bad as first thought. The over-representation of indigenous people in Australia's prisons may be due to the fact that they are unemployed and not that they are indigenous. The answer is, therefore, to get the indigenous people jobs.[83] Turning to education, Walker found that those 'who are both indigenous and an early school leaver are 127 times more likely to be in prison than those without such characteristics. The poorly-educated Aboriginal or Torres Strait Islander person has almost 14 times greater chance of imprisonment than his better educated cousin'.[84]

One cannot fault the suggestion that more needs to be done to open up educational and employment opportunities for the indigenous people of Australia. But what is disturbing is the suggestion that follows from the work of Walker and from that of Hood (although the latter is not directly relevant to indigenous Australians) that lack of employment and poor education have been accorded weight in the decision to imprison an indigenous offender where a non-custodial sentence was an option open to the court. This amounts to ethnocentrism and its perpetuation. Whether or not an indigenous offender is sent to prison is determined by reference to cultural norms that are not the norm experienced by the indigenous people. These cultural norms do not account for indigeneity. And so I have come full circle. Whilst judges may purport to take account of cultural difference in sentencing to what extent to they do so? And what is it they exactly mean by cultural difference?

---

81 Walker, J, 'The Over-representation of Aboriginal and Torres Strait Islander People in Prison' (August 1994) *Criminology Australia* 13. See also Cove, J, 'Aboriginal Over-representation in Tasmania' (1992) 25 ANZ Journal of Criminology.

82 Walker, J, *op cit*, at 14.

83 Walker states that: '[I]f unemployment amongst Aboriginal and Torres Strait Islander people were reduced to that of the non-indigenous population and if rates of imprisonment reflected this change, these figures suggest that the indigenous prison population could fall from 2,200 to down around 530.' (See Walker, J, *op cit*, at 15.)

84 Walker, J, *op cit*, at 15. He concludes that '[I]f levels of education amongst Aboriginal and Torres Strait Islander people were improved to that of the non-indigenous population and if rates of imprisonment reflected this change, these figures suggest that the indigenous prison population could fall from its current figure of 1391.9 per 100,000 persons aged over 15 (30 June 1992) to the figure of 164.3 per 100,000 reducing the actual numbers of Aboriginal and Torres Strait Islander prisoners from 2,200 to 262'.

> The official record-keepers saw all, recorded all, and rarely knew well or at all the people they wrote about.[85]

CONCLUSION

I return specifically to the theme that I have attempted to weave throughout this chapter, that of treating as equals people who, by virtue of[86] circumstances beyond their control, are unequal. That is not to ignore the possible existence of racism practised wittingly or unwittingly in sentencing by the judiciary. The perception of the indigenous people and anecdotal evidence demands that the judiciary continually be the subject of scrutiny in this regard. But what I have advocated is that in the absence of a proven body of judicial knowledge of indigeneity, and as the Nation slowly creeps toward true reconciliation wherein the indigenous people are accorded the dignity that by right is every persons and share equally in all political, economic, cultural and civil domains, counsel must assume responsibility for educating the judiciary and for neutralising ethnocentrism. In the light of the gross over-representation of indigenous people in custody it is a weighty responsibility.

85 RCIADIC National Report, 1991, Canberra: AGPS.

86 *Ibid.*

CHAPTER NINE

ABORIGINAL LAND RIGHTS IN SOUTH AUSTRALIA

Anthony Moore

MABO AND BASIC PRINCIPLES OF AUSTRALIAN LAND LAW

The decision of the High Court of Australia in *Mabo v Queensland (No 2)*[1] has attracted enormous public and academic comment. The decision relates to probably the most sensitive social issue of Australian society – the relationship between Aboriginal and non-Aboriginal persons. The decision also involves a dramatic overturn of doctrines considered to be long-established and fundamental to the structure of legal principles applied by Australian courts. Whilst the decision is about the entitlement of the plaintiff and those represented by the plaintiff to an interest in land, the decision has potential ramifications for almost every area of law. The judgments of the members of the court have a highly political nature. This characterisation is not to attack the judgments but to highlight the essence of the court's consideration. As the final arbiter of common law doctrine in Australia, the High Court must be concerned with the moral coherence of the basic principles enunciated by the court as much as it must be concerned with their logical coherence. For a court of final review the concern for coherence must override the conclusions of errant precedents or accidents of history. In essence *Mabo* is a statement that the principles of the Australian legal system cannot withstand the immorality of the proposition that Australia is a settled territory because there was no legal system in force prior to the claim of sovereignty by the British Crown.

From the perspective of land rights, the denial of the existence of land rights in favour of those Aboriginal inhabitants who occupied the land prior to the claim of sovereignty by the British Crown rested on two principles – the nature of the territory at the time of being claimed and the principle of tenure. The principle of tenure in its basic form is that all land vests in the Crown and all rights of individuals to interests in land derive from a grant of an interest by the Crown and involve a tenurial relationship between the individual and the Crown. The form of tenure is described as free socage tenure. An element of unreality afflicts the statement as to the overriding interest of the Crown because the tenurial relationship between the individual and the Crown carries no consequences. There are no incidents or obligations owed by the individual to the Crown and special rights of the Crown in relation to the land – the right to acquire the land compulsorily and the right to claim the land when the holder dies without a will and without any relatives to claim the land – are claimed not by virtue of the tenurial rights but from statutory powers that are not confined to interests in land. The principle of tenure must be distinguished from that of sovereignty whereby the Crown has

1 *Mabo v Queensland (No 2)* (1993) 63 ALJ 442. Comments include Nettheim, G, 'Judicial Revolution or Cautious Correction? *Mabo v Queensland*' (1993) 16 UNSWLJ 1; Wheeler, 'Common Law Native Title in Australia – An Analysis of *Mabo v Queensland (No 2)*' [1993] FLR 271; Stephenson and Rampala (eds), '*Mabo* – A Judicial Revolution', 1993, Brisbane: University of Queensland Press; Butt, P, '*Mabo v Queensland:* A Summary' (1993) 67 ALJ 442; Bartlett, R, *The Mabo Decision,* 1993, Sydney: Butterworths.

legislative and executive authority with respect to the territory. This authority allows for the making of laws recognising, transferring or extinguishing rights in land.

The exercise of legislative and executive power has allowed the recognition of interests in land whose source is inconsistent with the need for an original grant from the Crown. Not only Aboriginal land claims but those of many of the early non-aboriginal land claimants are based on an association with the land.[2] In New South Wales official government policy was to confine settlement fairly closely to the area surrounding Sydney Harbour. However much development was undertaken by those who defied official government policy and went out and exercised control over the lands of the interior. The feature of the claims of these squatters was that they were able to acquire the political power (the squattocracy) to legitimise their land takings. Australian preference for small land holdings has been constantly at odds with the economic power of large land-owners. That battle was fought not only in early New South Wales but in the later selection movement and the closer settlement attempts to reward the heroes of the two world wars. In South Australia the development of Kangaroo Island after the Second World War is but one example of this conflict. Whatever the preferences of government, Australian geography has dictated victory by the large land-holders.

The doctrine of tenure is only significant for Aboriginal land rights if any claims to the land derived from association with the land prior to the claim to sovereignty by the British Crown are denied. The denial of those claims depends upon the characterisation of the territory at the time sovereignty is claimed. The standard distinction is that between settled and conquered territory.[3] In the case of a settled territory existing laws and thus rights flowing from those laws are not recognised whereas in the case of a conquered territory existing laws continue to apply until displaced by an exercise of sovereignty. The basis of the distinction is a matter of constitutional rather than property law. It is possible to argue that the distinction is not one determined by the judiciary but reflects an executive determination. As a matter of the substance of the distinction, characterisation as a settled territory is said to rest on the absence of any existing legal system. At the same time legal systems were conceived as a product of societies which cultivated the land rather than those which nomadically drew succour from the land. In modern environmental terms, civilisation equates to environmental degradation. Settlement was contrasted with the act of conquest and in turn conquest was conceived in terms of battle on formed lines rather than the attrition of small-scale killings and the impact of introduced disease.

It is because of the primary issue of the characterisation of the territory that *Mabo,* whilst a case about the existence of land rights, is even more so a case about constitutional law. Land rights flow from *Mabo* not because they are accommodated as part of the common law as some form of exception to the tenurial principle, but because legal rights are recognised as flowing from the legal system in force prior to the claim of sovereignty by the British Crown. This legal system is recognised and enforced not as part of but something outside the common law. This recognition cannot be simply a matter of land law.

2 Castles, AC, *An Australian Legal History*, 1982, Sydney: Law Book Company, pp 175–76.

3 *Ibid*, pp 515–20.

The doctrine of tenure

The application of the doctrine of the tenure in Australia is traditionally ascribed to the 1848 decision in *AG (New South Wales) v Brown.*[4] In that decision a challenge was made to the exercise by an individual of the taking of minerals from land. The land had been granted to the individual, but the right to take minerals had been excepted from the grant. The challenge by the Crown in that case was upheld, on the basis that rights to land derived from the grant by the Crown. However, the Crown could make the grant subject to such exceptions or limitations as it desired. Although the grant provided the private rights to the land it could also qualify those rights in such ways as the Crown saw fit. The court rejected an argument that there was an inconsistency between the fact of the grant itself and the exceptions from the grant. The decision can be seen as paradoxical: whilst the tenurial relationship of itself imposes no burdens upon the individual land holder in favour of the Crown, the terms of the grant by the Crown may be subject to such conditions and exceptions as the Crown sees fit. Thus rights to minerals have in Australia been divorced from ownership of the surface land.

The application of the doctrine of tenure in Australia, and acceptance of the principle that Australia was a settled territory was confirmed by the decision of the Privy Council in 1899 in *Cooper v Stuart.*[5] That decision has been traditionally seen as inconsistent with any claim by Aborigines or Aboriginal groups to rights in land based upon their traditional association with the land.

In *Milirrpum v Nabalco Pty Ltd and the Commonwealth*[6] Blackburn J reiterated the proposition that the doctrine of tenure was part of the law of Australia and explained clearly its significance for Australia:[7]

> All the Australian cases to which I was referred ... affirm the principle, fundamental to the English law of real property, that the Crown is the source of title to all land; that no subject can own allodially, that only an estate or interest in it which he holds mediately or immediately of the Crown. On the foundation of New South Wales, therefore, and of South Australia, every square inch of territory in the colony became the property of the Crown. All titles, rights and interest whatever in land which existed thereafter in subjects of the Crown were the direct consequence of some grant from the Crown.

4 (1847) 1 Legge 312; see Buck, A, '*Attorney-General v Brown* and the Development of Property Law in Australia' (1994) 2 Aust Prop LJ 128.

5 (1889) 14 AC 286.

6 (1971) 17 FLR 141; [1972–73] ALR 65.

7 (1971) 17 FLR 141 at 245.

Policies towards Aboriginal peoples[8]

Although in the early stages of British settlement there were some official statements of concern for the well-being of the Aboriginal peoples, there was very little recognition of the social and cultural identity of these peoples. From the 1860s the official policy towards the Aboriginal population was that of 'protection'. This policy involved isolating and segregating full-blood Aborigines on reserves and restricting contact and breeding between them and outsiders. The purpose of the reserves, therefore, was not to restore the relationship between the Aborigines and the land. Rather it was a means of isolating the Aboriginal population. In some cases the administration of the reserves and much of the role of missionaries was unsympathetic to the traditional way of life of Aborigines.

By the 1950s the policies of both national and State governments were based on the concept of assimilation. It was assumed that all Aborigines would aspire to the same way of living as other Australians. Assistance was provided for Aborigines and attempts were made to remove formal discrimination. But a distinct and surviving Aboriginal culture was not recognised.

Some movement towards the recognition of self-government of reserves by Aborigines occurred in the 1960s. In South Australia the Aboriginal Land Trusts Act 1966 set up land trusts to administer the Aboriginal reserves in the state. These trust arrangements have not been regarded as enhancing the position of Aboriginal peoples. One of the problems affecting the trust was that their administration was seen to be subject to extensive ministerial control.

The *Gove Peninsula* case

A new effort at the legal assertion of land rights in favour of traditional Aboriginal occupants came in the late 1960s in the Gove Peninsula. The discovery of minerals led to new interest in the land by non-Aboriginal developers and conflict with traditional occupants. The resulting litigation produced the decision in *Milirrpum v Nabalco Pty Ltd and the Commonwealth*[9] referred to above. Aboriginal groups based at Yirrkala on the Gove Peninsula in the Northern Territory brought an action in the Northern Territory Supreme Court to assert their continuing ownership of their traditional lands. They challenged the validity of mining leases granted over their land by the Commonwealth government. In the determination of those claims Blackburn J held that the doctrine of communal native title did not form, and had never formed part of the law of any part of Australia, and that such a doctrine had no place in a settled colony. In any event he concluded that the mining leases granted by the Commonwealth to Nabalco Pty Ltd were valid exercises of the executive power of the Commonwealth government and thus overrode any communal native title rights. He further held however that the

8 Material in this section and the following two sections are based on the account in Bradbrook, AJ, MacCallum, SV, and Moore, AP, *Australian Real Property Law*, 1991, Sydney: Law Book Company, pp 27–33.

9 (1971) 17 FLR 141.

Aboriginal clans in the Gove Peninsula had established a recognisable system of law and that this system of law provided for a relationship between the clans and the land. On the other hand Blackburn J did not consider that the relationship between the clans and the land constituted a proprietary relationship in any sense known to the common law. In any event he concluded that the plaintiffs had not established that their predecessors had, at the time of the acquisition of their territory by the Crown as part of the colony of New South Wales, the same links to the same areas of land as those claimed by the plaintiffs.

The decision of Blackburn J was strongly criticised by many writers.[10] In particular they attacked the finding that New South Wales was a settled colony and that the doctrine of communal native title was never part of the Australian common law. However the decision is significant in that it recognises that the Aboriginal clans had a recognisable system of law, and that system of law involved a relationship between the clans and the land. That relationship differed from forms of proprietary interest of land known to the common law particularly because it did not involve the total exclusion of other groups and because the ownership was not individualised but held on a communal basis. The findings in *Milirrpum,* however, undercut the basis for the description of Australia as a settled colony in that they reject the view that there were no systems of law operating prior to the assertion of sovereignty by the British Crown.

Statutory Aboriginal land rights

Following the *Milirrpum* decision, the focus for the grant of Aboriginal land rights switched to the political arena. In 1967 a referendum had amended the Australian constitution[11] so that the Commonwealth parliament had power to pass laws specifically for the benefit of Aboriginal people. In 1973 the newly elected Australian Labour Party government commissioned Mr AE Woodward QC as Aboriginal Land Rights Commissioner. He was to inquire into and report on the 'appropriate means to recognise and establish the traditional rights and interests of Aborigines to and in relation to lands'. In particular the Commissioner was to report on arrangements for vesting title to, and granting rights in, land in the Northern Territory already reserved for the use and benefit of Northern Territory Aborigines. He was also to inquire into the desirability of establishing appropriate procedures for the examination of claims to Aboriginal traditional rights and interests in land in the Northern Territory outside Aboriginal reserves. By the time of a decision as to appropriate action on the basis of the Commissioner's report to the national government, there had been a change of government and the conservative Liberal-Country Party coalition government was in power. That government introduced and obtained the passage of the Aboriginal Land Rights (Northern Territory) Act 1976.

In line with the Commissioner's recommendations the 1976 Act provided for the setting up by the Commonwealth of at least two land councils. The councils were to

10 These responses are set out in Bradbrook, AJ, MacCallum, SV, and Moore, AP, *op cit*, p 28.

11 Section 51(xxxi) empowers the Federal government to make laws with respect to the people of any race for whom it is deemed necessary to make special laws.

nominate the trustees who should administer the land vested in the Aborigines, and were to provide administrative services and give direction in certain matters. The councils were to represent Aborigines in negotiations with the government in relation to land rights, to protect the interests of traditional owners in all negotiations concerning the use of land, and co-ordinate and make traditional claims to vacant Crown lands. The making of traditional land claims was to be based on the spiritual attachment of Aboriginal clans to an area of land over which they were entitled to forage under Aboriginal law. Only unalienated Crown land could be the subject of a land claim. In 1980, the Act was amended[12] to provide that if the land council agreed to mining, that agreement was to be valid even if the consent of the local Aboriginal communities had not been obtained.

In South Australia Aboriginal land rights were conferred by the Pitjantjatjara Land Rights Act 1981 and the Maralinga Tjarutja Land Rights Act 1984. The Pitjantjatjara Land Rights Act transferred just under 100,000 square kilometres of land to the Pitjantjatjara people and the Maralinga Tjarutja Land Rights Act involved a 50,000 square kilometre tract of land. The statutes set up statutory Aboriginal corporations to be the holders of special titles to traditional lands. All members of the relevant Aboriginal community are members of the corporate body. The body's principal functions are to administer the land vested in it; to ascertain the wishes and opinions of all traditional owners in relation to the management, use and control of the land; and to seek, where practicable, to give effect to those wishes and opinions. The body corporate has wide powers to permit or deny access to lands. No mining operations can proceed without the consent of the body corporate, although unreasonable refusal of consent may lead to arbitration. South Australia has not set up any open-ended procedures for claims to vacant Crown lands until very recently.

Whilst the national government with respect to the Northern Territory and the South Australian government had made significant steps in the protection of the rights of Aboriginal peoples with their traditional lands, the response was not matched in other parts of Australia. In 1985 the national Australian Labour Party government published a 'Preferred National Aboriginal Lands Rights Model'. This model included a commitment to the principles that Aboriginal land would be held under inalienable freehold title, and sacred sites would be protected. A previous Australian Labour Party commitment to Aboriginal control of mining on Aboriginal land was altered to a proposal that the relevant government have the power to determine mining applications in cases where miners and Aboriginal communities could not agree on the terms and conditions under which mining was to occur. The government would receive recommendations from a tribunal before making these decisions. It would also be up to the government to determine the proportion of royalties payable to Aborigines. The preferred model was constrained by the national government's concern to reduce prospects of national/state conflict over land rights legislation. Despite the fact that the preferred model itself contained concessions towards development interests, in 1986 the

12 Aboriginal Land Rights (Northern Territory) Amendment Act 1980 (Cth).

proposal was allowed to die. The failure of the national government to insist upon basic standards for Aboriginal land rights placed the onus for resolving the issue back with the courts. In particular, legislation in Western Australia and Queensland failed to make any commitment to land rights conforming to the model or to the standards applied in 1976 in the Northern Territory by the national Liberal-Country Party government.

The *Mabo* case

In the period following *Milirrpum v Nabalco and the Commonwealth*,[13] the High Court gave an indication[14] that it was willing to consider the issue of the recognition of native title in Australia. That opportunity arose in *Mabo v Queensland*.[15]

The claim in that case involved land known as the Murray Islands which comprise three islands with an area of nine square kilometres in the Torres Strait. The claim was instituted by three of the Meriam people who inhabit the islands. The native inhabitants live in village communities. The land is occupied in small properties which have been handed down from generation to generation. In 1879 the islands were annexed to Queensland. In 1882 the Queensland government reserved the islands for native inhabitants. Also in that year the Queensland government leased to a missionary society an area of two acres on one of the islands. In 1931 the government leased two of the islands to non-residents to allow a sardine factory to be established, but the lease expressly precluded interference with the natives' use of the islands. The action by the Meriam people was commenced in 1982.

In 1985 the Queensland Parliament passed the Queensland Coast Islands Declaration Act 1985. That Act declared that on annexation to Queensland in 1879 the lands vested in the Crown in right of the State of Queensland free from all other rights, interests and claims whatsoever. In *Mabo v Queensland (No 1)*[16] this Act was held to be invalid as inconsistent with the Racial Discrimination Act 1975. The High Court held that the 1985 Act extinguished all traditional land rights which would otherwise have survived annexation to Queensland. The High Court held that the Act deprived the Meriam people of their property but left unimpaired the rights of those whose property did not originate from the laws and customs of the Meriam people. Under s 10 Racial Discrimination Act persons of one race could not be granted by law property rights of a more limited nature than those granted to other races. The Meriam people were granted a more limited property right.

The matter was then further heard by Moynihan J in the Queensland Supreme Court. He reserved a number of questions for determination by the High Court pursuant to s 18 Judiciary Act 1903. In argument on these questions, the Queensland

13 (1971) 17 FLR 141.

14 In *Coe v Commonwealth* (1979) 24 ALR 118 the High Court stated that the issue of recognition of land rights of occupants prior to the assertion of sovereignty by the British Crown was an issue that had not been the subject of any authoritative ruling by the High Court.

15 Ultimately resolved as *Mabo v Queensland (No 2)* (1993) 66 ALJR 408.

16 (1988) 166 CLR 186.

government claimed that when the Murray Islands were annexed, the Crown acquired the absolute beneficial ownership of the islands, and that no other rights could exist over the islands unless granted by the Crown. The native inhabitants argued that their customary native title was not extinguished upon annexation, and that nothing since annexation had extinguished that title.

The High Court held that the acquisition of sovereignty by the British Crown over territory in Australia did not automatically extinguish customary native title. The common law could accommodate native customary title as something in existence prior to the acquisition of sovereignty. The Crown's sovereignty conferred upon it the ultimate title but this ultimate title did not necessarily confer beneficial ownership. The court held that existing customary native title was not extinguished. The Crown's sovereignty carried beneficial ownership only over areas where no native title to the land in fact existed. The Crown's ultimate sovereignty empowered it to appropriate land to itself or alienate land to others. But until the land was appropriated or alienated any traditional native interests in the land that existed under native law or custom when the colony was established continued in existence. The mere acquisition of sovereignty was not an exclusion of the existence of the native title.

The High Court held that as had been shown in *Nabalco* there was a subtle and elaborate system of rules in force amongst indigenous peoples of Australia prior to the acquisition of sovereignty by the British Crown. It was therefore false to describe Australia as a settled colony on the basis that it was without settled inhabitants or settled law. Since that description was false the rule that Crown ownership subsisted in the lands of the acquired territory because there was no other proprietor could not be sustained. The title of the Crown should be recognised where the Crown exercised its right to grant land or its sovereign power to appropriate for itself full ownership of parcels of land. But otherwise the doctrine of tenure did not require wholesale beneficial ownership of the land to the exclusion of indigenous inhabitants.

Native title reflects the entitlement of indigenous inhabitants to their traditional lands, in accordance with their laws and customs. The nature and extent of native title is essentially a question of fact as to what were the incidents conferred by the traditional laws and customs. Native title may possess characteristics unknown to the common law. To prove the existence of native title, there must be an established entitlement to occupy or use particular land. That entitlement must have sufficient significance to demonstrate a locally recognised special relationship between the users and the land. The relationship between the indigenous inhabitants and the land need not amount to possession as known to the common law. The use of the land need not involve exploitation of the land by way of permanent improvements upon the land. The relationship can flow from a nomadic lifestyle and need not involve more than the use of the land to obtain food. Native title is customarily held by communities, but in rare cases may be vested in individuals. Native title cannot normally be alienated but remains with clan or group which exercises control.

It is possible for a clan or group to relinquish their title to land by ceasing to have any relationship with that land.[17] It is not clear what amounts to an abandonment of title. It is clear that laws and customs of people change from time to time and the influx of Europeans has imposed tremendous pressures. The maintenance of traditional ownership depends on the maintenance of an identifiable community living under the laws and customs of that community and as part of those laws and customs the community observes a relationship with the land. Once abandoned, native title cannot be revived.

The Crown's status as the ultimate owner and the sovereign authority gives the Crown the power to extinguish native title. Any Crown grant or alienation that is clearly inconsistent with the continued exercise of native title over the land extinguishes the title to the extent of the inconsistency. Thus a grant in fee simple which confers a total right of occupation extinguishes a native title. However in cases of leases by the Crown and the grant of mining rights the question of extinction involves a comparison of the extent of title claimed by the native group as against the nature of the claim under the interest later granted by the Crown. The High Court has emphasised that the extent of the native title is defined not by the common law but by the system of law of the native peoples themselves. Because there are many systems of law of the native peoples, there can be no single definition of the extent of that title. Similarly the range of Crown leases in Australia is extensive and their common incidents vary very significantly. The question of extinguishment therefore depends upon the consistency of two things which take different forms in different places. It is certainly true that a number of Crown leases are expressed so that the rights conferred should not disturb the traditional exercise of movement across that land by native groups. There may well then be no inconsistency between the native title and such a Crown lease.

The issue of extinguishment was raised by the existence of the two leases in *Mabo;* the first to the London Missionary Society (later transferred to the Australian Board of Missions), the second for the sardine factory. The first lease conferred an absolute right of possession and all members of the High Court considered that this lease extinguished native title. The sardine factory lease however contained a condition protecting the use by the Murray Islanders of their tribal gardens and plantations and of their fishing operations on adjacent reefs. Brennan J indicated his opinion that even this lease extinguished native title.[18] He considered that the lease conferred possessory rights on the lessee and a reversionary interest to the Crown. These rights left no room for the continued existence of rights and interest derived from Meriam laws and customs. On the other hand,[19] Deane and Gaudron JJ contended that the lease neither extinguished nor had any continuing adverse effect upon any rights of the native inhabitants because it recognised and protected their usufructuary rights.

17 This matter is further discussed in *Coe v Commonwealth* (1993) 118 ALR 193. The issues of the extent to which the ongoing relationship must be a physical one and the burden of proof as to whether title has been extinguished are ones on which differing positions have been put forward. See also *Mason v Triton* (1994) 34 NSWLR 572.

18 (1993) 66 ALJR 408 at 433–34.

19 Their discussion is at (1993) 66 ALJR 408 at 455. In *Pereroultja v Tickner* (1993) 42 FCR 32 the Full Federal Court held that a freehold grant to an Aboriginal land trust did not extinguish native title because the purpose of the grant was to give effect to and preserve native title.

With respect to the grant of mining rights, the position resulting from the nature of Crown grants in Australia[20] is that the fee simple interest does not carry with it rights to minerals in the land. Consequently, a later grant of mining rights is not inconsistent with the common law fee simple interest. However native title may, in this respect, be more extensive than the common law fee simple interest. In particular any disturbance of the land pursuant to mining rights which would affect sacred sites may well be inconsistent with the native title which regulates and protects access to the sacred sites. Even so the grant of mining rights over land, even if inconsistent with native claim in total would seem only to detract from part of that claim and not extinguish it fully.

One significant constraint upon the capacity of State or territory governments to extinguish native title is the Racial Discrimination Act 1975. Under this Act any State law or executive action which discriminated against any native group would be invalid. Therefore, as almost a universal principle, to extinguish native title without compensation when title for other persons would only be extinguished with compensation would seem to amount to discrimination and therefore to be invalid. The significance of this proposition can be seen in the invalidation of the Queensland Coast Islands Declaration Act in *Mabo v Queensland (No 1).*[21]

Native Title legislation[22]

Following the decision in *Mabo* the Federal government passed the Native Title Act 1993. This Act provides a procedure whereby native title may be claimed and its validity assessed. It also validates past Commonwealth government actions and allows the states and territories to validate past actions of their governments. The objects of the Act are set out in s 3. They are:

(a) to recognise and protect native title;

(b) to establish ways in which future acts affecting native title can proceed, and to set standards for them;

(c) to establish a mechanism for determining claims to native title; and

(d) to validate past acts that are invalid because of the existence of native title.

Native title is defined as the rights and interests of Aboriginal peoples or Torres Strait Islanders as observed under traditional custom and as recognised by the common law of Australia.[23] Rights and interest comprising native title include hunting, gathering or fishing.

20 This position is illustrated by the decision in *AG v Brown* (1847) 1 Legge 312 (see footnote 4).

21 (1988) 166 CLR 186.

22 Much of the material in this section is drawn from French J, *A Lawyer's Guide to Native Title*, 1995, Adelaide: Adelaide University Continuing Legal Education Paper No 97 and Butt, P, 'The Native Title Act: A Property Law Perspective' (1994) 68 ALJ 285.

23 Section 61 Native Title Act 1993 (Cth).

Under the Act an application can be made for a determination as to whether native title exists.[24] The application will normally be made to the National Native Title Tribunal. Application for a determination can be made by the persons who claim the native title, or by the Commonwealth minister, or by the minister of a State or Territory where the whole of the area is within the jurisdiction of that State or Territory. An application can also be made by any person having an interest in the whole of the area over which the determination is sought. Thus a person whose interests are adverse to native title can seek a ruling as to the existence of native title.

Once an application is made the first act is that of determining whether to accept it.[25] An application containing the required information must be accepted unless the registrar of the tribunal considers that the application is vexatious or frivolous or that prima facie the claim cannot be made out. After acceptance the registrar must give notice of accepted applications to all persons whose interest may be affected by a determination. These persons may include anyone with a proprietary interest in the land registered in a Torrens or other register. A person whose interest may be affected by a determination that native title exists is entitled to oppose the application.

The National Native Title Tribunal can determine whether native title exists, and what rights are comprised by the particular title.[26] The tribunal can make such a determination where the application is not opposed or where the application is opposed but the parties reach agreement. Where the application is opposed and the parties have not reached agreement a mediation conference must be held to try to resolve the matter. If at this conference the parties reach agreement the tribunal can make a determination about the existence or otherwise of native title. This determination must be consistent with the terms of the agreement.

In cases where the tribunal is unable to make a determination, or on the application of any person whose interests are affected by a determination, the Federal Court has jurisdiction to make a determination.[27] In reaching a determination the Federal Court is not bound by technicalities, legal forms, or rules of evidence. The court may be assisted by assessors and may direct the holding of public conferences to help resolve the relevant issues.

In South Australia a separate procedure for the determination of native title is provided by the Native Title (South Australia) Act 1994. Under this Act jurisdiction to determine the existence of native title is conferred upon the Supreme Court and the Environment Resources and Development Court.[28] In proceedings involving a native

24 In *Wik Peoples v Queensland* (1994) 120 ALR 465 Drummond J held that a determination under the Act operated *in rem* in that it declares the status of native land over the land as regards the whole world not just for the parties to the action.

25 Section 63. In *Re Waanyi Peoples Native Title Determination* (1994) 129 ALR 100, French J (President of the Tribunal) ruled the function under s 63 was a low-level negative screening test and the applicant had to show evidence of the elements necessary to make out the claim. The applicant did not have to establish a *prima facie* case but rather that a *prima facie* case could be made out.

26 Sections 70, 71 and 73.

27 Section 167.

28 Section 5 Native Title (South Australia) Act 1994.

title question, the relevant court is directed[29] to make use of the expert assistance of Native Title Commissioners appointed under the Environment Resources and Development Court Act 1993. In proceedings relating to native title the relevant court is directed to proceed with a minimum of formality, and is not bound by the rules of evidence, and must act according to equity good conscience and the substantial merits without regard to legal technicalities and forms.

Applications under the South Australian Act[30] may be made by any person who claims to be entitled to native title in land. An application may be made by a representative Aboriginal body on behalf of persons who claim native title in land. The State minister or the Commonwealth minister may make an application. In addition an application may also be made by a person whose interests would be affected by the existence of native title in land. On the hearing of an application for a native title declaration, any interested person must be allowed to introduce evidence and make submissions. An interested person includes a person whose interests would be affected by the existence of native title.

Validation of government actions

The Commonwealth Native Title Act 1993 validates past actions by the Commonwealth government which were at least partially invalid because of the way in which they affected native land rights.[31] It also provides for State legislation which might similarly validate actions by State governments.[32] South Australia has passed legislation based upon this provision: Native Title (South Australia) Act 1994. Similar legislation has been passed in New South Wales, Queensland, Victoria and the Northern Territory: Native Title (New South Wales) Act 1994, Native Title (Queensland) Act 1993, Land Titles Validation Act 1993 (Victoria) and Validation of Titles and Actions Act 1994 (NT).

Western Australia enacted legislation dealing with native title but on lines very different to that of the Commonwealth legislation and the models in the other States and the Northern Territory. The Land (Title and Traditional Usage) Act 1993 (WA) purported to extinguish native title and substitute statutory rights flowing from the Act. This Act was held to be inconsistent with both the Racial Discrimination Act 1975 and the Native Title Act 1993 by the High Court in *Biljabo v Western Australia*.[33] The legislation thus has no effect and to the extent that any action of the Western Australian government affecting native title is invalid that invalidity remains.

The Commonwealth legislation only validates past acts which were to some extent invalid. In the case of acts of the Commonwealth government, invalidity would

29 Section 7.

30 Section 19.

31 Section 14 Native Title Act 1993 (Cth).

32 Section 19.

33 (1995) 128 ALR 1.

normally result from an acquisition of property without just compensation thus infringing s 51(xxi) of the constitution. Past acts are further limited to acts which would have been valid but for the existence of native title. The past is in general defined as acts occurring prior to 1 January 1994 though some later exercise of rights flowing from earlier legislation may also be regarded as past acts.

The past acts are placed in four categories described as A, B, C and D. Category A acts are grants of freehold estates and commercial, agricultural, pastoral or residential leases. Category B acts are grants of leasehold interests other than commercial, agricultural, pastoral or residential leases, and other than mining leases. Category C acts are grants of mining leases. Category D acts are any other acts.

The Commonwealth legislation validates the acts by the Commonwealth government.[34] In respect of Category A acts the legislation provides that the act extinguishes the native title involved. Category B acts extinguish native title to the extent of any inconsistency. Category C acts and Category D acts do not extinguish native title but suspend the rights flowing from the native title during the currency of the activity allowed by the Commonwealth act.

Validation of Commonwealth acts creates an entitlement to compensation for the holders of native title affected.[35] With respect of Category A and Category B acts the compensation is payable with respect to the title extinguished. With respect to Category C and Category D acts where native title is suspended compensation is payable only on conditions.

The South Australian legislation follows the Commonwealth model. The legislation expressly adopts the definition of past acts and the Categories A, B, C and D of the Commonwealth legislation.[36] The legislation deems past acts of the State of South Australia to have been at all times valid and extinguishes native title affected by a Category A past act and to the extent of inconsistency by a Category B past act.[37] The South Australian legislation also preserves any reservation or condition contained in a past Act where that reservation or condition was for the benefit of Aboriginal peoples and preserves any rights or interests of Aboriginal peoples other than rights conferred by native title.[38]

The Commonwealth Native Title Act 1993 also provides for the validation of future acts.[39] Future acts include legislative and executive activity and the creation, variation, extension, renewal or extinguishment of any legal or equitable rights. The acts must affect native title in relation to land or water. The future is defined in relation to the making of legislation as acts after 1 July 1993 and in relation to other activity as acts after 1 January 1994.

34 Sections 14–16.

35 Section 17.

36 Section 31 Native Title (South Australia) Act 1994 (SA).

37 Sections 32–36.

38 Section 38.

39 Sections 23 and 223 Native Title Act 1993 (Cth).

Future acts are classified as permissible future acts and impermissible future acts.[40] Impermissible acts are those which are not permissible acts as that category is defined. Permissible acts are defined as acts of three types: acts of low impact; legislative acts that are non-discriminatory; and non-legislative acts which would be valid if the title involved was an ordinary title (a fee simple interest).[41] Illustrations of low impact acts provided in the explanatory memorandum and include the grant of a permit to hold an event or of a bee-keeping licence. The illustration of a non-discriminatory legislative act is the making of legislation permitting mining on land irrespective of whether there is native title in the land. The illustration of a non-legislative act able to be made with respect to land subject to a fee simple interest is the grant of a mining lease over that land. An impermissible future act is invalid to the extent that it affects native title. A permissible future act entitles native title holders to compensation where there is no provision for just terms under the acquisition statute or brings into operation the right to negotiate system.

The right to negotiate system applies where the permissible future act involves the creation of a right to mine or the extension of the area over which, or period during which, a mining right has effect.[42] The system also applies to compulsory acquisition of interests held under native title where the purpose of acquisition is to confer interests on parties other than the government.[43] Notice of intention to do the act (ie create the right to mine) must be given to any native title claimant for the land involved.[44] Notice must also be given, in South Australia, to the Environment, Resources and Development Court or the National Native Title Tribunal.[45] All parties have the right to make submissions to the government about the proposed act.[46] A party may request mediation by the court or tribunal. In the absence of agreement through negotiation or mediation a party may request a determination from the court or tribunal.[47] The court or tribunal may determine that the proposed act may be done, may not be done, or may be done subject to conditions.[48]

CONCLUSIONS

The decision in *Mabo* may be seen as emphasising the power of the common law to resolve crucial social issues. In the writer's view a stronger argument can be made that the decision reflects the power of the courts to utilise a bill of rights. In *Mabo* a crucial

40 Section 236.

41 Section 235.

42 Section 26.

43 Section 28.

44 Section 29.

45 Section 30.

46 Section 31.

47 Section 36.

48 Section 38. A right of appeal lies to the Federal Court with respect to a determination on a question of law: s 169(i).

element was the existence of the Commonwealth Racial Discrimination Act 1975. This Act allowed the High Court to invalidate the Queensland Coast Declaratory Act 1985. Unless this Act was invalidated the issues of whether Australia was truly a settled territory and the scope of the doctrine of tenure could not have arisen.

The *Mabo* decision has now assumed a dominant position in the framing of social values in Australia. Such is the respect paid to the decision that the Commonwealth Native Title Act 1993 and the legislation in States and Territories (other than Western Australia) substantially provide only procedural devices whereby the substantive principles derived from *Mabo* can be developed. In Western Australia the attempt to pursue an independent course was based not so much on a rejection of *Mabo* as an assertion that land rights are a matter of State determination. Of course this assertion involves the legally inaccurate analysis that the Australian constitution divides subject-matters between the national and State governments as opposed to the true position whereby the State's powers are those left over after the exercise of Commonwealth powers and the key provision is the inconsistency section.[49] In any event it is disingenuous to describe *Mabo* as concerned with land rights rather than the rights of indigenous peoples.

If the dominance of *Mabo* is readily explicable in terms of social culture, deficiencies of a system whereby land rights for indigenous peoples are defined by the common law process must be acknowledged. That process involves the enunciation of principle at the highest level by a High Court which adheres to a process of individual judgments and thus differing shades of meaning for even agreed results. Consequently *Mabo* is unable to resolve whether the sardine factory lease would extinguish native title. The case by case process means that the scope of native title and the ways in which it is affected will only be defined over an extremely long time.

The development of a doctrine of native title depended on an understanding of the cultures of the indigenous peoples of Australia. The factual findings in *Milirrpum v Nabalco and the Commonwealth* were fundamental to the development of this understanding. The opportunity for a clear and bold resolution of native land rights existed in the 1980s and was lost by the national government. Against that inaction *Mabo* was inevitable and the Native Title Act 1993 (Cth) and related State legislation at least provide a means for steps forward.

49 Section 109 Australian Constitution.

CHAPTER TEN

HUMAN RIGHTS AND THE EXTINGUISHMENT OF NATIVE TITLE

Michael Dodson

INTRODUCTION

In 1992 the decision in *Mabo (No 2)*[1] was delivered by the High Court of Australia. There is no denying that the recognition of native title which resulted from that case was a monumental step forward not only for the recognition and protection of indigenous interests in land but for indigenous rights generally. However, a crucial feature of that decision was the finding that the sovereign government carries the right to extinguish native title. The manner in which a government can remove the property interests of its citizens raises a number of human rights issues. This is particularly so where the interference with property interests threatens the cultural heritage of those dispossessed.

In the Preamble to Australia's National Action Plan the Australian government has clearly expressed its position on international human rights:

> In seeking to advance human rights through its foreign and domestic policies, the Australian Government subscribes to the view that human rights are *inherent,* that is, they are the birthright of all human beings; *inalienable,* insofar as they cannot be lost or taken away; and *universal* in that they apply to all persons, irrespective of nationality, status, sex or race. Australia rejects the view that there is any hierarchy of human rights.[2]

These fundamental human rights, which are inherent, inalienable and universal to all human beings, are articulated in numerous international instruments, many of which have been signed and ratified by Australian governments.

I have already argued that the 'willingness and commitment of Australian governments to respond to the High Court's recognition of native title in a manner consistent with the full protection of our human rights, will be a significant test of Australia's commitment to human rights and a guide to the integrity of our nation at an international level'.[3] This is not only the responsibility of governments and those charged with the responsibility of overseeing the Native Title Act 1993 (Cth), but it is also the responsibility of the judiciary in the development and interpretation of the common law. This is especially so given that an important feature of the Native Title Act

1 *Mabo v The State of Queensland (No 2)* (1992) 175 CLR 1 ('*Mabo (No 2)*').

2 *National Action Plan Australia*, 1994, Canberra: AGPS, Preamble, p 3.

3 Aboriginal and Torres Strait Islander Social Justice Commissioner, *Native Title Report: January–June 1994*, 1995, AGPS, p 53.

is the manner in which it leaves a number of issues, such as the content of native title[4] and the circumstances in which it is extinguished,[5] to be resolved by the common law.

In this chapter I will focus on the issue of common law extinguishment of native title and some of the international human rights standards relating to indigenous ownership of land. It is my view that native title must be recognised and protected in a manner that is consistent with Australia's international obligations. Unfortunately the manner in which extinguishment is being asserted by governments that are reluctant to acknowledge the ownership of land by indigenous peoples, the manner in which quasi-judicial determinations[6] appear to be facilitating those views, and the indications of the manner in which the courts will interpret extinguishment,[7] give rise to concerns over the degree to which fundamental human rights standards are being met.

EXTINGUISHMENT AND *MABO (NO 2)*

The issue of extinguishment is currently the most crucial of the unresolved legal issues arising from *Mabo (No 2)*. All the judges held that upon the claiming of sovereignty, the new sovereign had the power to extinguish native title. However, it is not clear where that power comes from. Brennan J argued that it was a concomitant of sovereignty,[8] Toohey J on the other hand voiced his doubts as to whether this was indeed the case.[9] Whatever the basis of the power to extinguish native title, the court was clear that if the new sovereign wished to extinguish native title it was competent to do so. However, there was not a unanimous voice as to when such action would be completely effective. *Mabo (No 2)* does not clearly state the circumstances in which native title will be extinguished, although there are a number of comments about extinguishment in the judgments.

Loss of laws and customs

Brennan J held that because native title is a title based on the laws and customs of indigenous people, loss of observance of those laws and customs would mean that title to land is extinguished.[10] Importantly, however, the court noted that our laws and customs

4 The definition of native title in the Native Title Act 1993 (Cth) ('NTA') is very broad and appropriately flexible, see s 223(1).

5 The NTA is clear that native title is extinguished where there is a validation under the Act (s 15(1)) however where the act affecting native title is valid without reliance on the legislation the effect of that act is left to the common law.

6 See for example *Re Waanyi Peoples Native Title Determination Application* (1995) 14 February 1995, QN 94/9, National Native Title Tribunal *per* French J ('*Waanyi* case').

7 See comments by the High Court in *Mabo (No 2)* and the *State of Western Australia v The Commonwealth* (1995) 16 March, No P4/1994 (unreported) High Court of Australia.

8 *Mabo (No 2)* 175 CLR 1 at 48 *per* Brennan J.

9 *Mabo (No 2)* 175 CLR 1 at 193–194 *per* Toohey J.

10 *Mabo (No 2)* 175 CLR 1 at 70 *per* Brennan J. Deane and Gaudron JJ (at 110) did not feel that they had to answer this question, but nevertheless expressed an opinion that at that time the abandonment of traditional customs and ways would not mean loss of native title rights, at least where the relevant community continues to occupy or use the land.

are not to be kept in a time warp and it was recognised that laws and customs can adapt over time, especially with the influence of western cultures.[11] This is consistent with judicial comments in other jurisdictions and necessary in order to conform with Article 27 of the International Covenant on Civil and Political Rights ('ICCPR').[12] Deane and Gaudron JJ also noted that where indigenous peoples abandon their traditional lands, our title ceases to exist.[13] However, they did not elaborate the circumstances in which this would occur.

Australia has a long and unpleasant history of forcibly removing Aboriginal children from their families and dispersing our communities from our traditional lands in the pursuance of policies of assimilation and integration. The effect of these policies has been severely detrimental to the laws and customs of many indigenous communities, but it will not in all cases necessarily mean that those laws and customs have been lost or abandoned nor will it mean that connections to land have been sufficiently broken to extinguish title.

Surrender

Native title can be surrendered to the Crown by agreement with the holders of native title. It is inalienable to anyone except the Crown. Such a surrender may give rise to a fiduciary duty.[14] The inalienability of native title was considered by Brennan, Deane and Gaudron JJ to be necessary to ensure that the integrity of the doctrine of tenures was maintained. In North America this was known as a right of pre-emption. It was said to ensure that there could be only one source of land grant.[15]

Extinguishment by legislation

The court reaffirmed the rule that had been applied elsewhere[16] that native title can be extinguished by legislation which shows a clear and plain intent to have that effect.[17] There do not have to be express words stating that extinguishment is to occur but the language must be clear and unambiguous.

11 *Mabo (No 2)* 175 CLR 1 at 61, 70, 110 *per* Brennan, Deane and Gaudron JJ. See also Toohey J (at 192) where he states that an 'indigenous society cannot, as it were, surrender its rights by modifying its way of life'.

12 *Lansman v Finland* Comm No 511/1992, adopted 26 October 1994, CCPR/C/52/D/511/1992.

13 *Mabo (No 2)* 175 CLR 1 at 110 *per* Deane and Gaudron JJ.

14 *Mabo (No 2)* 175 CLR 1 at 60 *per* Brennan J. This is similar to the approach adopted by Dickson J, with whom Beetz, Choudinard and Lamer JJ agreed in *Guerin v R* (1984) 6 WWR 481. In *Guerin* the rest of the court comprising of Wilson J, with whom Ritchie and McIntyre JJ agreed, argued that a fiduciary obligation arose from the nature of the native title itself. This was the approach adopted by Toohey J, in *Mabo (No 2)* 175 CLR 1 at 203–05.

15 *Johnson v McIntosh* (1823) 8 Wheat 543. See also *Mabo (No 2)* 175 CLR 1 at 59, 88 *per* Brennan, Deane and Gaudron JJ. For a lengthy discussion of this see McNeil, K, *Common Law Aboriginal Title*, 1989, Oxford: Oxford University Press, pp 231–35.

16 See for example *R v Sparrow* (1990) 70 DLR (4th) 385.

17 *Mabo (No 2)* 175 CLR 1 at 64, 195 and 111 *per* Brennan, Toohey J, Deane and Gaudron JJ.

There is also some authority to suggest that native title can be extinguished by legislation through necessary implication. For example, in the Canadian case of *Delgamuukw* it was noted that 'intention can be declared *expressly or manifested by unavoidable implication*'.[18] Extinguishment in the latter case should be inferred only if the interpretation of the statute permits no other result.[19] However, at the same time it has been noted that mere inconsistent legislation is not enough to extinguish native title in the absence of intent.[20] There is a degree of flexibility in the interpretation of all statutes, but the judges in *Delgamuukw* noted that the clear and plain intent test should be applied with as much vigour as possible.[21]

I do not believe that anything less than legislative intent with clear and unambiguous words should be sufficient to extinguish native title.[22]

Extinguishment by inconsistent grant

The court also held that native title can be extinguished by inconsistent grant. The court held that where an inconsistent grant exists native title is extinguished to the extent of the inconsistency.[23] The application of this test involves little reference to the requirement of clear and plain legislative intent to extinguish when the grant was made. This is particularly so in the judgment of Brennan J who said:

> A crown grant which vests in the grantee an interest in land which is inconsistent with the continued right to enjoy a native title in respect of the same land necessarily extinguishes the native title. The extinguishing of native title does not depend on the actual intention of the Governor in Council (who may not have adverted to the rights and interests of the indigenous inhabitants or their descendants), but on the effect which the grant has on the right to enjoy the native title.[24]

Brennan J noted that there is a general rule that the Crown cannot derogate from a grant once made.[25] However he reasoned that because native title is not a Crown grant it does not receive similar protection.[26] He held therefore that an inconsistent grant would be effective to extinguish native title.

In *Central Control Board (Liquor Traffic) v Cannon Brewery Co Ltd*[27] Lord Atkinson argued that:[28]

18 *Delgamuukw v British Columbia* (1993) 104 DLR (4th) 470 at 523 *per* MacFarlane JA.

19 (1993) 104 DLR (4th) 470 at 525, see also Lambert JA (at 665).

20 (1993) 104 DLR (4th) 470 at 664 *per* Lambert JA, referring to *R v Sparrow* (1990) 70 DLR (4th) 385.

21 (1993) 104 DLR (4th) 470 at 523 *per* MacFarlane JA.

22 Aboriginal and Torres Strait Islander Social Justice Commissioner (*op cit*, at footnote 3) p 85.

23 *Mabo (No 2)* 175 CLR 1 at 68, 69 and 111 *per* Brennan Deane and Gaudron JJ.

24 *Mabo (No 2)* 175 CLR 1 at 68 *per* Brennan J.

25 Brennan J referred to Stead v Carey (1845) 1 CB 496 at 523 for this proposition see *Mabo (No 2)* 175 CLR 1 at 64.

26 *Mabo (No 2)* 175 CLR 1 at 64.

27 [1919] AC 744 referred to in *Mabo (No 2)* 175 CLR 1 at 195, 111 *per* Toohey J, Deane and Gaudron JJ.

28 As quoted by Toohey J in *Mabo (No 2)* 175 CLR 1 at 195.

> ... an intention to take away the property of a subject without giving to him [*sic*] a legal right to compensation for the loss of it is not to be imputed to the Legislature unless that intention is expressed in unequivocal terms.

Toohey J argued in *Mabo (No 2)* that:[29]

> It need hardly be said that where an executive act is relied upon to extinguish traditional title, the intention of the legislature that executive power should extend this far must likewise appear plainly and with clarity.

Deane and Gaudron JJ argued that in the absence of express legislation to the contrary, the extinguishment of native title without compensation would be wrongful.[30] Their approach was however baldly refuted by Mason CJ and McHugh J who in their brief judgment stated:[31]

> ... neither of us nor Brennan J agrees with the conclusion to be drawn from the judgments of Deane, Toohey and Gaudron JJ that, at least in the absence of clear and unambiguous statutory provision to the contrary, extinguishment of native title by the Crown by inconsistent grant is wrongful and gives rise to a claim for compensatory damages.

A further question which has been left unclear is what amounts to inconsistency. It would appear from *Mabo (No 2)* that a grant of freehold is inconsistent with native title and would therefore extinguish native title.[32] However, the effect of lesser interests is unclear. Brennan J said that a lease is inconsistent with the continuance of native title by virtue of the mere fact that there is a reversion to the Crown at the end of the term.[33] In the case of a number of leases granted on the Murray Islands, he suggests that it does not matter that there were limited reservations in the leases[34] preserving certain rights of indigenous peoples.[35]

29 *Mabo (No 2)* 175 CLR 1 at 196.

30 *Mabo (No 2)* 175 CLR 1 at 111 *per* Deane and Gaudron JJ.

31 *Mabo (No 2)* 175 CLR 1 at 15 *per* Mason CJ and McHugh J.

32 *Mabo (No 2)* 175 CLR 1 at 69 and 110 *per* Brennan, Deane and Gaudron JJ.

33 *Mabo (No 2)* 175 CLR 1 at 68 *per* Brennan J. This approach has drawn criticism from French J in the *Waanyi* case (1995) 14 February 1995, QN 94/9 at 25–28. For a brief critique of Brennan J's approach see Aboriginal and Torres Strait Islander Social Justice Commissioner (*op cit*, at footnote 3) p 94.

34 It is common practice in many states for leases to contain reservations in favour of indigenous peoples to carry on certain parts of their traditional laws and customs. This is the case in Western Australia, South Australia and the Northern Territory. For further discussion see Brennan, F, 'Pastoral leases, Mabo and the Native Title Act 1993', in Edmunds, M (ed), *Land, Rights, Laws: Issues of Native Title*, Issues Paper No 1, 1994, Canberra, Native Title Research Unit, AIATSIS; Amankwah, H, '*Mabo:* Extinguishment of Native Title and Pastoral Leases Revisited' (1993) 63 *Aboriginal Law Bulletin* 13; Reynolds, H, 'The *Mabo* Judgment in the Light of Imperial Land Policy' (1993) 16 *University of New South Wales Law Journal* 27; Aboriginal and Torres Strait Islander Social Justice Commissioner (see above footnote 3) pp 95–97.

35 *Mabo (No 2)* 175 CLR 1 at 72–73 *per* Brennan J.

Deane and Gaudron JJ considered that the grant of a lease containing a reservation may not necessarily be inconsistent with native title but a lease conferring exclusive possession would.[36] Toohey J decided not to answer the question.[37]

'Extinguishment' of native title and human rights

The approach of the majority in *Mabo (No 2)* is in my opinion troublesome. The extent of these problems is highlighted by consideration of indigenous perspectives and international human rights standards. The standards enunciated in international instruments define the minimum standard of protection which native title holders are entitled to enjoy. These instruments include the Universal Declaration of Human Rights, the International Covenant on Economic, Social and Cultural Rights ('ICESCR'), the International Covenant on Civil and Political Rights ('ICCPR') and the International Convention on the Elimination of All Forms of Racial Discrimination. Indigenous peoples are entitled to enjoy the human rights enunciated in these instruments to the same extent as all other Australians. Any aspect of the common law which derogates from these rights will render Australia in breach of those international obligations.

There are also more specific standards relating to the human rights of indigenous people evolving at an international level. In particular, the International Labour Organisation Convention No 169 ('ILO 169') although not yet ratified by Australia and the Draft Declaration on the Rights of Indigenous Peoples ('Draft Declaration') are equally important in assessing international standards with regard to indigenous human rights, even though they are not binding on Australia. The Draft Declaration is particularly relevant in providing a useful indication of what the international indigenous community perceives as the appropriate standards which apply.

Certain well-established human rights are of special relevance to indigenous land ownership and are worth noting in detail. They are human rights which Australia has bound itself to respect:[38]

---

36 *Mabo (No 2)* 175 CLR 1 at 110 *per* Deane and Gaudron JJ.

37 *Mabo (No 2)* 175 CLR 1 at 197 *per* Toohey J.

38 In addition to the rights listed here there is the clearly expressed right of all peoples to self-determination (see for example Article 1 of the ICCPR and Article 1 of ICESCR). A detailed discussion of this is not within the scope of this chapter. It is sufficient to note, as I said in the Native Title Report, that the common law recognition of native title and the laws and customs upon which it is based, has the potential to facilitate the full exercise of the right to self-determination which has long been denied to indigenous peoples. Australia would be impairing the human rights of indigenous peoples if it hinders the full exercise of the right to self-determination of indigenous peoples, Aboriginal and Torres Strait Islander Social Justice Commissioner (*op cit*, at footnote 3) p 72.

FREEDOM FROM DISCRIMINATION AND EQUALITY BEFORE THE LAW

Of the major instruments to which Australia is a party, the right to freedom from discrimination appears in the Charter of the United Nations, the ICESCR, the ICCPR and is the subject matter of the International Convention on the Elimination of All Forms of Racial Discrimination. Also relevant are the Declaration on the Rights of Persons Belonging to National or Ethnic, Religious and Linguistic Minorities, particularly Article 4; Article 2 of the ILO 169 and Articles 1 and 2 of the Draft Declaration.

Freedom from discrimination has been directly applied to equality before the law and property rights. Article 26 of the ICCPR states:

> All persons are equal before the law and are entitled without any discrimination to the equal protection of the law. In this respect, the law shall prohibit any discrimination and guarantee to all persons equal and effective protection against discrimination on any ground such as race, colour, sex, language, religion, political or other opinion, national or social origin, property, birth or other status.

Article 5 of the International Convention on the Elimination of All Forms of Racial Discrimination provides that:

> … States parties undertake to prohibit and to eliminate racial discrimination in all its forms and guarantee the right of every one, without distinction as to race, colour, or national or ethnic origin, to equality before the law, notably in the enjoyment of the following rights:
>
> (a) The right to equal treatment before the tribunals and all other organs administering justice …
>
> (d) Other civil rights, in particular …
>
> (v) The right to own property alone as well as in association with others;
>
> (vi) the right to inherit …'

This provision was central to the protection of indigenous property rights in *Mabo (No 1)*. There, in finding the Queensland Coastal Island Declaratory Act 1985 discriminatory, Toohey and Gaudron JJ noted:[39]

> A person who is a member of the Miriam people is entitled to own and inherit those property rights in the same way and to the same extent as any other Australian.

However, in my view, the common law treatment of native title in *Mabo (No 2)* is in effect discriminatory. It does not deliver equality before the law to indigenous people nor does it provide the equal protection of our property interests.

39 *Mabo v Queensland* (1988) 166 CLR 186 at 217 *per* Brennan, Toohey, and Gaudron JJ *('Mabo (No 1)')*.

To my knowledge no other form of title is able to be extinguished by an executive action without the unambiguous consent of parliament. In *Mabo (No 2)* Toohey J stated:

> A sovereign can, by a positive act, seize private as well as public property in the act of acquiring sovereignty and the seizure is non-justiciable. But seizure of private property by the Crown in a settled colony after annexation has occurred would amount to an illegitimate act of state against British subjects since in a settled colony, where English law applies, there is no power in the Crown to make laws, except pursuant to statute. Emergency powers aside, the common law required legislative authority for compulsory acquisition of property.[40]

It is my view that a purported grant that lacks the requisite degree of statutory authority is ineffective to dispose of any interest in land. Native title should not receive lesser protection than other property interests. It is perhaps a legal nicety that the courts assume that the indigenous peoples of Australia became subjects of the Crown in 1788. But, if that is going to be the assumption, then a law which treats the property of one group of subjects in lesser regard than the property of all other subjects is patently unacceptable.

It is certainly difficult to think of any other property interest which could be extinguished by a wrongful act, as Deane and Gaudron JJ held, regardless of whether any compensation is payable. There is no justification for such a position.

It has been noted that the common law has a long history of recognising customary rights to land and those rights were thought worthy of the same protection as titles derived from Crown grant. Thus in AG for the *Isle of Man v Mylechreest* it was stated with regard to the effect of Crown grants on the customary tenure on the Isle of Man that:

> The ... language of the grants is quite large enough to carry the full title to the soil of the Isle, including minerals ... so far as the Crown could grant them. But, on the other hand, the Lordship could only be granted subject to the rights which the customary tenants might then have acquired by custom or otherwise in their tenements ...[41]

There is also North American jurisprudence to suggest that native title should be given the same protection as other interests. In *US v Shoshone Tribe* it was noted that indigenous rights of occupancy should be 'as sacred and as securely safe-guarded as is fee simple absolute title'.[42] This included protection from the interference with their interests in land without the authorisation of Parliament. As Felix Cohen observed:[43]

> ... while a grant of land in Indian possession may convey a legal fee, such a grant does not impair the Indian title, which the grantee must respect until it has been duly terminated by treaty, agreement, or other authorised action of Congress or the Indians.

---

40 *Mabo (No 2)* 175 CLR 1 at 184.

41 *AG for the Isle of Man v Mylechreest* (1879) 4 App Cas 294 at 302. See also McNeil, K, *Common Law Aboriginal Title*, 1989, Oxford: Oxford University Press, pp 237–41 and Aboriginal and Torres Strait Islander Social Justice Commissioner (*op cit*, at footnote 3) pp 86–89.

42 *US v Shoshone Tribe* (1938) US 111 as quoted in Cohen, F, 'Original Indian Title' (1947) 32 *Minnesota Law Review* 55.

43 Cohen, F, *op cit*, p 53, referring to *Buttz v Northern Pacific Railroad* (1886) 119 US 55.

That native title in Australia is susceptible to extinguishment in a discriminatory manner is ironic given the strong pronouncements against discrimination in *Mabo (No 2)*, particularly by Brennan J. In rejecting the view that Australia was *terra nullius*, the High Court acknowledged the influence of international standards which no longer tolerate the denial of human rights at the hands of flawed legal doctrines. The view is expressed most clearly from the judgment of Brennan J:[44]

> Whatever the justification advanced in earlier days for refusing to recognise the rights and interests in land of the indigenous inhabitants of settled colonies, an unjust and discriminatory doctrine of that kind can no longer be accepted. The expectations of the international community accord in this respect with the contemporary values of the Australian people. The opening up of international remedies to individuals pursuant to Australia's accession to the Optional Protocol to the International Covenant on Civil and Political Rights ... brings to bear on the common law the powerful influence of the Covenant and the international standard it imparts. The common law does not necessarily conform with international law, but international law is a legitimate and important influence on the development of the common law, especially when international law declares the existence of universal human rights. A common law doctrine founded on unjust discrimination in the enjoyment of civil and political rights demands reconsideration. It is contrary both to international standards and to the fundamental values of our common law to entrench a discriminatory rule which, because of the supposed position on the scale of social organisation of the indigenous inhabitants of a settled colony, denies them a right to occupy their traditional lands.

Brennan J also observed that if:[45]

> ... it were permissible in past centuries to keep the common law in step with international law, it is imperative in today's world that the common law should neither be nor be seen to be frozen in an age of racial discrimination.

The discriminatory treatment of indigenous property interests has now been remedied by the Racial Discrimination Act 1975 (Cth). In *Western Australia v The Commonwealth* the High Court held that:[46]

> The Racial Discrimination Act does not alter the characteristics of native title, but it confers on protected persons rights or immunities which, being recognised by 'the tribunals and all other organs administering justice', allow protected persons security in the enjoyment of their title to property to the same extent as the holders of titles granted by the Crown are secure in the enjoyment of their titles.

This principle of non-discrimination is also further entrenched by the Act with regard to the future protection of native title interests.[47] However, neither of these legislative

44 *Mabo (No 2)* 175 CLR 1 at 42 *per* Brennan J.

45 *Mabo (No 2)* 175 CLR 1 at 41–42.

46 *State of Western Australia v The Commonwealth* (1995) 16 March, No P4/1994 *per* Mason CJ at 27–28. See also *Mabo (No 1) per* Brennan, Toohey and Gaudron JJ.

47 See ss 7 and 235 Native Title Act. It should be remembered however, that the Act also allows for the discriminatory validation of past grants at the expense of native title rights. See Aboriginal and Torres Strait Islander Commissioner (*op cit*, at footnote 3) pp 67–68.

measures will assist indigenous peoples whose titles have been deemed to be extinguished by some administrative act prior to 1975.

FREEDOM FROM ARBITRARY DEPRIVATION OF PROPERTY

The right to own property free of arbitrary deprivation has been expressed in a number of international instruments. The most fundamental of these is Article 17 of the Universal Declaration on Human Rights which provides that:

> 1. Everyone has the right to own property alone as well as in association with others.
> 2. No one shall be arbitrarily deprived of his property.

In theory at least, the reference to property in this context is broad enough to cover indigenous land ownership, although many States have refused to acknowledge traditional land systems as such. Indeed, the main struggle for many indigenous peoples is to have their titles recognised as a form of property that is worthy of protection. In this context, Article 1(2) of the ICCPR is cast in broader terms. Article 1(2) provides:

> All peoples may, for their own ends, freely dispose of their natural wealth and resources without prejudice to any obligation arising out of international economic co-operation, based upon the principle of mutual benefit, and international law. In no case may a people be deprived of its own means of subsistence.

There has been a great deal of difficulty in coming to terms with communal land ownership concepts in international law. This has added to the difficulty of protecting indigenous property rights in domestic institutions where land interests have been denigrated by courts and referred to as permissive occupancies or rights to occupy.[48] Rarely have they been given the status of property. There is no justification for this, but where those recalcitrant interpretations of indigenous land ownership prevail the human right for a people not to be deprived of its means of subsistence is certainly broad enough to cover the rights of indigenous people.

The human right not to be arbitrarily deprived of property was central to the protection of native title rights belonging to the Murray Islanders in *Mabo (No 1)*.[49] In that case the High Court also noted that arbitrary does not only mean illegally, it also includes 'unjustly'.[50]

In my opinion, the discriminatory treatment of native title at common law amounts to an arbitrary deprivation of property. This is particularly so given that the majority of

48 The much criticised United States decision of *Tee-Hit-Ton Indians v United States* (1955) 348 US 272 exemplifies this. In Australia see *Milirrpum v Nabalco* (1971) 17 FLR 1 and *Mabo (No 2)* 175 CLR 1 *per* Dawson J.

49 *Mabo (No 1)* (1988) 166 CLR 186 at 217 *per* Brennan, Toohey and Gaudron JJ.

50 *Mabo (No 1)* (1988) 166 CLR 186 at 217. See also *State of Western Australia v The Commonwealth* (1995) 16 March, No P4 of 1994 *per* Mason CJ, Brennan, Deane, Toohey, Gaudron, McHugh JJ, pp 25–28.

the court held that native title could be extinguished without giving rise to compensation. Furthermore, the reasoning of the majority appears to lead to a situation whereby native title can be extinguished by an executive act where there is no clear and plain legislative authority to do so. This degree of vulnerability is extraordinary and provides compelling support to the argument that the Crown is under a fiduciary duty to indigenous peoples, as suggested by Toohey J in *Mabo (No 2)*.[51] Indeed, that native title will be deemed to be extinguished even where there is a wrongful act is certainly within the meaning of arbitrary. Any deprivation of property without authority, whether such action is deemed wrongful or not, constitutes an arbitrary deprivation.

Protection of indigenous cultural heritage

Interference with indigenous peoples' land directly affects and damages our cultural heritage. This is a natural consequence of the special relationship that most indigenous societies have with the lands upon which we reside. Land is essential not just to gain a level of economic independence. It is also central to religious and social activity. In this regard the human right to have our cultural heritage recognised and protected is intertwined with our need to have the land ownership recognised and protected.

The most frequently cited statement of the human right to protection of cultural practices comes in the form of Article 27 of the ICCPR. Article 27 provides that:

> In those States in which ethnic, religious or linguistic minorities exist, persons belonging to such minorities shall not be denied the right, in community with other members of their group, to enjoy their own culture, to profess and practise their own religion, or to use their own language.

While it may be suggested that Article 27 only requires that States tolerate minorities, the Human Rights Committee, in a recent comment, affirmed the view that the enjoyment of rights protected by Article 27:[52]

> ... may require positive legal measures of protection and measures to ensure the effective participation of members of minority communities in decisions which affect them.

The cultural rights protected by Article 27 have been given very broad interpretation.[53] The Human Rights Committee has provided some elucidation of the subject matter of Article 27 and the extent of the protection it provides. It has been held to extend to 'the right of persons, in community with others, to engage in economic and social activities

51 *Mabo (No 2)* 175 CLR 1 at 203–05 *per* Toohey J.

52 Adopted by the Committee at the 50th session on 6 April 1994 (Doc CCPR/C/21/Rev 1/Add 5). As referred to in Aboriginal and Torres Strait Justice Commissioner (*op cit*, at footnote 3) p 146. See also Cholewinski, R, 'State Duty Towards Ethnic Minorities: Positive or Negative?' (1988) 10 *Human Rights Quarterly* 344, and Blades, A, 'Article 27 of the International Covenant on Civil and Political Rights: A Case Study on Implementation in New Zealand' [1994] 1 *Canadian Native Law Reporter* 1 at 13.

53 McGoldrick, D, 'Canadian Indians' Cultural Rights' (1991) 40 ICLQ 665. See also Anaya, SJ, 'Indigenous Rights Norms in Contemporary International Law' (1991) 8 *Arizona Journal of International and Comparative Law* 17.

which are part of the culture of the community to which they belong'.[54] It has also been noted that 'historical inequities' will constitute a violation of Article 27 for as long as they continue.[55] The Human Rights Committee have specifically indicated that the cultural rights protected under Article 27 include 'a particular way of life associated with the use of land resources, especially in the case of indigenous peoples'.[56]

Other strong statements in the international arena for the protection of cultural rights have come in the form of the UNESCO Declaration of the Principles of International Cultural Cooperation,[57] ILO 169, the Draft Declaration of the Rights of Indigenous Peoples, Articles 2 and 4 of the Declaration on the Rights of Persons Belonging to National or Ethnic, Religious and Linguistic Minorities, Article 30 of the International Convention of the Rights of the Child, Article 15 of the International Covenant on Economic, Social and Cultural Rights, Principle 22 of the Rio Declaration on Environment and Development, and Chapter 26 of the United Nations Agenda 21.

The present construction of native title in the Australian common law risks authorising the infringement of indigenous peoples' right to enjoy our culture. This danger comes from the common law approach to extinguishment which is removed from the reality of the existence of our laws and customs and only recognises native title where no inconsistent extinguishing act has occurred. This is exacerbated by the broad definition given to what is inconsistent.

In many cases, despite past dealings with various parcels of land, indigenous people have continued the exercise of our laws and customs. This is particularly so on pastoral leases where indigenous people were used as a cheap source of labour and worked on their traditional country. Indeed, even though there has been occupation by the grantee of an interest, some indigenous people have remained on their lands and have maintained continuity in the exercise of their traditional activities.[58] The present judicial construction of extinguishment appears incapable of accommodating this on-going co-existent attachment. It would render it, and the laws and customs upon which it is based, invisible.

The injustice of such non-recognition is graphically highlighted by the National Native Title Tribunal's refusal to accept an application for native title in the *Waanyi*

54 *Lubicon Lake Band v Canada Communication,* No 167/1984 reproduced in (1991) 11 *Human Rights Law Journal* 311.

55 See above footnote 54.

56 Comment adopted by the Committee at the 50th session on 6 April 1994 (Doc CCPR/C/21/Rev 1/Add 5). As referred to in Aboriginal and Torres Strait Justice Commissioner, *op cit,* p 146.

57 Article 1 states:

1. Each culture has a dignity and value which must be respected and preserved.
2. Every people has the right and duty to develop its culture.
3. In their rich variety and diversity, and in the reciprocal influence they exert on one another, all cultures form part of the common heritage belonging to all mankind.

As quoted in Anaya, SJ, *op cit,* p 17.

58 Aboriginal and Torres Strait Islander Social Justice Commissioner, *op cit,* pp 80–81, 89–92 and 95–97.

case.[59] In that case Frank Hann, the grantee of a 21-year pastoral lease which took effect in 1883, abandoned the property in 1895 or 1896, transferring his interest to the Bank of New South Wales. The bank later surrendered the interest to the crown and it was gazetted as a camping and water reserve.[60] The Waanyi people always remained in the area and claim to have maintained their traditional attachment to the land. French J, President of the National Native Title Tribunal, held that the short-term leasehold interest was sufficient to completely extinguish native title. The irony of the situation is succinctly stated by Henry Reynolds:

> It would be hardly surprising if the Waanyi people, as French [J] surmised, found his decision perverse and the law itself burdened by moral shortcomings. It is highly selective in its application. It has a very long arm but it is choosy as to what it picks up. It can reach back to 1882 and determine that a pastoral lease granted to Hann extinguished their rights to their traditional land despite the fact that Hann went off to Western Australia and never came back, while they stayed on in their country.[61]

The word 'extinguishment' is a misnomer. As long as indigenous laws and customs exist, native title is not extinguished. The common law may not recognise those rights, but governments and lawyers should not fool themselves that a declaration of extinguishment will make the laws and customs of indigenous people disappear. The simple reality is that such a law will not dispose of the grievances of indigenous peoples. We know our land is ours. A fence is not so grand a structure that it can automatically destroy our relationship with our land. A piece of paper cannot destroy a culture, except perhaps in the sometimes perverse imaginings of lawyers. As one Aboriginal man bluntly told the Parliamentary Joint Committee on native title:[62]

> That land out there is our land and the pieces of paper mean nothing. This land is ours and it will go on being ours.

This deep disjuncture between the realities of indigenous people and the Australian legal system requires reconciliation. The fact that native title appears to be construed by the courts so that it can be extinguished by snippets of archaic administrative action when our laws and customs still exist exemplifies contemporary injustice. It does not exemplify the reconciliation of indigenous and non-indigenous interests based on justice. By relying on legal theory the courts turn a blind eye to indigenous realities. The absurd extreme of this is that a lease could be granted and never used by the grantee, but it will still be deemed by the courts to destroy rights derived from thousands of years of culture. Likewise a lease could have expired and even though no inconsistency arose in fact, the

59 *Per* French J.

60 For a good summary of this case and the facts see Nettheim, G, 'Moral Shortcoming: Waanyi Peoples and Native Title' (1995) 73 *Aboriginal Law Bulletin* 10.

61 Reynolds, H, '*Mabo* Offers Logic Without Morality' *Australian,* 28 February 1995, p 5.

62 Richard Franklin speaking to the Parliamentary Joint Committee on Native Title, Melbourne, 10 March 1995, *Official Hansard Report*, p 897.

court will deem native title rights as extinguished. This is not because of any actual conflict in land use, but because of the mere fact that a lease was issued. Of course, like the Waanyi, indigenous people could continue observing their laws and customs in relation to land long after the interest has expired, but to the common law such practices are invisible. It is understandable that indigenous peoples have difficulty in comprehending the justice in processes which operate in such an arbitrary manner. It is understandable why one Aboriginal man has commented, 'We have respect for their law. But they have no respect for our law'.[63]

The test for extinguishment should be whether the laws and customs are still being recognised by indigenous peoples. Even if it is to be accepted that a subsequent grant can affect native title interests, even without the clear and unambiguous consent of parliament, then it is not necessary that native title need be deemed 'extinguished' as a result. In my view, if the laws and customs still exist at the expiry of the interest then native title should still be recognised. This is not a radical proposition. It would not curtail any existing non-indigenous interests in land. Nor is it completely foreign to the common law. It is analogous to the non-extinguishment principle in the Native Title Act.[64] In *R v Sparrow* it was held that native title rights could be regulated without those interests being extinguished.[65] It may be more equitable to conceptualise valid grants affecting native title as having a regulatory effect on native title for the period of the interest rather than being construed as extinguishing acts. This would be particularly relevant to a more just approach to leases. The existence of a lease is not inconsistent with native title. Even where a lease provides exclusive possession, that exclusive possession applies only for the term of the lease. The existence of the lease should be understood as having the effect of regulating native title rights for the period. There should be no bar to native title rights continuing in full when the interest expires, provided that the laws and customs which give content to native title continue to be observed. At the same time there should be greater scope for the recognition of the co-existence of various interests when there is no actual inconsistency in land use.

Indigenous grievances will continue despite the assertion of legality of extinguishment. Indeed it is the continuing observance of traditional laws and customs despite the non-recognition of those systems in Australian courts that has made native title claims possible today. This must be borne in mind by those who seek to deem native title extinguished in as many instances as possible. Our laws and customs are real. They are tenacious. They do not disappear at the whim of western jurisprudence and will continue to be observed regardless of what the common law says. We are entitled to have our laws and customs protected. Claims for protection of culture are no less legitimate where tribunals assert that the title to land was 'extinguished' in some distant legal past by an obscure administrative transaction. Failure to adequately protect those laws and customs will amount to a breach of Australia's international obligations.

63 McNaught Ngallametta as quoted in Daley, H, 'Report on the Wik Mediation', 7 December 1994, Nine Network (interview).

64 See s 238 Native Title Act.

65 *R v Sparrow* (1990) 70 DLR (4th) 385 at 400 *per* Dickson CJC and La Forest J.

International human rights standards clearly establish a measure by which the nature of the extinguishment of indigenous property interests can be gauged. It is true that the protection of fundamental human rights have not been on the international agenda for the entirety of Australia's history, nor indeed when many of the Acts which have been asserted to have extinguished native title had been made. That does not detract from their importance in identifying the nature of dispossession and extinguishment of native title. The contemporary assertion of the past operation of discriminatory common law rules has the effect of entrenching the common law in an age of racial discrimination, the very result which Brennan J argued against in *Mabo (No 2)*.

THE NEED FOR AN NEW APPROACH

While the decision in *Mabo (No 2)*, by recognising that existence of indigenous peoples' property rights, was a gigantic step forward for indigenous people, the conceptualisation of those rights and the limitations placed upon them potentially undermine the ability of the decision to deliver indigenous people more than token recognition. There is a real need to reconceptualise the extinguishment of native title in a manner which conforms with Australia's international human rights obligations.

There is ample scope for such a reconsideration in current approaches to judicial interpretation. While an international treaty does not become part of the domestic law until it has been implemented through legislation, it is permissible to refer to international instruments in order to remove ambiguities or uncertainties in statutes and the common law.[66] More recently, the important influence that international law plays in the development of the common law has also been acknowledged.[67] In particular, the courts appear more willing to refer to international instruments in the development of the common law where human rights are involved,[68] or where there is a complaints process to an international forum[69] as is the case with the Optional Protocol to the ICCPR.[70]

Indeed, through agreeing to a formal complaint mechanism to an international body all arms of the Australian government have become more accountable for breaches of human rights. Breaches of human rights will be difficult to hide from international

66 See for example *Deitrich v The Queen* (1992) 177 CLR 292, although note the doubts of Dawson J (at 349) with regard to the common law. See also *Mabo (No 2)* 175 CLR 1 at 42 *per* Brennan J and *Minister of State for Immigration and Ethnic Affairs v Ah Minh Teoh* (1995) 7 April, FC 95/013 (unreported) High Court *('Teoh')*.

67 *Deitrich v The Queen* (1992) 177 CLR 292 at 321 and 360 *per* Brennan and Toohey JJ. *Mabo (No 2)* 175 CLR 1 at 42 *per* Brennan J, with whom Mason CJ and McHugh J agreed; *Teoh* (1995) 7 April, FC 95/013 at 11 and 45 *per* Mason CJ and Deane J (with whom Gaudron J agreed on this point) and McHugh J.

68 *Teoh* (1995) 7 April, FC 95/013 at 11 and 45 *per* Mason CJ and Deane J (with whom Gaudron J agreed on this point). *Mabo (No 2)* 175 CLR 1 at 42 *per* Brennan J, with whom Mason CJ and McHugh J agreed.

69 *Mabo (No 2)* 175 CLR 1 at 42 *per* Brennan J, with whom Mason CJ and McHugh J agreed.

70 See discussion in Caleo, C, 'Implications of Australia's Accession to the First Optional Protocol to the International Covenant on Civil and Political Rights' (1993) 4 *Public Law Review* 175.

scrutiny and will potentially lead to Australia's embarrassment on the international stage. Interestingly, in its recent consideration of a report submitted by the United States, under Article 40 of the ICCPR, the Human Rights Committee recommended that the United States take steps 'to ensure that previously recognised aboriginal Native American rights cannot be extinguished'.[71]

The potential effectiveness of international complaints procedures, such as the optional protocol to the ICCPR, in exposing governments should not be underestimated. Indigenous peoples in other jurisdictions have already shown a willingness to use the optional protocol to complain about infringements by the States in which they reside. Article 27 of the ICCPR has been very relevant to indigenous peoples using this procedure.[72] Furthermore, given the concerns by indigenous peoples as to the legitimacy of the institutions which determine the ambit of our legal rights, it is not surprising that as Douglas Sanders notes, 'indigenous populations persist in the belief that their rights are not simply a matter for domestic law'.[73]

It is axiomatic that universal human rights must be respected in the domestic arena if they are to have any living meaning. The failure of governments to respect our human rights will only prompt indigenous peoples to take their grievances to international bodies. It is my view that the Australian common law in relation to extinguishment, as discussed in *Mabo (No 2)*, needs to be carefully reconsidered so as to accord more accurately with international human rights standards.

Of course reassessing the common law in this regard does not remove any obligation from Parliament to respect indigenous peoples' human rights. Indeed, I do not believe that Parliament should extinguish native title without the consent of indigenous peoples. The existence of international obligations require that all arms of government respect indigenous peoples' human rights. Governments can not hide in the thickets of their own legal institutions and do nothing when those institutions are operating in a discriminatory manner. Similarly, the judiciary should not sidestep Australia's obligations to protect human rights by entrenching fundamentally discriminatory doctrines in the common law and then leave it to governments to remedy those injustices.

71 CCPR/C/79/Add 50 p 8.

72 For example see *Lovelace v Canada* Comm No 6/24, (1981) UN Doc A/36/40; *Kitok v Sweden* (1985) Comm No 197, (1988) UN Doc A/43/40; and *Ominyak and The Lubicon Lake Band v Canada* (1984) Comm No 167, reproduced in (1990) 11 *Human Rights Law Journal* 305: all of which are referred to in Blades, A, 'Article 27 of the International Covenant on Civil and Political Rights: A Case Study on Implementation in New Zealand' [1994] 1 *Canadian Native Law Reporter* 1. See also *Lansman v Finland* (1992) Comm No 511, CCPR/C/52/D/511/1992, adopted 26 October 1994.

73 Sanders, D, 'Aboriginal Rights: The Search for Recognition in International Law', in Boldt, M, and Long, JA (eds), *The Quest for Justice: Aboriginal Peoples and Aboriginal Rights*, 1985: Toronto, University of Toronto Press, p 303.

CONCLUSION

It is important not to lose sight of what extinguishment of native title is. It is an act of colonialism. In *Mabo (No 2)* the validity of the assumption of such power was not seriously questioned, although some discussion was provided by Toohey J.[74] Brennan J was willing to accept that the power to extinguish was an attribute of sovereignty.[75] The assertion of sovereign power to extinguish native title is deeply resented by indigenous peoples and it is a continuing source of grievance. It is no less an act of colonial racism today than it was 207 years ago and the mere fact that it has been sanctioned by the common law will add little to the legitimacy of the exercise of that power in the eyes of those being dispossessed.[76] As an old man from Ngukurr remarked on hearing the details of *Mabo (No 2)* decision: 'Different story. Same ending.'

The crucial test for the Australian people is to see extinguishment of native title for what it is. It is the racist appropriation of property by the dominant culture on the basis that it has the power to do so. It is fundamentally a racist appropriation. Governments and industries must look to solutions to land conflicts in a manner that respects indigenous human rights. This involves moving away from legal theories based on discrimination and looking at the day-to-day reality of indigenous peoples. As long as our laws and customs continue then we are entitled to have those laws and customs protected including our title to land. There will be justifiable resentment when our human rights are not acknowledged or protected.

That indigenous laws and customs continue despite assertions of 'extinguishment' does not mean that the decisions of Australian courts relating to the 'extinguishment' of native title are not significant. These decisions are critical. They are critical because they set the parameters for what can and can not be done to indigenous people and their land with the sanction of the non-indigenous legal system. A determination that native title is extinguished authorises the government to deprive indigenous peoples of their traditional lands and to justify such deprivation on the basis that the actions are 'legal'. While judicial pronouncement about the existence or non-existence of native title do not destroy ownership in indigenous law, the dispossession that follows on such pronouncements can and does impair the extent to which we can exercise our laws and customs. This in turn limits our ability to assert our property rights. The problem of legitimacy arises when the basis for authorisation is isolated from the reality of those being dispossessed.

The problem of extinguishment arises from the collision of two systems of law. The resolution implicit in court determinations that native title is extinguished is that the

74 *Mabo (No 2)* 175 CLR 1 at 193–96 *per* Toohey J.

75 He observed that:

> 'Sovereignty carries the power to create and to extinguish private rights and interests in land within the Sovereign's territory. It follows that, on a change of sovereignty, rights and interests in land that may have been indefeasible under the old regime become liable to extinction by exercise of the new sovereign power. The sovereign power may or may not be exercised with the solicitude for the welfare of indigenous inhabitants but, in the case of common law countries, the courts cannot review the merits, as distinct form the legality, of the exercise of sovereign power' *per* Brennan J (at 63).

76 Aboriginal and Torres Strait Islander Social Justice Commissioner, *op cit*, pp 8–79.

Australian legal system prevails and the indigenous legal system should be subordinated. This power relationship is a political fact that the court will not examine. But the avoidance of the issue will not make it go away. There may be nothing the court can do to remedy the perception that, for indigenous people, the true foundation of the Australian legal system is blunt power and not justice, force and not consent. But human rights standards provide the courts with a basis for working out principles of extinguishment that may be perceived as a legitimate compromise between the interests of indigenous and non-indigenous people. An approach to extinguishment based on respect for human rights provides a way for the courts to reconcile the two laws and produce decisions on extinguishment that do not merely repeat the gestures of colonialism.

CHAPTER ELEVEN

MABO AND ITS RAMIFICATIONS FOR THE FUTURE OF INDIGENOUS AUSTRALIANS

Frank Brennan

The editors of this book have invited contributors and readers to share their sense of responsibility 'in supporting the journey toward maturity as one Nation, the journey toward reconciliation'. The recent national debate and law on native title involved the Commonwealth Parliament, the High Court and the Australian people in a protracted consideration of the two laws and the two perspectives on land which have underpinned the clash between Aboriginal and non-Aboriginal Australia. The Acts of the Parliament, the decisions of the court and the debates among the people have contributed to a better understanding of the past and its contemporary relevance and a surer foundation for a future in which all Australian land-holders and users can be done right, according to law, without fear or favour, affection or ill-will.

Eddie Mabo's tombstone opening on 3 June 1995 at Townsville was a reminder to all Australians that Eddie Mabo was a Torres Strait Islander who gave his life to a dream of recognition and liberation for himself and his people wanting guaranteed access to and control of their traditional lands. On a national speaking tour before the ceremony, his wife, Bonita, recalled that Eddie's 10-year legal battle for land rights on his island of Mer, in the Murray Islands, 'cost him every spare cent, all his leisure time. It cost him his health and his life'. His dying words to his wife were 'land rights'. Eddie's initiative provided the first opportunity in the history of the Australian federation for the High Court to consider the traditional claims of indigenous Australians to land rights, regardless of any land grants which governments or parliaments may have made to them. Previously, Blackburn J of the Supreme Court of the Northern Territory had ruled that Aborigines had no rights to land recognised by the common law as surviving the acquisition of sovereignty by the Crown.[1]

The full bench of the High Court has now given three decisions relating to native title. In *Mabo (No 1)* the court, by a four to three majority, ruled that the Queensland Parliament's attempt to defeat Eddie's litigation by retrospectively legislating any native title rights out of existence fell foul of the Commonwealth's Racial Discrimination Act 1975. In *Mabo (No 2)* the court, by a six to one majority, ruled that native title could survive the acquisition of sovereignty by the Crown and still existed on lands with which indigenous people maintained their connection under their own system of law and over which the Crown had not granted an interest to others who would be able to exclude traditional owners from access. In *State of Western Australia v Commonwealth* the court, by seven to zero, affirmed the principle that native title was part of the common law of Australia, applying on the Australian mainland as in the Torres Strait. Six judges said:[2]

1 *Milirrpum v Nabalco Pty Ltd* (1970) 17 FLR 141.

2 *WA v Commonwealth* (1995) 128 ALR 1 at 20 *per* Mason CJ, Brennan, Deane, Toohey, Gaudron, McHugh JJ.

> Once it is realised that the common law theory which underlay the acquisition of sovereignty in 'settled' colonies at the time of settlement of Western Australia regarded the territory of a colony inhabited by indigenous people to be 'desert uninhabited', an inference that the British Crown intended a general extinguishment of native title cannot be drawn. Extinguishment would have been seen to be an unnecessary step to take. The Crown's colonial policy was capable of being implemented without a general extinguishment of native title. Therefore the presumption remains that native title in Western Australia was not extinguished in the course of acquiring that Colony.

The same reasoning applies to all colonies established on the Australian continent. Native title to land survived until the Crown dealt with the particular land in a manner inconsistent with the continued legal recognition of native title. Dawson J, who had previously been the sole dissenter on the survival of native title after the assertion of sovereignty, acknowledged that the two earlier cases had decided issues of fundamental importance and that it was desirable 'that the law now follow a constant course in order to achieve maximum certainty with the least possible disruption'.[3] The law of native title is here to stay. It is the common law of the land. In all Australian colonies, the exertion of sovereignty by the Crown – that act of State which established each colony – resulted in the application of the common law and 'the radical title to the land, which vested in the Crown under the common law, was burdened by existing native title at the time of vesting'.[4] Native title could be extinguished in one of three ways. The traditional owners could abandon their land and lifestyle. The Crown could alienate the land to others by grant of freehold or lease. The Crown could appropriate the land to itself and use it in a manner inconsistent with the continuance of native title.

Those cases were the first time indigenous Australians have used litigation in the highest court of the nation to achieve significant gains above and beyond what the Crown or Parliament was prepared to concede to them by way of land grants. It gave rise to much public misunderstanding about the role of the courts in the democratic process. After these cases and on the occasion of his swearing in as Chief Justice of Australia, Sir Gerard Brennan, who wrote the lead judgment in *Mabo (No 2)*, noting that the judicial oath required justice to be done according to law, said, 'In appellate courts, the law may authorise a tension between abstract justice and a rule of law to be resolved by an alteration of the rule'. He continued:

> Insistence on the rule of law has a corollary which is implicit in the terms of the judicial oath. If right is to be done according to law, right will be done only if the law be just. Such tension as there is between justice and the rules of law surfaces most acutely in litigation before the High Court.

Conceding the inevitability that the decisions of the High Court would be seen by some 'to have a legislative flavour' he insisted:

> But this court is not a parliament of policy; it is a court of law. Judicial method is not concerned with the ephemeral opinions of the community. The law is most needed

3 *WA v Commonwealth* (1995) 128 ALR 1 at 70 *per* Dawson J.

4 *Ibid.*

> when it stands against popular attitudes, sometimes engendered by those with power, and when it protects the unpopular against the clamour of the multitude. But judicial method is concerned with the equal dignity of every person, his or her capacity to participate in the life of the community, to contribute to society and to share in its benefits; it is concerned with the powers entrusted to governments and the manner in which those powers are exercised. Judicial method starts with an understanding of the existing rules; it seeks to perceive the principle that underlies them and, at a deeper level, the values that underlie the principle.

In those three cases, the High Court acknowledged the principles of Crown and parliamentary sovereignty, the separation of powers and non-discrimination against persons on the basis of their race. The court espoused the value of equal respect for persons and cultures and the values of the rule of law. Persons who espouse the same values and enunciate the same principles may still have differing attitudes to outcomes. Not all opponents of the *Mabo* decisions are racist. Some of them have a very absolute understanding of Crown sovereignty and see little scope for judicial review. Critics of the High Court's approach have claimed that the judges go beyond their function when they base their decisions on their perception of the contemporary values of the community. These critics usually confuse values with attitudes. When the Commonwealth Parliament debated the Native Title Bill, Government and Opposition members and all minority senators espoused the principle of non-discrimination and the value of equal respect for persons and cultures. Their disagreement was over the application of the agreed principles informed by the shared values to the vexed issues of balancing native title rights against development rights and according the states the opportunity to tailor their own responses while measuring up to a national standard. There is an ongoing debate about the limits of judicial activism, the extent to which judges of the ultimate court of appeal are free to reverse previous understandings of the common law, doing justice at the cost of certainty.

Some commentators argue that the *Mabo* litigation opens the door to extensive judicial rewriting of the relationship between Aborigines and the Crown, between indigenous persons and all other citizens, between customary law and 'the whitefella law', including common law and statute. The three decisions set the limits to the judicial correction available to Aboriginal groups wanting to set right the injustices of the past. It is not enough for Aborigines to demonstrate a past injustice for judges then to correct the present state of the common law. The judicial method, the province of parliament and its control of the purse strings all place external and self-imposed limits on the activity of judges even of the High Court. Though the judges have ruled that the Crown did not extinguish all native title at the time sovereignty was asserted, they conceded that the Crown did have power to extinguish all title at that time. By majority they decided this could have been done without consent or compensation. The Crown being sovereign had the power to appropriate any person's property without compensation, whatever their race. The fact that the Crown would usually pay compensation to a property holder did not create a legal requirement for compensation nor a fetter on the Crown's sovereign discretion. The Crown had lawfully extinguished native title over lands throughout Australia parcel by parcel even when no compensation was paid.

Common law native title is a very fragile form of title when compared with Crown grants made under legislation of a state parliament which usually provides for acquisition only for a prescribed public purpose and on payment of compensation. In the early years of colonisation, the Crown was not fettered by the Acts of colonial legislatures. With the advent of responsible government, state parliaments were able to place restrictions on Crown activities. After Federation the Commonwealth constitution placed restrictions on the sovereign powers of state parliaments when their laws came into conflict with valid laws of the Commonwealth Parliament. Since the passage of the Australia Acts 1986 'the constitution can now be abrogated or amended only by the Australian people in whom, therefore, the ultimate sovereignty of the nation resides'.[5] To date, the sovereign Australian people have not amended the constitution to provide any specific protection of native title nor to provide compensation for past extinguishment of native title. The Commonwealth Parliament's Racial Discrimination Act guarantees that, after 1975, persons of a particular race who do not enjoy a right to the same extent as others under a State law do achieve parity by operation of the Commonwealth law.[6] In *State of Western Australia v The Commonwealth* six of the judges said:[7]

> Where under the general law, the indigenous 'persons of a particular race' uniquely have a right to own or inherit property within Australia arising from indigenous law and custom but the security of enjoyment of that property is more limited than the security enjoyed by others who have the right to own or inherit other property, the persons of the particular race are given by s 10(1), security in the enjoyment of their property 'to the same extent' as persons generally have security in the enjoyment of their property. Security in the right to own property carries immunity from arbitrary deprivation of the property. Section 10(1) thus protects the enjoyment of traditional interests in land recognised by the common law. However, it has a further operation.
>
> If a law of a State provides that property held by members of the community generally may not be expropriated except for prescribed purposes or on prescribed conditions (including payment of compensation), a State law which purports to authorise expropriation of property characteristically held by the 'persons of a particular race' for purposes additional to those generally justifying expropriation or on less stringent conditions (including lesser compensation) is inconsistent with s 10(1) Racial Discrimination Act.

Since 1975, native title-holders have enjoyed the same security from interference with their property rights by state governments or state parliaments as enjoyed by holders of Crown grants.

---

5 Brennan CJ, Swearing in as Chief Justice, (1995) 21 April, Transcript, p 15.

6 Section 10(1) Racial Discrimination Act 1975 provides:

> If, by reason of, or of a provision of, a law of the Commonwealth or of a State or Territory, persons of a particular race, colour or national or ethnic origin do not enjoy a right that is enjoyed by persons of another race, colour or national or ethnic origin, or enjoy a right to a more limited extent than persons of another race, colour or national or ethnic origin, then, notwithstanding anything in that law, persons of the first-mentioned race, colour or national or ethnic origin shall, by force of this section enjoy that right to the same extent as persons of that other race, colour or national or ethnic origin.

7 *WA v Commonwealth* (1995) 128 ALR 1 at 24 *per* Mason CJ, Brennan, Deane, Toohey, Gaudron, McHugh JJ.

There is no way that the High Court will question the propriety of the original assertion of Crown sovereignty over territory in the Australian colonies. It is an act of State which is not justiciable in a domestic court set up by the sovereign. From 1788 to 1986, there has been a gradual change to the font of sovereignty from the Crown to the people. The Queen (her heirs and successors) is the head of State under the constitution which is the entrenched, lawful expression of the will of the people. The constitution is the supreme expression of the people's will. The organs of government created under the constitution – the head of State, the House of Representatives, the Senate and the High Court – are the primary organs for the exercise of sovereign power. Aborigines now share the sovereignty of the people equally with all other citizens. Arguments for an Aboriginal sovereignty distinct from the popular sovereignty which underpins the legitimacy of the constitution or which seeks to limit the powers of the constitutionally authorised organs of government will not be entertained by the High Court whose own authority is derived from the constitution which presently makes no special provision for the place of Aborigines. Isabel Coe was unsuccessful in her attempt to have the High Court concede the discrete Aboriginal sovereignty of the 'Wiradjuri nation' in a claim asserting the incapacity of the New South Wales Crown or Parliament to interfere with native title in the Wiradjuri region.[8] She attempted to have the High Court adopt some of the terminology of the US constitution and Supreme Court decisions. Mason CJ said *Mabo (No 2)* was 'entirely at odds with the notion that sovereignty adverse to the Crown resides in the Aboriginal people of Australia'. He also rejected her claims that the Wiradjuri were 'a domestic dependent nation' or 'a free and independent people'. He concluded that they had no rights and interests 'other than those created or recognised by the laws of the Commonwealth, the State of New South Wales and the common law'. So too was Denis Walker unsuccessful in his claim that the Commonwealth and state parliaments have no power to legislate in a manner affecting Aboriginal people without their request and consent. He was trying to invoke the customary law of the 'Bundjalung nation' to answer criminal charges of assaulting police and maliciously discharging a loaded firearm to prevent lawful apprehension.[9]

Aboriginal attempts to expand the effect of the *Mabo* decisions such that the common law as declared by the High Court would include recognition of Aboriginal law other than the law relating to land are not likely to succeed. The obstacle will be the court's regard for the sovereign power of governments and parliaments. The principle of non-discrimination will necessitate a recognition that laws affecting citizens' activities and which make no reference to Aborigines apply to them as to any other citizens. In every instance the statutory law would cover the field and extinguish any previously operative customary law. Customary law in the fields of criminal law, family law and contract law will require statutory recognition or at least some legislative directive to the judiciary to accommodate such law or its underlying principles.

Since 1975 native title has enjoyed the same protection from government interference as Crown grants of freehold and leasehold. Since 1 January 1994 native title

8 *Coe v Commonwealth* (1993) 118 ALR 193 *per* Mason CJ.

9 *Denis Walker v The Queen* (1994) 22 December, No S176, High Court of Australia, *per* Mason CJ.

in all jurisdictions has enjoyed the further protection of the Commonwealth's Native Title Act 1993. In *State of Western Australia v Commonwealth* the High Court said the Native Title Act:[10]

> ... removes the common law defeasibility of native title, and secures the Aboriginal people and Torres Strait Islanders in the enjoyment of their native title subject to the prescribed exceptions which provide for native title to be extinguished or impaired. There are only three exceptions: the occurrence of a past act that has been validated, an agreement on the part of the native title-holders, or the doing of a permissible future act.

The Native Title Act also provides native title-holders with two additional rights not available to ordinary freeholders. They have a special right to negotiate when a miner seeks access or when a government wants to acquire the land so as to vest title in a third party. If agreement is not reached, either party can refer the matter to an independent tribunal which can be overridden by the minister making a decision in the public interest. Furthermore, in exercise of their native title rights and interests, they can hunt, fish and gather on their traditional lands or in their traditional waters without obtaining the usual licence or permit for such activity provided they do not use the produce for commercial purposes.[11]

For two centuries government authorities dealt with land in Australia as if native title did not exist. In built-up areas, native title will have been extinguished because the land has been subject to Crown grants and because traditional owners have lost the necessary connection with their land. The Land Fund and Indigenous Land Corporation (ATSIC Amendment) Act 1994 now guarantees indigenous Australians $45 million a year for land purchases and land management, including land improvement, 'to help redress the dispossession of Aboriginal persons and Torres Strait Islanders'. In this way, the Parliament has started to address the moral claims of Aborigines for compensation for past dispossession. Native title is likely to exist in remoter parts of Australia. For example, Western Australia is the largest state, of which 35% is and always has been classified as 'vacant Crown land'. As this land has never been the subject of Crown grant, it may still be subject to native title. That issue cannot be resolved to the satisfaction of developers who may need to negotiate with the native title-holders until they know who they have to deal with. Any person wanting to conduct an activity on 'vacant Crown land' can no longer act with lawful authority just by receiving permission from a state official. There may be native title-holders who now have to be treated in the same way as a freeholder in the same jurisdiction would be treated.

The Commonwealth's Native Title Act guarantees Aboriginal claimants access to the National Native Title Tribunal ('NNTT') for a determination of native title. The claimants could also use a state tribunal provided it has received Commonwealth authorisation complying with the national standard for such a tribunal. There has to be some fine tuning of the relationship between the NNTT and the Federal Court because

10 (1995) 128 ALR 1 at 42. For details on the operation of the Act see Brennan, F, 'Parliamentary responses to the *Mabo* decision', in Stephenson, MA (ed), *Mabo: The Native Title Legislation*, 1995, St Lucia: University of Queensland Press, pp 1–25.

11 Section 211 Native Title Act 1993.

under the constitution the federal judicial power can be exercised only by a court. The NNTT cannot make a binding, authoritative and enforceable determination independent of the Federal Court. Even though the High Court upheld the substance of the Native Title Act in March 1995, the judges did point out that 'No question as to the constitution, procedure, findings or determinations of the National Native Title Tribunal has arisen for decision'.[12] A month earlier the court struck down amendments in the Sex Discrimination and Other Legislation and Amendment Act 1992 and the Law and Justice Legislation Amendment Act 1993 which made a determination of the Human Rights and Equal Opportunity Commission binding, authoritative, and enforceable, thereby invalidly purporting to invest judicial power in the Commission.[13]

A further 16% of Western Australia is reserve land gazetted for use by the Crown for various public purposes. It is a mixed question of law and fact whether such land has been classified and used in such a way as to exclude any native title-holders who may still have claims under their local system of Aboriginal law. 1% of Western Australia is state forest and timber reserves which may still permit the continuation of native title. Only 7% of the state is freehold which undoubtedly extinguishes native title as does another 3% of non-pastoral leases. The remaining 38% of the state is covered by pastoral leases. As in the Northern Territory and South Australia, Western Australian pastoral leases contain a reservation allowing continued Aboriginal access to the pastoralist's land.

The three cases decided by the full bench of the High Court have not required a determination whether native title survives on any pastoral leases. In *Mabo (No 2)* some of the High Court judges had cause to consider whether native title could survive on land subject to fixed term lease for a sardine factory. The lease contained a reservation that the lessee was 'not in any way to obstruct or interfere' with the Islanders' traditional use of gardens and plantations. Brennan J (Mason CJ and McHugh J concurring) took the approach that native title was always extinguished by a lease just as it was by a grant of freehold, regardless of any reservation contained in the lease. Native title could survive on land subject to lesser interests such as a miner's authority to prospect. Brennan J's rationale was:[14]

> By granting the lease, the Crown purported to confer possessory rights on the lessee and to acquire for itself the reversion expectant on the termination of the lease. The sum of these rights would have left no room for the continued existence of rights and interests derived from Meriam laws and customs.

When Isabel Coe laid claim to a third of New South Wales, including vast pastoral holdings in the Wiradjuri region, Mason CJ said the plaintiff confronted 'a formidable obstacle' – given the 'Brennan approach' that with the grant of a lease – 'the Crown's title is thus expanded from a mere radical title and, on the expiry of that term becomes a *plenum dominium*'.[15]

12 *WA v Commonwealth* (1995) 128 ALR 1 at 42 *per* Mason CJ, Brennan, Deane, Toohey, Gaudron, McHugh JJ.

13 *Brandy v Human Rights and Equal Opportunity Commission* (1995) 127 ALR 1.

14 (1992) 175 CLR 1 at 73.

15 *Coe v The Commonwealth* (1993) 118 CLR 193 at 205–06.

The Brennan approach seems to draw a distinction between lands subject to Crown grants and those remaining under Crown control as reserves or trusts. Native title can be extinguished only by action of the Crown or Parliament. It is not extinguished by other persons. If the Crown gives a person the power to do things which are inconsistent with the continuation of native title, the grant of power extinguishes native title. So while the question whether native title survives on Crown land is a mixed question of law and fact, the question whether native title survives on a Crown grant is only a question of law. It is immaterial whether the land-holder has in fact acted in a way contrary to the ongoing existence of native title. The only issue is whether the Crown has given the land-holder the legal authority to act that way. Has the Crown granted the land-holder rights to interfere with what would have been native title rights? If so, the Crown has extinguished native title by making the grant even though the land-holder has done nothing in fact to interfere with traditional Aboriginal access and use of the land.

Most Western Australian pastoral leases are subject to a reservation allowing Aboriginal access for sustenance on unenclosed and unimproved parts of the land. By improving or enclosing the land, the pastoralist has the power to exclude Aboriginal access. Therefore native title was extinguished on such leases when the lease was granted. This approach has support from McHugh J and presumably from Dawson J who in *Western Australia v The Commonwealth* said:[16]

> [T]he reasons for judgment of Brennan J, with whom Mason CJ and McHugh J agreed, departed least from what I regarded as established law and, for my present purposes, may be accepted as containing the basic principles for which *Mabo (No 2)* now stands as authority.

Deane and Gaudron JJ said they would leave the issue of the possible effect of the sardine lease on native title 'until another day'. But in passing, they did say:[17]

> It would seem likely that, if it was valid, it neither extinguished nor had any continuing adverse effect upon any rights of Murray Islanders under common law native title.

Toohey J's general reasoning in *Mabo (No) 2* would support this approach. Now that Mason CJ has retired, the most educated guess is that the High Court's view on the survival of native title on pastoral leases with reservation clauses would depend on the new judge, Gummow J, the other six being evenly divided.

Though Northern Territory pastoral leases are subject to a reservation permitting Aboriginal access for hunting and gathering, no access is permitted within 2 km of a homestead. In South Australia Aboriginal access for hunting, gathering and camping is permitted but not within a kilometre of any building or 500 m of any dam.[18] Given that

16 (1995) 128 ALR 1 at 68.

17 (1992) 175 CLR 1 at 117.

18 For further detail on the effect of these complex reservations in pastoral leases, see Stephenson, MA, 'Pastoral Lease and Reservation Clauses', in Stephenson MA (ed), *Mabo: The Native Title Legislation*, 1995, St Lucia: University of Queensland Press, pp 104–19; Brennan, F, 'Pastoral Leases, *Mabo* and the Native Title Act 1993', in Edmunds, M (ed), *Land, Rights, Laws: Issues of Native Title*, Issues Paper 1 and 3, 1994, Canberra: Native Titles Research Unit, AIATSIS.

the construction of a homestead by a pastoralist would exclude Aboriginal access in an area around the homestead, the Crown grant of such a title probably extinguishes native title. However, in *State of Western Australia v The Commonwealth*, the High Court had cause to make an exhaustive survey of the history of Western Australia subsequent to the establishment of the colony to determine whether the Crown at the time of the assertion of sovereignty had 'the antecedent intention to be from the beginning the absolute owner of land within the colony'.[19] Having referred to the reservations in pastoral leases, six of the judges observed:[20]

> So far as these vignettes of history reveal, those involved in establishing the British colony of Western Australia knew that there were Aborigines who, by their law and customs, were entitled to possession of land within the territory to be acquired by the Crown and settled as a Colony.

So, it is arguable that these reservations maintain native title on land until the pastoralist, in fact, acts with lawful authority so that native title can no longer be enjoyed over the surrounds of the pastoralist's improvements.

The Western Australian government claims that up to a third of the pastoral leases in that state were granted between 4 March 1933 and 21 January 1935 when the applicable Land Act Amendment omitted all reference to reservations. The registrar of the NNTT has taken the view that leases executed during that time 'conferred exclusive possession and therefore extinguished native title. Once extinguished, native title cannot be revived.'[21] The Brennan line of extinguishment on all leases, whether pastoral or not, whether containing reservations or not, is consistent but the Deane/Gaudron approach extends a modicum of justice to another group of Aborigines who otherwise suffer complete dispossession without guaranteed compensation.

Whether or not native title survived on pastoral leases with reservations was a purely academic question until the passage of the Native Title Act 1993. Now native title-holders have a right to negotiate the terms on which a miner may have access to native title land and on which the government may acquire the land for vesting in a third party. Even if a pastoral lease is held by a person or corporation which is not Aboriginal, the miner would still have to deal with any native title-holder who still has access to the land. This issue awaits urgent resolution before the High Court. The uncertainty affects especially the mining industry in Western Australia where 38% of the state is pastoral lease and mineral production exceeds $10,000 m a year with capital expenditure of over $2,000 m a year, employing more than 30,000 people. Premier Richard Court has yet to set up a nationally-approved state apparatus for determining native title and hearing development applications. He issued thousands of development applications of doubtful validity up until March 1995 when the High Court predictably struck down his Land

19 (1995) 128 ALR 1 at 17.

20 (1995) 128 ALR 1 at 19.

21 National Native Title Tribunal, media release PR94/21, 11 December 1994.

(Titles and Traditional Usage) Act 1993 passed in November 1993.[22] The High Court said 'the WA Act purported to extinguish native title, creating administratively defeasible rights in its place'.[23] It was contrary to the Racial Discrimination Act 1975 and inconsistent with the valid Native Title Act 1993.

Many Aborigines migrated to pastoral leases up until the 1960s finding employment on under-award wages. Often Aboriginal groups came to identify with particular pastoral properties *having* left their traditional country. Others were fortunate to work on properties which included their traditional country. Many Aborigines in the north of Australia carry the name of the property on which they were 'born in the cattle'. Over time, pastoral property boundaries often became the boundaries for living and ceremonial purposes as well as work purposes. The local Aboriginal law adapted to the circumstances of the group. But it was not always a one-way process. Anthropologist Nancy Williams has observed in relation to the East Kimberley that:[24]

> ... the history of pastoral leases indicates that boundaries altered through both coalescence and subdivision from their first gazettal in the last quarter of the 19th century to the middle of the 20th so that they increasingly came to resemble, if not be isomorphic with, those of the Aboriginal traditional land-owners.

Given the comprehensive dispossession these people would suffer if native title was extinguished on all pastoral leases, the Commonwealth Parliament provided for Aborigines to be restored as native title-holders if they were the holders of the pastoral lease. Ever since the establishment of the Aboriginal Land Fund Commission, replaced by the Aboriginal Development Commission and now by the Aboriginal and Torres Strait Islander Commission (ATSIC), there have been Commonwealth funds available for the purchase of cattle properties for local Aborigines. The problem is that the lease is invariably held by a corporation and native title can be restored only if all the shareholders are successful native title claimants.[25] When these corporations were created and vested with title, there was no requirement that the shareholders be traditional owners. After two centuries of colonial dislocation and one century of pastoral activity, there may be various levels of Aboriginal tradition *which has evolved with the circumstances in relation to* kin and country. The need to restructure such land holding corporations may cause antipathy between various Aboriginal groups claiming an interest in a pastoral operation on the traditional country of only one group. The cost of this antipathy would be worthwhile only if there was some tangible gain to be made in negotiations with a mining company wanting access to the land.

Even where there is no land holding corporation holding a pastoral lease, the government policy of requiring Aboriginal groups to be incorporated *before* being

22 See Brennan, F, '*Mabo:* Options for Implementation – Statutory Registration and Claims Processes', in Sanders, W (ed), *Mabo and Native Title: Origins and Institutional Implications* 1994, Canberra: Centre for Aboriginal Economic Policy Research, pp 31–45.

23 *WA v Commonwealth* (1995) 128 ALR 1 at 45 *per* Mason CJ, Brennan, Deane, Toohey, Gaudron, McHugh JJ.

24 Williams, N, personal communication, 17 August 1995.

25 Section 47 Native Title Act 1993.

eligible for ATSIC funding often exacerbates differences between groups. These differences could fester even more once there is a requirement to establish a native title claim before traditional owners are able to secure living areas for their families and are authorised to protect their lands and sites from outside interference. Even when there is little prospect of financial gain requiring the regular division of royalty equivalents or rents, tensions between claimants can be problematic. For example, the Purnululu Aboriginal Corporation (PAC) has successfully lodged a claim to the Bungle Bungle massif and surrounding national park and conservation reserve in the East Kimberleys of Western Australia. The area is presently managed by CALM, the state government's conservation and land management organisation. The Aboriginal members of PAC decided to make the claim 'following more than 10 years of frustrated efforts to gain agreement with CALM' on a plan for joint administration of the national park which is now the centrepiece of the government's tourist advertising campaign for the Kimberleys.[26] While watching the success of the joint management plans for the Kakadu and Uluru National Parks in the Northern Territory, these traditional owners claim to have been marginalised attending 'endless but futile meetings with successive state governments to gain recognition of Aboriginal people as equal partners in the management of the National Park'. The PAC is now confident that 'No activity can be initiated in the claim area without negotiation with the traditional owners'.[27] A native title claim gives them some political muscle when it comes to dealing with the state government, provided of course there is agreement as to who the traditional owners are.

The native title claim, though lodged by the Kimberley Land Council ('KLC') acting on instructions from PAC, is in the name of four persons who claim to hold native title with 'all descendants, maternal and paternal, actual and putative' of 12 named deceased persons. The Chairperson of the Mindi Mindi Aboriginal Corporation, which split from PAC in 1992, has issued public statements claiming the area comes within the Malnjin-Djaru traditional lands and that 'the PAC and their Kitja group don't have the right to claim over the area'.[28] Failing agreement, such inter-Aboriginal disputes will have to be settled by the NNTT, the Federal Court and state tribunals. Past rivalries among local Aboriginal groups will now be played out in land disputes where the gains over government and developers could be substantial. The Commonwealth government is now funding representative bodies such as the KLC to assist local Aboriginal groups with their land claims. The task of these representative bodies is invidious when the local groups cannot agree to settle their differences if only to strengthen their joint position against outsiders. Because of the history of dispossession, dislocation and disempowerment, some of these disputes are unresolvable. Failing perfect justice, all players will have to work for a durable compromise which creates sufficient certainty so governments and developers can treat in good faith with a representative group who 'speak for country'.

26 Butters, J, Vice-Chairperson of PAC, media release, Kimberley Land Council, 22 December 1994.

27 Butters, J, Vice-Chairperson of PAC, media release, Kimberley Land Council, 30 March 1995.

28 Edwards, B, quoted in the *Kimberley Echo*, 20 April 1995.

Prior to *Mabo,* Aborigines in the Northern Territory, Queensland and New South Wales were able to claim some lands which would be granted by the Crown under some form of statutory title usually described with the shorthand expression 'inalienable freehold'. In South Australia and Victoria, the parliaments had provided some one-off grants of such titles, South Australia having granted 18% of the state under the Pitjantjatjara and Maralinga land rights legislation. The High Court has left open the question whether such grants made for the benefit of Aborigines on the assumption that native title did not exist did themselves extinguish native title.[29]

There will continue to be considerable uncertainty about the benefits of native title until four developments occur. First, the Commonwealth needs to fine tune the relationship between the Federal Court and the NNTT at least to ensure that the tribunal does not exercise judicial power and also to permit the Federal Court to answer legal questions in the course of mediation by the tribunal or court staff. Second, the High Court has to decide whether native title has been extinguished on all pastoral leases. Though there are compelling considerations of justice for non-extinguishment, the theory of Crown sovereignty and the defeasibility of native title only by action of the Crown or by native title-holders acting in accordance with customary law point to wholesale extinguishment whatever the reservations in land legislation or leases. Third, the High Court has to decide if native title is extinguished on lands subject to beneficial grants made to Aborigines including traditional owners. Fourth, the Federal Court and NNTT need to have processed some claims to completion so future claimants and interested parties can know the rules of the game. Some commentators have also called for a test case on the Crown's fiduciary duty to native title-holders and other Aborigines whose ancestors were dispossessed by the Crown without compensation or consent. Elsewhere I have argued this would be a dead end.[30] The High Court has been quite categorical in holding that native title could be extinguished before 1975 without compensation, consent or consultation. That leaves little scope for a special duty of trust owed by the Crown to native title-holders. Whatever scope there is would be filled since by the operation of the Racial Discrimination Act which guarantees native title-holders equal treatment with the holders of Crown grants.

Especially in the remoter parts of Australia, there is understandably an abysmal ignorance and mistrust of the 'whitefella' talk about native title. Though the Commonwealth is resourcing representative bodies, land councils outside New South Wales and the Northern Territory have not previously had the resources to employ professional staff or even to cover their areas building trust and rapport with local Aboriginal communities who are content in what, to them, is their self-evident, irrefutable, undisturbed ownership of their country prior to the arrival of miners and

29 In *Pareroultja v Tickner* the Federal Court held that a grant of fee simple to a land trust under the Aboriginal Land Rights (Northern Territory) Act 1976 was not inconsistent with the continuance of native title as it would protect the native title. Refusing special leave to appeal, Mason CJ took the unusual step of indicating that the High Court was not to be taken as agreeing with the Federal Court on this issue. In *Mabo (No 2)* Brennan J said that a deed of grant in trust could be a special measure under the Racial Discrimination Act.

30 Brennan, F, '*Mabo* and the Racial Discrimination Act' (1993) 15 *Sydney Law Review* 206–22.

developers. Even the basics of *Mabo* are unknown to many communities expected to be the primary beneficiaries of native title. Unless told, they have no reason to suspect that they are entitled to compensation for any interference with their native title after October 1975, but not before. Unless a miner has arrived or unless a tourist development is on offer, they see little reason to seek a registration of native title, having a 'whitefella judge' certify what they have always known, that it is their country. When the miner comes, native title-holders in the more remote parts of Queensland and Western Australia, having heard about royalty cheques in the Northern Territory, are likely to be disappointed to learn that they do not have a veto over development. It is only the veto that gives them the economic bargaining power to move off the bottom of the welfare ladder.

The uncertainties about the existence of native title can provide claimants with some increased bargaining power over impatient developers seeking approvals. Native title-holders dealing with government and developers now hold some trump cards when they sit down to negotiate an outcome. Litigation, or even the threat of it, is a useful complement to the time honoured media campaigns highlighting the 'whitefella's' disregard for the Aboriginal perspective on proposed developments.

Prime Minister Keating was right to concede that few Aborigines would gain recognition of title to lands additional to those granted in jurisdictions which already had land rights legislation. Most of those dispossessed lost their lands well before 1975. The land fund doubles the amount which was available to ATSIC for land purchases in recent Federal budgets. The fund will now be perpetual, being self-sustaining in 10 years. Pastoral leases purchased from the fund will be convertible to native title bringing the right to negotiate into play, but lands purchased in the Northern Territory will not be convertible to inalienable freehold carrying the right of veto.[31]

Mabo and the Native Title Act do not provide any universal panacea for Aborigines seeking justice for the manifest adverse effects of sustained dispossession without compensation or consent. *Mabo* was a restricted and responsible exercise of judicial power. The Native Title Act was a modest addition by Parliament to the most restrictive of the majority judgments in *Mabo*. The tribunal process and the prospect of regional agreements about land use and service delivery provide the possibility of negotiated outcomes being accepted as durable solutions to intractable problems, because all parties have the opportunity to come to the table with both something to negotiate about and something to negotiate with. If the whole process becomes bogged down in legalistic determination of rights, native title will prove to be a hollow log obstructive to developers and of little use to native title-holders. French J, President of the NNTT, indicated his concerns when dismissing the Waanyi claim to traditional country which is the site of CRA's proposed century zinc mine south of the Gulf of Carpentaria. Holding that native title was extinguished by the grant of pastoral leases in 1883 and 1905, he conceded to the unsuccessful Aboriginal claimants:[32]

31 Section 191(u) Land Fund and Indigenous Land Corporation (ATSIC Amendment) Act 1994.

32 Quoted in *Koori Mail* (1995) 22 February.

> The process must seem perverse to those who maintain their association with their country and upon whom indigenous tradition confers responsibility for that country. The operation of past grants of interests to irrevocably extinguish native title, regardless of the current use of the land, reflects a significant moral shortcoming in the principles by which native title is recognised.

The political reality of the situation was stated by Queensland premier, Wayne Goss: 'I think the bottom line out of all this is that the company now has a secure basis to proceed with the project as far as any native title is concerned'. The last word on a 200-year grievance by indigenous people cannot be set down by a tight legislative response to a High Court decision in which the judges rightly restrict their role to determining a case, accepting the act of state and subsequent dispossession effected without compensation to be within power.

Where grievances relate to lands now held by others under Crown grant, rectification without occasioning further injustice is possible only by providing resources for the dispossessed to purchase lands on the open market. Where denial of land rights was accompanied by and justified by a denial of the land-owners' law, culture and even humanity, the wrongs committed by the state often for the benefit of new settlers cannot be set right just by land grants and monetary compensation. Having acknowledged the prior land rights, law and culture of Aborigines, the High Court has opened a window of opportunity for all Australians to review our constitutional arrangements and social policies so that Aborigines and Torres Strait Islanders may be guaranteed their due place in Australian society. The Social Justice Package, which is to complement the Native Title Act and the land fund, provides the opportunity for Aborigines locally, regionally and nationally to negotiate their future security in the nation state.[33]

The *Mabo* decisions and the Native Title Act have complicated the law of the land in Australia. They have accorded a modicum of land justice and compensation to some traditional owners previously denied adequate access and control of their lands. The uncertainties and tensions of a federal system of responsible government in which the role of the judiciary is circumscribed have provided new opportunities for all parties to agitate for the protection of their own interests and to co-operate in the national interest. For the first time, Aboriginal participation was not only possible but essential so that all parties could own the outcome. Now that all parties are at the table, the true test of our shared commitment to nation building begins. Reconciliation can be based on a shared future; it cannot be built on a divided past.

Aborigines and Torres Strait Islanders do not live on land alone. Eddie Mabo lived his adult life and died, in Townsville on the Australian mainland, a lifestyle away from his beloved island of Mer in the Torres Strait. He gave his life to 'land rights', the cause on his dying lips, the last words to his beloved. He objected to government wanting to vest his traditional country under the control of a council of his people elected by his people resident in the Murray Islands. He wanted recognition of his law, of his culture, of himself and his people who have been a law making and law abiding people for

33 See Brennan, F, *One Land, One Nation*, 1995, Brisbane: University of Queensland Press.

millennia. For him, land rights was not a Crown grant of vacant Crown land to his people even if it would give legal security and the protection of the State to his land. For him, land rights was the Crown's recognition that he and his people already had rights to land under their law, following their customs – a law belatedly recognised, respected and adopted by the colonisers. The High Court agreed so did the Commonwealth Parliament. The nation must now learn to live with the law of the land to which Eddie Mabo dedicated his life. The lessons will reverberate in human relationships and political structures well beyond the complex legalities of the incidents of native title.

CHAPTER TWELVE

RECONCILIATION AND THE CONSTITUTION

Belinda Wells and John Doyle

> There is no reconciliation without self-determination ... Australia will never be reconciled with Aboriginal and Torres Strait Islander peoples until they are genuinely free to choose their own destiny, whatever that may be.[1]

During the early 1970s the Australian government officially abandoned its assimilation policy towards Aboriginal and Torres Strait Islander peoples. There was talk of the need to protect the distinctive cultural heritage and identity of these peoples, and to promote their ability to influence their own destinies – what the government now refers to as 'self-determination'.[2]

At two points during the 1980s, there was discussion of a treaty between indigenous and non-indigenous Australians. The second of these initiatives culminated in the signing of the 'Barunga Statement' on 12 June 1988, which said firmly: 'The government affirms that it is committed to work for a negotiated Treaty with Aboriginal people.'[3]

However in 1995, as we write, there is no treaty or agreement between all the indigenous and non-indigenous people of Australia. It is true that there has been some recognition in parliamentary resolutions[4] and in statutory preambles of the prior occupation of Aborigines and Torres Strait Islanders, and of their 'dispossession and dispersal from their traditional lands by the British Crown'.[5] There has been statutory protection of cultural heritage and some land rights, and prohibition of racial

1 Professor Daes, Chairperson of the United Nations Working Group on Indigenous Populations, *The Position of Indigenous People in National Constitutions* (speeches from the conference in Canberra, 4–5 June 1993) 1993, Canberra: AGPS, p 62.

2 The Australian government has in recent years been prepared to accept that indigenous peoples have a right of *internal* self-determination, albeit in a relatively narrow sense: see Brennan, F, 'Self-Determination: The Limits of Allowing Aboriginal Communities to be a Law Unto Themselves' (1993) 16 *University of New South Wales Law Journel* 245, pp 256, 260–61.

3 The Barunga Statement, para 1. The statement was signed by Aboriginal leaders and by the Australian Prime Minister, Mr Hawke, and the Minister for Aboriginal Affairs, Mr Hand, on 12 June 1988: see Brennan, F, and Crawford, J, 'Aboriginality, Recognition and Australian Law: Where to From Here?' (1990) 1 PLR 53, pp 54–56.

4 In particular, the 'Bonner Resolution', which was passed unanimously by the Senate on 20 February 1975, and the '1988 Resolution' which was passed in both the House of Representatives and the Senate as 'the first motion put to the vote in the first sittings in the new Commonwealth Parliament House', but which did not secure bipartisan support: see McRae, H, Nettheim, G and Beacroft, L, *Aboriginal Legal Issues*, 1991, Sydney: Law Book Company, pp 295–96.

5 Preamble to the Council for Aboriginal Reconciliation Act 1991. See McRae, Nettheim, Beacroft, *op cit*, at footnote 6, pp 296–97 for discussion of preambles to State Acts, and for the terms of the proposed preamble to the Aboriginal and Torres Strait Islander Commission Act 1989 (Cth). The Act was passed without the preamble.

discrimination.[6] The Australian government and some indigenous people consider that the principle of self-determination has been upheld (at least to some extent) in the creation of the Aboriginal and Torres Strait Islander Commission (ATSIC) and its regional councils, and in the adoption of a handful of regional agreements.[7]

Our constitution, however, does not reflect any of these values. It has never done so. At the time of enactment, its two references to the indigenous peoples were designed to exclude them from the federal polity.[8] After the 1967 referendum, in which these two references were omitted, the only constitutional provisions of special application to Aboriginal and Torres Strait Islander peoples were ss 25 and 51(xxvi) – where the references were implicit only. Section 25 constitution is an anachronistic provision which is considered below.[9] Section 51(xxvi) confers power on the Commonwealth legislature to make laws with respect to 'the people of any race for whom it is deemed necessary to make special laws'. This is the extent of the constitutional recognition of the special position of the Aboriginal and Torres Strait Islander peoples in our society.

Since 1991, however, there has been a new impetus towards discussing a formal recognition of indigenous heritage, culture and rights. The High Court's landmark decision in *Mabo v Queensland (No 2)*[10] in 1992 has shaken the Australian community from its languor in relation to indigenous issues. The decision to recognise native title and to reject the doctrine of *terra nullius* has inspired indigenous leaders, and has stirred politicians, lawyers, and resource companies into action. More specifically, the Council for Aboriginal Reconciliation Act 1991 was enacted with bipartisan support not long after the conclusion of the Royal Commission into Aboriginal Deaths in Custody. The Act established a Council for Aboriginal Reconciliation, and prescribed its functions. One of its main functions is under s 6(g):[11]

6 For example, the Aboriginal and Torres Strait Islander Heritage Protection Act 1984 (Cth), the Aboriginal Land Rights (Northern Territory) Act 1976 (Cth), the Aboriginal Heritage Act 1988 (SA); the Native Title Act 1993 (Cth), the Pitjantjatjara Land Rights Act 1981 (SA) and the Maralinga Tjarutja Land Rights Act 1984 (SA); and the Racial Discrimination Act 1975 (Cth) and the Equal Opportunity Act 1984 (SA).

7 However, other indigenous Australians and their organisations 'have been critical of the suggestion that ATSIC represents a move towards self-determination': see *Controlling Destinies*, Issue Paper 8 of the Council for Aboriginal Reconciliation (CAR), 1994, Canberra: AGPS, pp 15–18; but *cf* Lois O'Donoghue in *Controlling Destinies*, pp 26–27 and *Walking Together: The First Steps*, Report of CAR to Federal Parliament 1991–94, 1994, Canberra: AGPS, (hereafter referred to as 'CAR Report'), p 171. On regional agreements, see *Controlling Destinies*, pp 42–45, and CAR Report, pp 254–56.

8 Sections 51(xxvi) and 127 of the Constitution: see text accompanying footnotes 31–34 below. See also s 25 of the Constitution.

9 See text prior and subsequent to footnote 148.

10 (1992) 175 CLR 1.

11 See also s 6(h):

> ... after that consultation, to report to the Minister on the views of Aborigines and Torres Strait Islanders and of the wider Australian community as to whether such a document or documents would benefit the Australian community as a whole, and if the Council considers there would be such a benefit, to make recommendations to the Minister on the nature and content of, and manner of giving effect to, such a document or documents ...

In the CAR Report, the Council has reported on its progress to date: *op cit*, pp 253, 170–179.

> ... to consult Aborigines and Torres Strait Islanders and the wider Australian community on whether reconciliation would be advanced by a formal document or formal documents of reconciliation.

At this stage the likely mechanisms for recognition of claims by indigenous peoples remain unclear. The possible mechanisms include common law, legislation, constitutional amendment, a separate, constitutionally entrenched Bill of Rights or Bill of Indigenous Rights, and a national agreement and/or regional agreements (either unimplemented, or implemented by an ordinary or entrenched statute). We may, like Canada, decide upon a combination of these.

In this chapter, we will discuss various mechanisms – particularly in light of developments in the United States, New Zealand, and (especially) Canada. However, we will focus on the possibilities for *constitutional* change.

We hold a particular view about the purpose of a constitution. In our view, the function of a constitution is not simply to allocate power to different organs and levels of government. The constitution of a community should also recognise and protect the values and principles that are regarded as fundamentally important by the people of that community. These principles should be regarded as of such importance that they will be entrenched against easy removal or change by subsequent generations.

In the mid- to late-1990s, there are a number of reasons why Australians are reconsidering the content of our constitution. We are approaching the centenary of our constitution in 2001. The Federal government is advocating constitutional amendments necessary to make Australia a republic, and there is support for an entrenched Bill of Rights. The decade of the world's indigenous peoples is underway. It is a pertinent time to consider whether our fundamental values are reflected in a constitution which makes no reference at all to the unique position in our society of Aboriginal and Torres Strait Islander peoples.

We make one final introductory point. The purpose of a document of reconciliation (of any type) should obviously be to reconcile groups within the Australian community – to assist them in appreciating their different perspectives. And so, we have opened our chapter by focussing on the over-arching concept of indigenous self-determination, and the claim that without internal self-determination there cannot be reconciliation. In this chapter we will focus on various rights whose recognition may contribute to realisation of that concept in the Australian context.

SOVEREIGNTY

We will begin by examining the existing legal framework. As we will see, in many areas there has already been, or is likely to be, significant change. However there appears to be (at least currently) one constraint which is non-negotiable.

We are referring to the legal principle which states that an acquisition of sovereignty by a sovereign nation such as Britain is non-justiciable. The acquisition is said to be an act of State which cannot be challenged in a municipal court. The High Court upheld this principle in *Mabo (No 2)*,[12] and most recently, in the case of *Walker v NSW*, Mason CJ reiterated the point so as to put the matter beyond doubt. He said:[13]

> *Mabo [No 2]* is entirely at odds with the notion that sovereignty adverse to the Crown resides in the Aboriginal people of Australia. The decision is equally at odds with the notion that there resides in the Aboriginal people a limited kind of sovereignty embraced in the notion that they are a 'domestic dependent nation' entitled to self-government and full rights (save the right of alienation) or that as a free and independent people they are entitled to any rights or interests other than those created or recognised by the laws of the Commonwealth, the State of New South Wales and the common law.

Sovereignty confers authority to exercise the executive, legislative and judicial powers of government. After the arrival of the British in the 18th century, the British and colonial governments, and later the Commonwealth and the States, were regarded as the sole repositories (within constitutional limits) of such authority.

It is said to follow from this, that the respective legislatures could enact statutes of general application which would extinguish any Aboriginal and Torres Strait Islander customary law which had 'survived British settlement'.[14] This was the main point at issue in the *Walker* case. The plaintiff had argued that upon Britain's acquisition of sovereignty, the colonists had received English law 'applicable to their own situation',[15] and this law applied *only* to the colonists. Specifically, he contended that 'the criminal statutes of New South Wales did not apply to people of Aboriginal descent'.[16]

Mason CJ, sitting alone, rejected this contention. He emphasised that there was a 'basic principle that all people should stand equal before the law'; and he said that the principle would be offended if 'different criminal sanctions' were applied 'to different persons for the same conduct'.[17] On a more technical note, he relied upon a rule of statutory construction: that legislation 'applies to all persons and matters within the territory to which it extends'.[18] His conclusion was dispassionate, and rejected any analogy with the recognition of common law native title in *Mabo (No 2)*.[19] Any customary criminal law that survived British settlement, he said, was 'extinguished by passage of criminal statutes of general application'.[20]

---

12 *Op cit*, at 31 *per* Brennan J (with whom Mason CJ and McHugh J agreed); see also *per* Deane and Gaudron JJ at 78–79. For a discussion of the theories of sovereignty as a 'political fact', and as a 'legal conception', see Morison, WL, 'The Future Scope of Australian Common Law' (1991) 13 Syd LR 335 at 336–38.

13 *Walker v NSW* (1994) 69 ALJR 111 at 112, in which he was repeating his statement in *Coe v Commonwealth* (1993) 68 ALJR 110 at 115.

14 *Walker v NSW* (1994) 69 ALJR at 113 *per* Mason C J.

15 *Op cit*, at 113, quoting from *Blackstone's Commentaries*, 5th edn, 1773, Bk 1, Chapter 4, p 107.

16 *Op cit*, at footnote 13.

17 *Ibid.*

18 *Ibid.*

19 *Ibid.*

20 *Ibid.*

It is difficult to predict whether in the future there will be greater pressure from Aboriginal people for political or legal recognition of Aboriginal sovereignty.

At present, no major political party in Australia, nor the Australian courts, would accept the contention that 'there is in Australia an Aboriginal nation [or nations] exercising sovereignty, even of a limited kind'.[21] Claims that continued Aboriginal sovereignty should be recognised and documented would be more likely to lead to disharmony within the Australian community, than to assist the process of reconciliation. At this stage, it may be that for most Aboriginal and Torres Strait Islander people, a claim in the language of 'self-determination' would suffice. In the present climate there would be little point in expressing their wishes in terms of 'Aboriginal sovereignty'.[22]

Nonetheless, we regard the Canadian experience on sovereignty as indicative of the sort of changes that may occur in Australia in the future. The Canadian experience suggests that the principle of the non-justiciability of an acquisition of sovereignty may not prove to be as unassailable as it seems at present. In Canada, principles such as those on sovereignty, which were 'once thought to be beyond legal and constitutional, if not moral, scrutiny', have been 'increasingly shown to be open to transformation and reform in the name of indigenous justice'.[23]

In Australia, as we are all aware, the High Court in *Mabo (No 2)* overturned the long-accepted principle that the British Crown, upon acquiring sovereignty, became the exclusive owner of all land in the Australian colonies. It did so on the ground of injustice. Yet, as Patrick Macklem pointed out, the notion of the 'discoverer' of lands acquiring absolute sovereignty over those lands, is equally unjust:[24]

> The principle that the 'discovery' of lands inhabited by an indigenous population vests sovereignty in the 'discovering' nation is (similarly) based on the proposition that indigenous people are insufficiently civilised or Christian to merit being viewed as competing sovereign powers. Fortified by the illusion of superiority, European powers claimed that the act of settlement in itself divests indigenous peoples of any and all sovereign authority over their land and their people.

Macklem made the following prediction:[25]

---

21 *Coe v Commonwealth* (1979) 24 ALR 118 at 129 *per* Gibbs J. Our addition in parentheses.

22 See, for example, Pearson, N, 'Reconciliation: To Be or Not to Be – Separate Aboriginal Nationhood or Aboriginal Self-determination and Self-government within the Australian nation?' (1993) 3(61) *Aboriginal Law Bulletin*, pp 14–17; Turner, P, *op cit*, at footnote 54; Dodson, M, *op cit*, at footnote 56; *cf* Mansell, M, 'Treaty Proposal' (1989) 2(37) *Aboriginal Law Bulletin*; and Mansell in *The Position of Indigenous People in National Constitutions*, *op cit*, pp 88–91.

23 Macklem, P, 'Indigenous Peoples and the Canadian Constitution: Lessons for Australia?' [1994] Pub LR 11 at 34.

24 *Ibid*, at 32 (our inclusion of the word 'similarly'). See also Watson, I, 'How Far is There to Travel in Achieving Rights?' [1993] *Law Society Journal* (NSW) 31 at 34.

25 *Ibid*, at 33. Macklem also suggests that '[s]ome softening of the view advanced by Brennan J in *Mabo* that the Crown is entitled to unilaterally extinguish Aboriginal title without compensation may well be in order'. He suggests that '[a] useful principle in this regard is the proposition that the Crown may owe Aboriginal communities fiduciary duties in certain circumstances'.

> Judging from recent events in Canada, invoking the time-honoured excuse that the courts do not have the authority to question the legitimacy of assertions of Crown sovereignty will not end the matter, for indivisible Australian sovereignty will be challenged, if not in a court of law, then in courts of public and international opinion.

Sovereignty of the people

Sovereignty in the sense of the exercise of powers of government over the people is a concept which might, however, offer Aboriginal and Torres Strait Islander peoples scope for pressing the issue of their relationship with the Crown. Prior to the retirement of Mason CJ, at least three members of the High Court had emphasised that the sovereignty of Parliament is ultimately derived from the people. In *Australian Capital Television Pty Ltd v Commonwealth*, for example, Mason CJ said:[26]

> The very concept of representative government and representative democracy signifies government by the people through their representatives. Translated into constitutional terms, it denotes that the sovereign power which resides in the people is exercised on their behalf by their representatives.

This theory of popular sovereignty was presumably based upon a notion that the people have delegated their sovereignty to their representatives in Parliament, either on a continuing basis, or in the past. It perhaps provides a new basis for arguments of indigenous sovereignty. For example, it could be said that if the theory 'does rest on some act of consent, albeit by our ancestors, as people who gave their assent to the constitution in one way or another (eg by voting, by choosing to live in Australia, etc), what is the act by which the Aboriginal people surrendered their inherent sovereignty?'[27]

THE CONSTITUTION AND INDIGENOUS PEOPLES

However, neither the Australian community nor our courts have discussed indigenous aspirations and needs through the language of 'sovereignty'. We have assumed that such terminology must refer to sovereignty in the international law sense and therefore pertains only to an independent nation State with a defined geographical area and population base, which has seceded from the remainder of Australia.

Views may change on this, as we move on from the formative stages of the reconciliation process. However, for the moment, the question that is posed is whether, in some *other* way our constitution currently recognises and protects the distinct identity and needs of Aboriginal and Torres Strait Islander peoples.

26 (1992) 177 CLR 106 at 137 *per* Mason CJ. See also *Nationwide News v Wills* (1992) 177 CLR 1 at 72 *per* Deane and Toohey JJ: 'the powers of government belong to, and are derived from, the governed, that is to say, the people of the Commonwealth'. See also Republican Advisory Committee's report, *An Australian Republic: the Options*, vol 1, 1993, Canberra: AGPS, p 1: 'Australia is a State in which sovereignty derives from the people', cited in Brennan, *op cit*, at footnote 28 p 36; and Dodson, M, 'Towards the Exercise of Indigenous Rights: Policy, Power and Self-determination' (1994) 35 *Race and Class* 65 at 75: '... despite their claims to the contrary, states are not sovereign. Peoples are sovereign'.

27 Doyle, J, '*Mabo*, Indigenous People and the Constitution', paper for the Legal Convention, September 1995, Brisbane.

The history of the constitutional treatment of indigenous issues is well known.[28] Aboriginal people played an extremely limited role in the adoption of the Commonwealth constitution. Except in South Australia, Aboriginal people were not able to vote for delegates to the Constitutional Conventions held during the 1890s.[29] With the exceptions of South Australia and Western Australia, women – whether Aboriginal or not – could not vote on the adoption of the constitution. By 1901, 'Aboriginal men, as British subjects, had the right to vote in all the colonies except Queensland and Western Australia', but 'the majority were not on the electoral rolls'.[30]

The preamble to the constitution gives no indication of the lack of participation by indigenous people and women in the system of representative democracy which it creates. The preamble is brief, inclusive, and purports to reflect a united, homogeneous society. It begins: 'Whereas the people' of the various colonies 'humbly relying on the blessing of Almighty God, have agreed to unite in one indissoluble Federal Commonwealth ...'.

The constitution, as adopted in 1901, contained two provisions which did refer specifically to Aboriginal people: ss 51(xxvi) and 127. Both singled out Aboriginal people for special treatment. Section 51(xxvi) conferred power on the Commonwealth to legislate with respect to 'the people of any race, *other than the aboriginal race in any State*, for whom it is deemed necessary to make special laws' (our italics).[31] A deliberate decision was made to allow Aboriginal issues to be regulated in an *ad hoc* manner by the states.

The second provision, s 127, provides a particularly clear indication of the degree to which Aboriginal people were regarded as excluded from the national polity. Section 127 provided as follows:

> In reckoning the numbers of the people of the Commonwealth, or of a State or other part of the Commonwealth, aboriginal natives shall not be counted.

Fr Brennan SJ explained that s 127 was drafted in order to assist the Commonwealth in providing an equitable distribution of funds to each state.[32] An obvious factor to be taken into account when calculating an appropriate distribution was the population of each state. However, there was no need to include Aboriginal people in such statistics: 'Aboriginals were not provided with government services; neither were they viewed as part of a state's economy.'[33]

28 See, for example, Brennan, F, *Securing a Bountiful Place for Aborigines and Torres Strait Islanders in a Modern, Free and Tolerant Australia*, 1994, Melbourne: Constitutional Centenary Foundation Inc, pp 6–7.

29 *Ibid.*

30 *Ibid.* Brennan, SJ, points out that 'non-Aboriginal women throughout Australia received the franchise' in 1902, but that '[i]t was not until 1965 that Queensland ... granted voting rights to adult Aborigines and Torres Strait Islanders': p 6.

31 As to the original purpose for including s 51(xxvi), see footnote 38 and accompanying text.

32 *Op cit*, at footnote 22 at 7.

33 *Op cit*, footnote 26.

Section 127 was evidence of the fact that at the time of federation there was no constitutional (or other) guarantee of equality for Aboriginal and Torres Strait Islander people. Indigenous people were regarded as being subject to Commonwealth and state laws, but had no right to insist on receiving equal treatment and benefits under those laws. Needless to say, nor did the constitution accord them any special rights over and above those few which were applicable to the Australian community at large.

In 1967, Australians voted overwhelmingly[34] to amend the constitution by deleting s 127 from it and by changing the scope of s 51(xxvi). Since then, the latter provision has conferred power on the Commonwealth to legislate with respect to:

> The people of any race, for whom it is deemed necessary to make special laws.

As a result, the Commonwealth and State legislatures have concurrent power to enact legislation with respect to Aboriginal and Torres Strait Islander issues.

Section 51(xxvi) – the 'race' power

Section 51(xxvi) was originally included in the constitution to give the Commonwealth power to regulate the entry, movement, labour conditions and so forth of 'alien races'[35] (a power previously enjoyed by the states).[36]

Since the power was extended in 1967 to cover Aboriginal and Torres Strait Islander people, the High Court has examined its scope in two cases: *Koowarta v Bjelke-Petersen*,[37] and *Commonwealth v Tasmania*.[38] The court has said that a person will be regarded as belonging to the aboriginal 'race' if the person is 'of aboriginal descent, albeit mixed', and if the person 'identifies himself as such and ... is recognised by the Aboriginal community as Aboriginal'.[39]

As interpreted by the High Court, the scope of s 51(xxvi) is broad in one respect, and narrow in another. It has been held that the provision is wide enough to enable the Commonwealth to enact laws which discriminate *against,* as well as in favour, of the people of a particular race.[40] For example, the power would 'enable the Parliament ... to regulate and control the people of any race in the event that they constitute a threat or

34 An 'unprecedentedly high 91% of the electors voted in favour' of the referendum proposal: McRae, Nettheim, Beacroft, *Aboriginal Legal Issues*, *op cit,* at footnote 5, p 313.

35 See Quick, J, and Garran, R, *Annotated Constitution of the Australian Commonwealth*, p 622, as cited in *Final Report of the Constitutional Commission* ('Final Report'), 1988, Canberra: AGPS, p 708.

36 The Commonwealth legislature could rely on s 51(xxvi) to enact special laws about 'the Indian, Afghan, and Syrian hawkers; the Chinese miners, laundrymen, market gardeners, and furniture manufacturers; the Japanese settlers and Kanaka plantation labourers of Queensland, and the various coloured races employed in the pearl fisheries of Queensland and Western Australia': Professor Harrison Moore, *The Constitution of the Commonwealth of Australia*, 2nd edn, 1910, p 464, as cited in Final Report, *ibid.*

37 (1982) 153 CLR 168.

38 (1983) 158 CLR 1.

39 *Commonwealth v Tasmania* (1983) 158 CLR 1 at 274 *per* Deane J.

40 See Final Report, para 10.360–10.362, *op cit*, and the footnotes referred to therein.

problem to the general community ...'.[41] Secondly, however, it is possible that the High Court would regard a law as supported by s 51(xxvi) only if it was a special law 'in the sense of having some special connection with the people of any race'.[42] This was the approach taken by Stephen J in *Koowarta.* As the Constitutional Commission pointed out in its Final Report, if such an approach were adopted, it is possible that the court would only uphold the validity of a law if it was itself satisfied that the law had been enacted in order to meet a special need, threat or problem 'posed by the people of the particular race'.[43]

In its Final Report in 1988, the Constitutional Commission recommended that the current wording of s 51(xxvi) be omitted, and replaced with the phrase 'Aborigines and Torres Strait Islanders'.[44] The Commission acknowledged that 'the nation as a whole has a responsibility for Aborigines and Torres Strait Islanders'.[45] However it took the view that a new provision should be adopted, which would not refer expressly to 'race', and which would 'be free of the possible limitations pertaining to 'special laws' which would apply' if the High Court adopted the approach taken by Stephen J in *Koowarta.*[46] The Commission did not regard it as appropriate to include in the new provision the phrase 'for the benefit of', or some similar qualification.[47]

Other constitutional provisions

There are other provisions in the constitution which may be relied upon for a purpose that is relevant to Aboriginal people.[48] One of these is s 51(xxxi), which confers power to legislate in relation to the acquisition of property by the Commonwealth on just terms. The Constitutional Commission considered the issue of whether s 51(xxxi) should be modified in order to accommodate the special situation of acquisitions of property by the Commonwealth for the purpose of disposition to Aboriginal people. It recommended against deletion of the 'just terms' guarantee in such circumstances.[49]

41 *Commonwealth v Tasmania* (1983) 158 CLR 1 at 158 *per* Mason J, as cited in Final Report, p 708.

42 *Koowarta v Bjelke-Peterson* (1982) 153 CLR 168 at 209–10 *per* Stephen J.

43 Final Report, p 709.

44 Final Report, pp 710–11, 718.

45 *Op cit*, at footnote 35 at 718. The Distribution of Powers Advisory Committee had put the point more forcefully: *op cit*, at footnote 35 para 10.392.

46 Final Report, p 719. The Commission emphasised that through its ratification of the International Convention on the Elimination of All Forms of Racial Discrimination ('CERD') and its enactment of the Racial Discrimination Act 1975 (Cth), Australia had shown that it no longer accepted race as a 'legitimate criterion on which legislation can be based': Final Report, p 711. In addition, the Commonwealth would still be able to regulate such matters as 'the entry and activities of aliens in Australia' under other heads of power, such as s 51(xix) ('naturalisation and aliens').

47 See Final Report, p 715.

48 For example, 'the external affairs power (s 51(xxix)), the power to acquire property (s 51(xxxi)), and the power to appropriate and grant money (ss 81 and 96)': see Final Report, p 713. In addition, the Constitutional Commission pointed out that the following provisions 'may have direct relevance to Aborigines if recommendations in the Australian Law Reform Commission's Report, *The Recognition of Aboriginal Customary Laws* concerning the recognition of customary marriages are adopted': s 51(ii) (taxation), s 51(xxi) (marriage), and s 51(xxiii) (invalid and old-age pensions): see Final Report, p 714.

49 Final Report, Chapter 9.

The Constitutional Commission did not address the issue of the direct inclusion in the constitution of provisions which would recognise and protect Aboriginal rights.[50] Discussion centred around the issue of whether there should be inserted into the constitution 'a provision along the lines of s 105A [of the constitution] ... which would confer a broad power on the Commonwealth to enter into a compact with representatives of the Aboriginal people'.[51]

We consider that the Constitutional Commission's consideration of these issues, and its discussion of an appropriate preamble to the constitution,[52] took place in a rather different atmosphere from that which prevails today. As a result, we intend now to move out from behind the existing framework provided by the constitution, and to explore the question of what rights, principles or other matters Aboriginal and Torres Strait Islander peoples might wish to see enunciated in a constitutional or other document. We will examine the precedents provided by international instruments, and various national approaches. We will consider the broad issue of what type of document we want our constitution to be, and the specific detail of whether and how it should be amended.

Equal rights

In February 1995, the Aboriginal and Torres Strait Islander Social Justice Commissioner Mr Mick Dodson, and the Chief Executive Officer of ATSIC, Ms Pat Turner, outlined in broad terms the rights which they regarded as worthy of protection.[53] They agreed that the 'recognition and enforcement of [two] different types of right ... are critical to the achievement of social justice for Aboriginal and Torres Strait Islander people'.[54] The first of these two broad categories was referred to as 'citizenship rights': that is, those rights which should be available equally to all people in Australia. The second category was made up of 'indigenous rights': that is, those rights which can only be claimed by indigenous peoples.

50 The Final Report, p 717, appears to indicate that the Commission and its Rights Committee had received submissions which advocated such an approach.

51 The Senate Standing Committee on Constitutional and Legal Affairs, *Two Hundred Years Later ...* (1983) pp 107, xii, and 115, as cited in Final Report, p 725. See discussion of this possibility below in the text accompanying footnotes 155–58.

52 Final Report, vol 1, p 104.

53 Both spoke during a session of the Australian Rights Congress in Sydney. See Chapter 10 by Dodson, M, in this volume for a more detailed discussion on rights.

54 Turner, P, unpublished address to a session of the Australian Rights Congress, 17 February 1995. In effect, Turner and Dodson asserted that Aboriginal and Torres Strait Islander peoples are entitled to the 'respect for the principle of equal rights and self-determination of peoples' provided for in Article 194 of the UN Charter. See also CAR Report, p 175.

We will begin by considering the first of these categories. Here, the issues are both whether the various civil, political, social, economic and cultural rights are available in Australia, and whether they are *equally* upheld in Australia.[55]

Mr Mick Dodson has emphasised the particular importance of social and economic rights for Aboriginal peoples. He acknowledged that the civil and political rights (such as those which relate to the criminal justice system) are obviously as fundamental for Aboriginal peoples as they are for all Australians. However, he said:[56]

> ... the most urgent and pressing concerns of indigenous peoples cluster around our social and economic rights: our rights to a decent standard of health, housing, water, education ... our survival rights.

In Australia we have legislation which prohibits discrimination on the ground of race in areas such as employment, housing, and the provision of goods and services.[57] But there is no legislation which imposes a positive obligation on our governments to ensure that certain rights are upheld: for example, an obligation on governments to provide an adequate standard of housing, education and health to every person within Australia. Aboriginal peoples have not in the past or in the present uniformly enjoyed such rights. As a result, whilst since 1967 they have enjoyed theoretical equality to participate in civil and political life, they have in practice been largely unable to participate. As Turner stated, there has not been 'equality in outcomes for indigenous Australians'.[58]

The Australian constitution does not include any explicit guarantee of equality in the enjoyment of rights. As mentioned above, the constitution contains only a handful of provisions which guarantee – within the Commonwealth sphere – certain rights or freedoms.[59] Whilst a majority of the High Court judges have been prepared to draw

---

55 As is well known, Australia has ratified various general international conventions on human rights, including the United Nations International Covenant on Civil and Political Rights ('ICCPR') and the International Covenant on Economic, Social and Cultural Rights ('ICESCR'). The Covenants provide that their provisions are to apply equally to all persons within the territory of the ratifying State (although the ICESCR allows some differential treatment of non-nationals), and that the State is to take all necessary measures (including legislative measures) to implement the principles set out in the Covenant. Australia has chosen to implement some, but not all, of the provisions by way of Commonwealth legislation, and accords constitutional protection to a couple of rights only (and then only partially): for example, freedom of religion (s 116), and the implied freedom of political communication.

56 Dodson, M, 'Adequacy of Protection for the Rights of Indigenous Peoples', unpublished speech delivered to a session of the Australian Rights Congress, 17 February 1995.

57 The Racial Discrimination Act 1975 (Cth), the Human Rights and Equal Opportunity Commission Act 1986 (Cth), and various State Acts prohibit such conduct and set up complaint, conciliation, and enforcement mechanisms.

58 Turner, P, *op cit*, at footnote 54, p 3. Dodson, M, has written: 'Juxtapose, on the one hand, the rhetoric of rights and commitment, the anti-discrimination laws and the government programmes and, on the other hand, the lived experience of peoples', *op cit*, at footnote 26, p 66. Elsewhere, he has provided several graphic examples of this 'lived experience'. In his words: 'Start with the right to life: we die, on average, twenty years earlier than other Australians. Our children die four to five times more often in childbirth and three times more often in infancy. Then go to the right to equality before the law: we are 26 times more likely to be taken into police custody than other Australians', *op cit*, at footnote 56, p 2.

59 These are generally regarded as s 51(xxxi) (acquisition of property on just terms), s 80 (jury trial for offences tried on indictment), s 116 (freedom of religion), and s 117 (prohibition against discrimination against the residents of other States).

implications such as 'freedom of political communication' and 'separation of judicial power' from the structure and provisions of the constitution, there has been less support for an implied right to equality before and under the law.[60]

If our constitution *was* amended so as to include some guarantees of social and economic rights or some type of equality right, it would be important to ensure that the *State* governments were equally subject to the guarantees.[61]

In addition, Turner regarded it as essential that the conventions of service delivery and special programmes be rethought, so that the participation of Aboriginal people becomes an integral part of the process.[62] Aboriginal peoples are seeking to break free of the passive, 'welfare recipient' model, and to assert 'the non-dependent core which is the heart of indigenous identity'.[63] This takes us into the complex and more contentious field of self-determination and indigenous rights.

SELF-DETERMINATION

International developments

For at least a decade, representatives from Aboriginal and Torres Strait Islander groups have been attending international discussions on indigenous rights. In particular, they have attended meetings convened under the auspices of the United Nations Sub-Commission on Prevention of Discrimination and Protection of Minorities. Some have been involved in formulating the principles set out in the UN Draft Declaration on the Rights of Indigenous Peoples.[64]

Article 3 of the Draft Declaration is in the same terms as Article 1(1) of the ICCPR and of the ICESCR. It provides as follows:

> Indigenous peoples have the right of self-determination. By virtue of that right they freely determine their political status and freely pursue their economic, social and cultural development.

60 See *Leeth v Commonwealth* (1992) 174 CLR 455 at 485–86, 501–02, 475–76, *per* Deane, Toohey, Gaudron, Brennan JJ; *cf* at 468 *per* Mason CJ, Dawson and McHugh JJ.

61 Since 1967, the Commonwealth government has had the power to control the delivery of many services to Aboriginal peoples through the exercise of s 51(xxvi) of the Constitution. Whilst ATSIC has taken over most of the responsibilities of the Commonwealth Department of Aboriginal Affairs, it remains the view of ATSIC's Chief Executive Officer that:

> ... in basic areas such as health, education, housing and essential service delivery, and the provision of basic community infrastructure, Aboriginal and Torres Strait Islander people are largely dependent on programs and services which fall within the jurisdictions of State, Territory and local governments. (See Turner, P, *op cit*, at footnote 54, p 4.)

62 She said that ATSIC would be addressing the issue of how this could be achieved in its report to the Commonwealth government on the social justice aspect of the government's response to *Mabo*: Turner, P, *op cit*, at footnote 54, pp 1, 5. ATSIC and CAR have now presented the government with their submissions on social justice issues: see, respectively, *Recognition, Rights and Reform*, 1995, Canberra: ATSIC and *Going Forward: Social Justice for the First Australians*, 1995, Canberra: AGPS.

63 Dodson, M, *op cit*, at footnote 56, p 7.

64 E/CN 4/Sub 2/ 1994/2/Add 1; 20 April 1994, drafted by the UN Working Group on Indigenous Populations.

It is followed by Article 4:

> Indigenous peoples have the right to maintain and strengthen their distinct political, economic, social and cultural characteristics, as well as their legal systems, while retaining their rights to participate fully, if they so choose, in the political, economic, social and cultural life of the State.

The Draft Declaration is still under consideration within the United Nations.[65] Its provisions enshrining the right to self-determination may be watered down as government representatives make their objections felt later in the process. Such governments fear that the right will be interpreted as encompassing a right to *external* self-determination – a right to secede from the nation State.[66]

Whatever occurs, the issues of indigenous rights and at least *internal* self-determination are now firmly on the international agenda. The United Nations Working Group on Indigenous Populations (WGIP) was established in 1982. In June 1989 the International Labour Organisation (ILO) adopted the ILO Convention 169.[67] The Convention recognised that indigenous peoples have distinct collective rights, such as rights to land, self-development, environmental protection, and cultural integrity. Several years later, at the 1992 Rio Summit, two of the central principles of ILO Convention 169 – self-development and cultural integrity – 'attained a global consensus'.[68] There followed the International Year of the World's Indigenous Peoples in 1993; and an agreement by the UN General Assembly to proclaim a 'Decade of the World's Indigenous Peoples', to commence on 10 December 1994.[69]

Professor Daes, the Chairperson of WGIP, which formulated the Draft Declaration, has defused much of the concern about the meaning of the term 'self-determination'. She has repeatedly affirmed the text of the 1970 UN Declaration of Principles on Friendly Relations,[70] and has emphasised that the right to self-determination will be met so long as governments are representative of and accountable to *all* of their constituents:[71]

---

65 See Barsh, 'Indigenous peoples in the 1990s: From object to subject of international law?' (1994) Harvard Hum RJ 33 at 55–56, 75. As presently drafted, there is an implementation provision, in which the United Nations undertakes to 'take the necessary steps to ensure the implementation of (the) Declaration including the creation of a body at the highest level ...' (see Article 41).

66 Note the distinction drawn by international law between the rights of 'externally colonised' peoples (a right to self-determination in the widest sense), and the rights of 'internally colonised' peoples such as Aboriginal and Torres Strait Islander peoples (no such right): see, for example, Dodson, *op cit*, at footnote 26, pp 68–70, and the discussion of the 'salt-water thesis' in *Controlling Destinies*, *op cit*, at footnote 7, pp 3–5.

67 Indigenous and Tribal Peoples Convention 1987, being a partial revision of ILO Convention 107 (adopted in 1957).

68 Barsh, *op cit*, at footnote 65, p 45. Barsh points out that as at June 1993 only five States had ratified ILO Convention 169.

69 Barsh, *op cit*, footnote 65, pp 69–70.

70 1970 Declaration of Principles on Friendly Relations and Cooperation Among States in Accordance with the Charter of the United Nations: see passage cited by Professor Daes, *op cit*, footnote 1, p 55.

71 *Op cit*, at footnote 1, p 55. For a description of the Australian government's attitude to the inclusion in the *Draft Declaration* of a right of self-determination, see Brennan, *op cit*, at footnote 2, pp 260–61. Professor Daes has also said that indigenous peoples are 'unquestionably' 'peoples' for the purposes of the self-determination provisions in the Draft Declaration, *op cit*, at footnote 1, pp 54–55.

> Once an independent State has been established and recognised, its constituent peoples must express their aspirations through the national political system, and not through the creation of new States. That is, unless the national political system becomes so exclusive and non-democratic that it no longer can be said to 'represent the whole of the population'.

Aboriginal representatives have supported such an approach,[72] but have also called for recognition of 'the weakness of democracy in adequately responding to aspirations of Aboriginal and Torres Strait Islander peoples'.[73]

Clearly, a system of representative government of the type found in Australia will not be sufficient, on its own, to ensure indigenous self-determination.[74] Professor Daes says that what is needed in all countries is 'a kind of belated State-building' in which indigenous peoples, 'after many years of isolation and exclusion', are recognised and incorporated 'in the fabric of the State, on agreed terms'.[75]

This, then, is a brief overview of the international context within which Aboriginal and Torres Strait Islander people are asserting and the Australian government is considering rights and measures associated with self-determination. If, in the future the Australian government ratifies ILO Convention 169 or the Declaration (once finalised), s 51(xxix) ('the external affairs power') will provide it with considerable scope for legislative implementation of the principles set out in these instruments. In the meantime, international developments are playing an influential role in disseminating the message of indigenous self-determination – not only to governments and indigenous peoples, but perhaps also to the wider community.[76]

Australia

We turn now to consider the more specific issue of self-determination within the Australian context.

Aboriginal and Torres Strait Islander peoples assert the right to self-determination on the basis that at the time of the arrival of the British just over 200 years ago, their ancestors had been living in Australia for thousands of years, with control over every

72 See, for example, the extracts from speeches made by Pastor Bill Hollingsworth, and Lois O'Donoghue, set out in *Controlling Destinies*, *op cit*, at footnote 7, pp 24–27.

73 'ATSIC's Response to Key Issues Seven and Eight', CAR Report, *op cit*, at footnote 7, p 176.

74 Such self-determination has been described as involving two elements: 'control' (of indigenous institutions, territories, and development) and 'consent' (and a right to participate in all decisions by non-indigenous institutions which affect indigenous peoples): *Controlling Destinies*, *op cit*, at footnote 5, p 8.

75 Professor Daes, *op cit*, at footnote 1, p 57. 'Because the non-indigenous State was founded on the basis of non-recognition of pre-existing indigenous rights and laws, indigenous peoples and the non-indigenous State lack an agreement about the basic principles of nationhood, the structure of government, the source of law, and the shaping and sharing of power, wealth and national resources': see Dodson, *op cit*, at footnote 26, p 73.

76 This has at least been the case in those countries in which there are no (non-indigenous) groups clamouring for special minority rights: Barsh, *op cit*, at footnote 65, pp 76–77. In Australia, for example, it could be said that the protest action against nuclear testing by the French at Mururoa Atoll was at least as much about indigenous self-determination, as about environmental protection.

aspect of their lives. Mick Dodson contrasts this basis with the basis underlying the rights asserted by other, non-indigenous, minority groups:[77]

> Our rights are structured on a fundamentally different ground. Literally, the ground of this country is the ground of our rights.

In a broad sense, the principle of self-determination is the common fabric through which is threaded the various strands of indigenous rights. As each thread is put into place, the fabric as a whole becomes stronger, more durable.

Three main strands of indigenous rights have been identified as:[78]

- *autonomy rights:* which focus upon the right of indigenous peoples to determine the way in which they live and control their social, economic and political systems;
- *identity rights:* which relate to the right to exist as distinct peoples with distinct cultures; and
- *territory and resource rights:* which encompass such things as land entitlements, the right to resources of that land, and the use of those resources.

Each of these strands is made up of many threads, and not all of them will be susceptible to the setting of precise and uniform legislative standards.

For example, in the area of 'autonomy rights', it may be more appropriate to implement the principle of autonomy through a series of regional agreements which are tailored to the wishes and needs of each particular Aboriginal community.[79]

Secondly, the 'identity rights' would include the right to protection of items and areas of cultural significance, which is currently regulated by State and Commonwealth legislation. However, this category would also include the right to recognition of Aboriginal customary law, which is an area that is largely unregulated (and therefore unrecognised). The Australian Law Reform Commission has recommended the recognition by our legal system of Aboriginal customary laws, but favoured the adoption of different approaches to different areas of the law, rather than a 'broad brush' approach.[80]

And, in relation to the third main strand of rights – 'territory and resource rights' – the Native Title Act 1993 (Cth) now represents legislative recognition of some, but not all, aspects of this category. Here, the common law may continue to play an important role in resolving areas of detail.

---

77 Dodson, *op cit*, at footnote 56, p 7. See also Barsh, *op cit*, at footnote 65, pp 81–82.

78 Turner, *op cit*, at footnote 54, p 6. Similarly, see Dodson, *op cit*, at footnote 56, p 6.

79 For an example of one form of implementation, see the description of the powers of the Cherbourg Aboriginal Council (including powers to pass by-laws, to appoint policemen, and to confer jurisdiction and powers on an Aboriginal Court) in Brennan, *op cit*, at footnote 2, pp 246–47; see also discussion at p 262.

80 ALRC, *The Recognition of Aboriginal Customary Laws*, ALRC Report No 31, 1986, Canberra: AGPS. Fr Brennan SJ makes the point that in view of the application (by the common law) of traditional Aboriginal law in *Mabo (No 2)*, 'there is now a strengthened argument for recognition by statutory or other means of other aspects of traditional or Aboriginal law': *op cit*, at footnote 3, p 248. See his discussion of issues relevant to the recognition of Aboriginal customary law on criminal responsibility, criminal procedure, and sentencing, *op cit*, at footnote 2.

It is important to recognise that many of the indigenous rights would be collective rights: by their nature, capable of assertion only by a group (or by an individual or individuals on behalf of a group).[81] The Australian legal system is largely unfamiliar with the idea of group rights. It will always be an extraordinarily difficult task to determine the appropriate balance between group rights and individual rights, both in a general sense (if some type of standard is to be drafted), and in a particular case.[82] For example, Dodson highlights the difficulties posed by an indigenous community's decision to protect its people from alcohol by declaring the community to be 'dry':[83]

> On the one hand are the rights of the community to determine how it will live, to protect its members from harm, and to preserve its culture – rights which are guaranteed under the International Covenant on Civil and Political Rights. On the other are the rights of the individuals to buy or to sell alcohol.

And so, it seems likely that different mechanisms will be advocated or thought appropriate for protecting different indigenous rights.

Nonetheless, Dodson emphasises that the indigenous rights *must* be recognised, and that that recognition must have constitutional force.[84] In his view, constitutional protection is necessary in order to prevent economic interests (for example, those of large resource companies) from too easily persuading the government of the day to override fundamental indigenous rights.[85] Constitutional recognition of such rights would clearly also play a symbolic and educative role, so that Australians will no longer think in terms of 'a hierarchy of rights, a hierarchy of knowledge', with Aboriginal rights and knowledge at the bottom – valued least.[86]

So, have other countries provided such constitutional protection of indigenous rights? We turn to look at the position in the United States, New Zealand, and Canada.[87]

81 Indigenous rights may also take the form of individual rights: see, for example, the various rights set out in the Draft Declaration.

82 For example, full implementation of a group's right to apply its traditional laws might entail non-observance of a particular individual's right to insist upon equality under the law and 'due process' (including separation of judicial power): see Brennan, *op cit*, at footnote 2, esp p 247.

83 Dodson, *op cit*, at footnote 56, p 10. See Human Rights and Equal Opportunity Commission ('HREOC'), *The Alcohol Report*, released on 11 July 1995. 'Certificates of exemption under the special measures provisions' of the Racial Discrimination Act, 1975 (Cth) will be issued by the Race Discrimination Commissioner to Aboriginal communities, but 'will be non-binding'. That is, they will only represent the opinion of the Race Discrimination Commissioner, 'and are open to judicial review': see the *Australian*, 11 July 1995, p 3.

84 Dodson, *op cit*, at footnote 56, p 11. See also Turner, *op cit*, footnote 54, p 9, who suggests that the Australian Constitution should be amended so as to recognise the 'special place (of) ... the indigenous peoples of Australia'; and the possibility of a Bill of Indigenous Rights should be considered.

85 Dodson, *op cit*, at footnote 54, p 12.

86 *Ibid*, p 2.

87 Another indigenous people who could have been considered here are the Sami, who live in Sweden, Finland, Norway and the Kola Peninsular of Russia: see ATSIC, *Native Title: International Responses*, 1994, Canberra: ATSIC, pp 10–11.

United States

The position of the indigenous people in the contiguous part of the United States is based upon a distinctive historical background. Both prior to and after the Declaration of Independence in 1776, numerous treaties were concluded between the US government and Indian nations. From the 1830, Indian tribes were regarded by the Supreme Court as 'political bod(ies) with the powers of self-government'.[88] For the most part, the tribes have thereafter exercised a limited form of sovereignty within their territories – even as the size of their domains was diminishing.[89]

The Indian tribes are expressly referred to in the Commerce Clause of the US constitution as a government whose commerce Congress may regulate. Professor Kickingbird has said that:[90]

> [As] governments, Indian tribes have the general power to:
>
> 1. make laws governing the conduct of persons, including non-Indians, in Indian country;
> 2. establish bodies such as tribal police and courts to enforce the laws and administer justice;
> 3. exclude or remove non-members from the reservation for cause; and
> 4. regulate hunting and fishing, land use and environmental protection.

The American experience of self-government – and the practicalities of 'limited sovereignty' and 'domestic dependent nation-status' – are of great interest. However, it should be noted that the scope of an Indian tribe's powers of self-determination is not constitutionally protected. As a result, subject-matters traditionally regulated by a tribe may become the object of regulation by Congress, or by State governments in conjunction with unsympathetic judgments from the Supreme Court.[91]

New Zealand

In New Zealand also, there was initial recognition by the European colonisers of the sovereignty of the indigenous people. This was said to result in only one treaty: the Treaty of Waitangi which was signed by Maoris and by representatives of the British Crown in 1840. In fact, there were two treaties: the English language version, and the Maori text. The latter text was 'not a straight translation of [the] English text'; it was

88 See the address by Professor Kickingbird in *The Position of Indigenous People in National Constitutions*, *op cit*, at footnote 1, pp 13–14.

89 *Op cit*, at footnote 1, pp 17–18. '... Indian tribes still possess those aspects of sovereignty not withdrawn by treaty or statute, or by implication as a necessary result of their dependent status': *United States v Wheeler* 435 US 313, 323 (1978), as cited in Fr Brennan SJ, *op cit*, at footnote 28, p 9. See also *Worcester v Georgia* 31 US 515 (1832) *per* Marshall CJ: Indian tribes 'had always been considered as distinct, independent, political communities, retaining their original natural rights'.

90 Professor Kickingbird, *op cit*, at footnote 1, p 15.

91 *Ibid*, p 19. In addition, the Supreme Court decided, some 40 years ago, that the Fifth Amendment to the Constitution, 'which provides that private property shall not be taken for public use without just compensation, did not apply to native title as it was only a right of occupancy not one of ownership': *Tee-Hit-Ton Indians v US* 348 US 272 (1955), as cited in ATSIC, *Native Title: International Responses*, *op cit*, at footnote 87, p 14.

'separately composed'[92] and signed in 1840, and then virtually ignored by non-Maoris until 1975.

For 130 years, the Treaty of Waitangi was regarded by the legal system as unenforceable in municipal courts. The New Zealand government derived support from Article 1 of the English language text which stated that the 'Maori signatories [had] ceded to the Queen all their rights and powers of sovereignty'.[93] It denied that Article 2 of the English text conferred enforceable land and resource rights on the Maori peoples.

In 1975 the Treaty was implemented, in part, by legislation. In the Treaty of Waitangi Act the two texts 'are published side by side and are there to be given equal status'.[94] The Waitangi Tribunal, which is set up under the Act, has power to make recommendations to the government (but not determinations) concerning the application of treaty principles to claims brought before it. The Tribunal has recommended, for example, that the Maori right to land and resources should not be confined to a right to engage in traditional practices recognised in 1840. In the Tribunal's view, the Treaty confers a 'right to development of resources and access to technology'.[95]

The Tribunal's recommendations typically form the starting-point for subsequent negotiations between the New Zealand government and the claimants. The Tribunal is not involved in these negotiations. In 1985 the jurisdiction of the Waitangi Tribunal was extended, so that it would have power to hear claims arising from events which had occurred in or after 1840.

Treaty principles have also played an important part in other forums. Since a significant decision by the New Zealand Court of Appeal in 1987, New Zealand courts have attempted to give substance to provisions in legislation which state that the legislation is to be applied 'in accordance with Treaty principles'.[96] The Treaty provision which guarantees Maori rights to land and resources such as fisheries, provided the impetus for a comprehensive settlement on fishing rights which the government and Maori agreed to in 1992.[97] The agreement was enacted as the Treaty of Waitangi (Fisheries Claims) Settlement Act 1992 (NZ).

However, the Treaty principles, and indigenous rights generally, are not constitutionally protected in New Zealand. The Waitangi Tribunal could be abolished,

---

92 Professor Sorrenson, *op cit*, at footnote 1, p 29.

93 *Ibid.*

94 *Ibid*, p 33.

95 Stokes, E, 'The Land Claims of First Nations in British Columbia' (1993) 23 VUWLR 171 at 175.

96 See, in particular, the landmark case of *New Zealand Maori Council v Attorney-General* [1987] 1 NZLR 641, in which the NZ Court of Appeal decided that 'the Government had to provide safeguards to protect Maori interests before transferring vast land assets to the state-owned enterprises' pursuant to the State-Owned Enterprises Act 1986: Brennan, *op cit*, at footnote 28, p 13.

97 '[T]he Crown [agreed to] provide Maori with capital to participate in a joint venture to purchase Sealord Products Ltd which held 26% of the nation's fishing quota. In return, Maori agreed to government proposals for amendment of the Fisheries Act thereby extinguishing fishing rights under the Treaty of Waitangi and reducing the Waitangi Tribunal's jurisdiction over fishing matters': see *Agreeing on a Document*, Issue Paper 7 of CAR, 1994, Canberra: AGPS, p 22.

or its powers severely circumscribed, by simple legislative amendment.[98] The New Zealand government has attempted to finalise Treaty claims.[99]

In any event, whilst it is worthwhile to have an independent, authoritative body such as the Tribunal, which adopts flexible and culturally appropriate methods of inquiry,[100] the impact of the tribunal is necessarily limited. The Tribunal has only had sufficient resources to deal with a handful of the claims that have been registered with it.[101] After a lengthy and potentially costly process, its recommendations may be ignored by the government.

More generally, it would be difficult for any body to turn back the full effect of the assertion of British sovereignty contained in Article 1 of the English text. The Maori text, ignored until 1975, did not include a ceding of sovereignty to the British. But the colonists proceeded to act upon their understanding of the Treaty, and to reject all suggestions of Maori self-government or of divided sovereignty of the type recognised in the United States.[102] Since 1867 the approach taken has been to set aside a small number of Maori seats within the New Zealand Parliament.[103]

To summarise, during the past 20 years the impact of the Waitangi Treaty principles has been considerable. The principles have been implemented in certain areas covered by statute, applied by courts in the interpretation of such statutes and perhaps also in developing the common law,[104] and been the subject of Waitangi Tribunal recommendations and the impetus for comprehensive settlement agreements. However, the Treaty principles have never been fully incorporated into municipal law – either by means of an ordinary statute, or by way of a statute that is constitutionally entrenched.

In particular, neither Treaty principles nor other indigenous rights are protected by the Bill of Rights Act 1990 (NZ) (which is an ordinary statute).[105]

98 See Professor Sorrenson, *op cit*, at footnote 1, pp 35–36. He reported (at p 36), however, that some conventions relating to the treaty seem to be developing. For example, 'governments appear to accept an obligation to adhere to the treaty and to consult Maori opinion before enacting legislation affecting Maori'.

99 In December 1994, the government released its 'fiscal envelope' proposal, in which all outstanding Maori land claims would be settled irrevocably, in return for a maximum sum of $1 billion 'available over about 10 years'. The proposal was abandoned, following vociferous Maori opposition: see Levy, 'Fighting Over the Land' (1995) 20(3) AR & LJ 113.

100 See Stokes, *op cit*, at footnote 95, pp 188–89.

101 'According to New Zealand lawyer Caroline Wainwright there have been over 330 claims registered and the Tribunal is equipped to conclude only about five claims per year': *Agreeing on a Document, op cit*, at footnote 97, p 23.

102 See Professor Sorrenson, *op cit*, p 30.

103 See Professor Sorrenson and Brennan, *op cit*, p 33 and 14.

104 However, judges 'have been cautious in making it so': see Professor Sorrenson, *op cit*, pp 36–37.

105 This is so despite the fact that the draft Bill of Rights contained in a White Paper on the issue provided that the Treaty of Waitangi would be the 'supreme law' of the country and that 'the rights recognised in the Treaty (would be) ... given comprehensive, indeed total, protection from legislative and executive disruption': see McHugh, PG, 'The Constitutional Role of the Waitangi Tribunal' [1984–85] NZLJ 224.

Canada

In Canada, by contrast, the 'existing Aboriginal and treaty rights of the Aboriginal peoples of Canada' are constitutionally protected. Section 35(1) of the Constitution Act 1982 provides that such rights are 'hereby recognised and affirmed'. In addition, indigenous people derive specific protection from s 25 of the Charter of Rights and Freedoms 1982 and general protection from the equality provisions in s 15 of the Charter. In our view, the existence of these constitutional provisions and of judicial decisions which interpret then, makes the study of the Canadian position particularly relevant.

In some respects, the Canadian legal framework prior to 1982 closely resembled that of Australia. As in Australia 'indigenous social and political organisation was deemed insufficiently civilised to merit sovereign recognition'.[106] As a result, the British Crown was regarded as having acquired sovereignty over the territory, and British law applied.[107] The various provinces ultimately agreed to become co-partners in a federation under an Act of the imperial parliament which set out the constitutional rules.[108] As in Australia, 'legislative regulation of Aboriginal people ... aimed at the eventual assimilation of Aboriginal people into colonial society.'[109]

However, in other respects, the background was rather different from that in Australia. From the beginning it was recognised that whilst the Crown had acquired sovereignty over a particular territory, it had not thereby acquired ownership of all land within the territory. This principle was implicit in the Royal Proclamation of 1763.[110] Further, it provided the impetus for the Crown to enter into 'approximately 500 treaties with Aboriginal people, both prior and subsequent to Confederation, covering more than half of Canada's land mass'.[111] Most of these treaties contain a clause in which the particular aboriginal people has agreed to 'cede, release, surrender, and yield up' their rights with respect to land; as a result, the courts have subsequently held that the group's common law rights to land have been displaced by 'treaty-based rights'.[112]

In addition, it is probably significant that the Federal government in Canada has had exclusive legislative power over 'Indians' since Confederation in 1867. (In Australia, as we have mentioned above, the Commonwealth has only enjoyed legislative power over Aboriginal peoples since 1967; and this is, of course, only *concurrent* power.) In 1982, the

106 Macklem, *op cit*, at footnote 23, p 14, including footnote 20, which demonstrates the racist attitudes underlying international law during the 1920s.

107 However, as Macklem points out, it was unclear initially whether all colonial laws applied to indigenous peoples: see Macklem, *op cit*, p 15, esp footnote 22 therein.

108 The British North America Act 1867. For a brief description of the Act, see Wilcox, *An Australian Charter of Rights?*, 1993, Sydney: Law Book Company, pp 28–29.

109 Macklem, *op cit*, p 17. And yet 'indigenous people did not possess the right to vote in Federal elections until 1960': Macklem, *op cit*, p 14.

110 The Royal Proclamation 1763 stated that the Crown 'reserve[d] (certain land) ... under our Sovereignty ... for the use of the ... Indians'. It also 'prohibit[ed] private purchases of Indian land throughout the Crown's North American colonies': Macklem, *op cit*, p 16.

111 Macklem, *op cit*, p 15.

112 *Ibid*.

Canadian constitution was 'repatriated' from England, and the Canadian Charter of Rights and Freedoms was enacted as part of the Constitution Act 1982.[113]

The Charter guarantees various civil and political freedoms and rights.[114] However, aside from minority language educational rights, the Charter does not include social, cultural and economic rights, for example rights to an adequate standard of health, education, and housing, and rights to preservation of cultural heritage and identity. We have noted above that it is these types of rights which Aboriginal and Torres Strait Islander peoples consider particularly important.

The Charter does include an equality provision, s 15, which may be used to attack discrimination in any type of federal or provincial law.[115] The provision has been relied upon by the Working Group on Aboriginal and Treaty Rights.[116]

The rights and freedoms in the Charter are 'guaranteed equally to male and female persons'.[117] However, various provisions specifically recognise and protect areas of difference within Canadian society.[118] In particular, s 25 provides that the Charter rights and freedoms 'shall not be construed so as to abrogate or derogate from any aboriginal, treaty or other rights or freedoms that pertain to the aboriginal peoples of Canada'.

We turn now to the issue of the recognition of 'Aboriginal and treaty rights'. These are guaranteed not by the Charter, but by s 35 of the Constitution Act 1982. Section 35 provides as follows:

> (1) The existing Aboriginal and treaty rights of the Aboriginal peoples of Canada are hereby recognised and affirmed.
> (2) In this Act, 'Aboriginal peoples of Canada' includes the Indian, Invit and Metis peoples of Canada.
> (3) For greater certainty, in sub-s 1 'treaty rights' includes rights that now exist by way of land claims agreements or may be so acquired.
> (4) Notwithstanding any other provision of this Act, the Aboriginal and treaty rights referred to in sub-s 1 are guaranteed equally to male and female persons.

113 See Wilcox, *op cit*, pp 33–37; see also Macklem, *op cit*, p 21, footnotes 70 and 71.

114 For example: freedom of religion, expression, and association, and democratic, mobility, criminal procedure, and equality rights.

115 Section 15 provides as follows:

(1) Every individual is equal before and under the law and has the right to the equal protection and equal benefit of the law without discrimination and, in particular, without discrimination based on race, national or ethnic origin, colour, religion, sex, age or mental or physical disability.

(2) Subsection (1) does not preclude any law, program or activity that has as its object the amelioration of conditions of disadvantaged individuals or groups including those that are disadvantaged because of race, national or ethnic origin, colour, religion, sex, age or mental or physical disability.

116 Wilcox, *op cit*, p 175, footnote 659.

117 Section 28 The Canadian Charter of Rights and Freedoms ('The Charter').

118 For example, freedom of 'conscience and religion' (s 2(a)) and freedom of 'thought, belief, opinion and expression' (s 2(b)) are protected. Section 27 provides that the Charter 'shall be interpreted in a manner consistent with the preservation and enhancement of the multicultural heritage of Canadians'. See also ss 2(c) and 2(d), and 29. Note that the rights and freedoms in the Charter are not absolute: see s 1.

Since 1982, the guarantee of 'existing aboriginal ... rights' has been one of the main sources of development in the protection of indigenous rights. The phrase is not defined in the constitution, and so it has been left to the courts to determine its scope. A significant recent decision was that of the Supreme Court of Canada in the case of *R v Sparrow*.[119] The court held that s 35(1) protects those practices which 'form an 'integral part' of an Aboriginal community's distinctive culture', including 'at least part of the bundle of rights traditionally associated with the common law of Aboriginal title'.[120] In the case at hand, for example, the court recognised that the fishing rights of the Musqueam nation came within the scope of the 'Aboriginal rights' recognised by s 35(1), and that they were 'existing' rights in the sense that they had not been 'extinguished' prior to 1982.

In *R v Sparrow* the court also made it clear that Aboriginal rights, like Charter rights, are not absolute. The Supreme Court held that a law may restrict their exercise if it exhibits a 'valid legislative objective'.[121] In future, it is likely that a government will also be required to demonstrate that its legislation satisfies other tests, for example that it infringes the Aboriginal right as little as possible, and that it is consistent with the fiduciary obligation owed to aboriginal peoples.[122]

Indigenous people in Canada have also used the judicial process to pursue one of their main objectives: self-government, in a variety of forms. At this stage, the courts have not accepted that the 'existing Aboriginal ... rights' recognised by s 35(1) include an Aboriginal right to self-government.[123]

In any event, Aboriginal self-government has also been pursued through the political process. Developments within the judicial and political spheres have tended to interact with each other, so that 'progress' in one form has had the effect of moving on the dialogue in the other.[124]

119 [1990] 1 SCR 1075.

120 Macklem, *op cit*, p 22. Section 35(1) would presumably also protect rights such as linguistic rights and hunting rights. Thus far, the section has been interpreted as extending protection only to natural resources that the people has *traditionally* used (and therefore as not encompassing rights to natural gas and oil). However this issue has not yet been considered by the Supreme Court of Canada.

121 [1990] 1 SCR 1075 at 1114, as noted in Macklem, *op cit*, p 22. However, it seems that the constitutional protection of the rights may mean that the rights may not be *extinguished* by legislation.

122 That is, 'the government is expected to act in the interests of Aboriginal people in Canada': see Macklem, *op cit*, pp 22–23.

123 In *Delgamuukw v ABC* (1991) 79 DLR (4th) 185 (BSCS) the Gitksan and Wet'suwet'en peoples of British Columbia argued that although the British Crown had acquired sovereignty over their lands, they had continued to own the lands and were 'entitled to govern the territory by reference to Aboriginal, not provincial, law'. In the Court of Appeal of British Columbia, three of the five judges held that s 35(1) does not recognise a right to self-government. However, the issue has not been considered by the Supreme Court of Canada: see Macklem, *op cit*, pp 23–25.

124 For example, Macklem points to the impact of the case of *Calder v AGBC* (1973) 34 DLR (3rd) 145, in which the Supreme Court recognised the existence of an inherent Aboriginal title to land. He considers that this decision 'led the Federal Government to announce that it was prepared to enter into negotiations with respect to territory which had not (previously) been the subject of a treaty between the Crown and Aboriginal people': Macklem, *op cit*, p 20.

Since judicial recognition of inherent indigenous title to land, a number of comprehensive agreements have been concluded between indigenous people and Federal and/or provincial governments. These agreements are usually the product of a process of negotiation initiated by the lodging of a statement of claim, in which the government is interested in addressing and settling a wide range of issues.[125] All of the agreements which have resulted from this process 'purport to extinguish Aboriginal title to land in exchange for monetary compensation, title to specified land, hunting, trapping and fishing rights over certain territory, and administrative authority with respect to social and political matters.'[126]

More generally, the Canadian government has enacted legislation, and has considered constitutional amendments which would uphold the principle of self-government. The legislation – the federal Indian Act 1985 – is seen by some as containing an imposed and generalised solution.[127] However, since the mid-1980s Canadian politicians have in addition been discussing the possibility of a constitutional right to Aboriginal self-government.[128] Aboriginal organisations have been vocal in support of such a right, both from within the legislature and by other means including the use of blockades over ancestral land.[129]

Perhaps the most significant initiative has been the Charlottetown Accord 1992.[130] The Charlottetown Accord proposed constitutional and other recognition of the

125 See Macklem, *op cit*, pp 20–21, including references to various specific agreements (p 20). A final agreement may be accompanied by implementing legislation.

126 The Nunavut Agreement is a recent product of a comprehensive claims process. In the agreement the government has promised to introduce legislation which will establish the territory of Nunavut (currently part of the Northwest Territories) as 'a self-governing political jurisdiction within the framework of the Canadian constitution'. The agreement 'establishes a Nunavut Social Development Council to assist in the development of social and cultural policies, an Inuit Heritage Trust, to assist in the preservation of archaeological sites, and a Nunavut Wildlife Management Board ...' According to Macklem '[m]ost commentators are of the view that Nunavut will eventually obtain the status of a province within the Canadian federation', *op cit*, at footnote 23, pp 20–21.

127 The Indian Act 1985 'creates "bands" out of Aboriginal communities and establishes the "band council" as the basic unit of indigenous governance'. It provides that 'band councils have the authority to pass by-laws in relation to local matters, including aspects of band membership, health, commerce, traffic, law and order, public works and zoning'. In effect, it seems that the Indian Act has created another tier of government with powers akin to those held by local governments in Australia. As in the case of local government by-laws, the by-laws passed by the band council must be consistent with the enabling Act (here, the Indian Act) and federal regulation: see Macklem, *op cit*, p 18.

128 For example, between 1983 and 1987 there were four Minister's Conferences at which such issues were discussed: see Macklem, *op cit*, p 26, footnote 92.

129 The Meech Lake Accord was opposed on the basis 'that it wrongly viewed Canada as founded by two peoples, the English and the French, and did not address Aboriginal demands that an explicit right of Aboriginal self-government be entrenched in the Constitution': see Macklem, *op cit*, p 26. For examples of particular blockades, see pp 26–27.

130 In addition, in 1991, the Canadian government established a Royal Commission on Aboriginal Peoples, with powers to examine and propose solutions in relation to 'all issues which it deems to be relevant to any or all of the aboriginal peoples of Canada' (and, in particular, in relation to those issues which fall within the 16 specific subject-matters outlined in the mandate): see Macklem, *op cit*, p 27.

Aboriginal peoples' 'inherent right of self-government within Canada'.[131] It also proposed various reforms which were unrelated to this issue. The package as a whole was rejected by the Canadian people in a national referendum in October 1992. Nonetheless, the process which culminated in the Accord indicates that in Canada there is substantial *political* recognition of the right of Aboriginal self-government, even if there is not yet *legal* recognition.[132] In addition, as Macklem points out, the Accord 'represents an important model for the constitutional recognition of Aboriginal self-government'[133] – a model with resonance in various areas of Australia.

In any event, even without the constitutional entrenchment of this principle, it seems clear that the recognition of indigenous rights in s 35 of the Canadian constitution has had and will continue to have a profound effect on the attitudes of the judiciary, the politicians, and the people of Canada.

AUSTRALIA – A DOCUMENT TO ASSIST RECONCILIATION?

In Australia, there are already 'reconciliation documents' of sorts. There are regional agreements which have been negotiated by governments, commercial enterprises, and indigenous peoples. The agreements have tended to be less comprehensive in their coverage of issues than their Canadian equivalents and have 'variable legal bases, some statutory, others not'.[134] Secondly, the people of the Torres Strait Islands are in the process of 'achieving greater autonomy through the development of a development plan' and through the creation of a new body, the Torres Strait Regional Authority.[135] The Native Title Act 1993 (Cth) encourages the development of regional agreements in relation to land and waters.[136]

In Canada, the rights (and the extinguishment of rights) set out in such agreements are constitutionally protected. They are more likely to encompass rights associated with

131 The aspect of the Accord which related to Aboriginal self-government was ambitious in its scope. 'The Accord proposed that the Constitution of Canada be amended to recognise that '[t]he Aboriginal peoples of Canada have the inherent right of self-government within Canada' and that this right be "interpreted in light of the recognition of Aboriginal governments as one of the three orders of government in Canada"': see Macklem, *op cit*, pp 27–28. The Accord further called for the federal, provincial and Aboriginal governments to conduct negotiations to determine 'the way in which Aboriginal self-government would take shape in particular instances'; and it proposed that all rights contained in resultant self-government agreements would receive constitutional protection. (Such rights would be regarded as treaty rights under s 35(1) Constitution Act 1982: see Macklem, *op cit*, p 29, especially at footnote 105.)

132 McNeil, K, 'The Constitutional Entrenchment of Aboriginal Treaty Rights', an address delivered to Flinders University Law School on 28 March 1995.

133 Macklem, *op cit*, p 28. He discusses the current avenues for recognition and application of the principle, given that constitutional reform is currently 'off the agenda': p 30.

134 *Controlling Destinies*, *op cit*, p 42. '[E]xamples can be found in the Great Barrier Reef Marine Park, the Mitchell River delta, and the Torres Strait, in Queensland, and in the Northern Territory, and elsewhere.'

135 *Controlling Destinies*, *op cit*, p 18.

136 Preamble and s 21 of the Native Title Act 1993 (Cth): see *Controlling Destinies*, *op cit*, pp 42–43.

indigenous self-government. Incorporation of such rights may, however, be within reach in Australia, since both Torres Strait Islanders and Northern Territory Aborigines are agitating for greater power 'to make decisions about social, cultural, economic, and environmental matters' within their regions.[137]

Regional agreements are able to include solutions which are appropriate to local needs. They tend to focus on land use and protection of cultural heritage, and may in the future include grants of local government-type powers.[138]

Recognition of Aboriginal and Torres Strait Islander perspectives on such issues contributes to indigenous self-determination. As we have discussed, there are many strands which make up self-determination, and not all are appropriate to all people in all circumstances. Self-government over a defined territory is a realistic goal for some discrete communities, but not for city-based indigenous people.[139] Some indigenous people regard programmes to combat alcoholism and to increase community employment as contributing to personal and collective self-determination, regardless of whether they are administered by an indigenous organisation or not.[140] Others reject any suggestion that Commonwealth-funded statutory authorities such as ATSIC can contribute, through their representative nature and their programmes, to indigenous self-determination.[141]

So, opinion will differ on the appropriate mechanisms for implementing general principles such as the right to self-determination and the need to protect cultural heritage. Nonetheless, in our view consideration should be given to according *legal* recognition to such principles. Politicians and public speakers may express views on the *moral* entitlements of Aboriginal and Torres Strait Islander peoples,[142] but greater

137 Mr Getano Lui, Chairman of the Torres Strait Island Co-ordinating Council, cited in *Controlling Destinies*, *op cit*, p 33. See also Professor Russell Matthews' comments on the financial viability of self-governing areas (pp 33–34), and Darryl Pearce's call for academics to develop detailed models of self-government, which would demonstrate how 'an Aboriginal self-governing entity [could] fit into the Territory or ... into the Commonwealth legislation' (pp 28–29).

138 Fr Brennan SJ reports that: '[t]o date some indigenous communities have been granted powers of local government together with some additional functions such as the provision of their own courts and police services', *op cit*, at footnote 28, p 33. For example, the Cherbourg Aboriginal Council exercises such powers: see Brennan, *op cit*, footnote 2, pp 246–47.

139 That is not to say that Aboriginal people in urban areas such as Redfern could not be accorded greater autonomy: for example, the power to govern matters relating to members of their community. See Brennan, *op cit*, at footnote 2, pp 262–63.

140 As to the Community Development Employment Projects (CDEP), operated through ATSIC, see *Controlling Destinies*, *op cit*, pp 37–38; on individual attempts to combat alcoholism, see pp 47–51.

141 See, for example, *Controlling Destinies*, *op cit*, pp 15–18. It is argued, for example, that ATSIC embodies the principle of self-management rather than self-determination. Self-determination, by contrast, 'incorporates the notion that indigenous organisations and representatives should be able to shape policy for their people and not simply manage government programmes, run co-operative enterprises and administer local government functions for communities which happen to be indigenous': see Brennan, *op cit*, at footnote 2, p 256.

142 For examples of speeches by politicians, see the statement made in 1972 by the then Prime Minister, Mr McMahon (discussed in the CAR Report, *op cit*, p 11, and the speech by the current Prime Minister Mr Keating on 10 December 1992 (extracted in (1993) 3(61) *Aboriginal Law Bulletin* 4–5).

attitudinal change is worked by rights which are not only legally recognised but legally *enforceable*.[143] The decision in *Mabo (No 2)*[144] and the impact of s 35 of the Canadian constitution are obvious examples of this.

A starting point would be to include in the constitution some acknowledgment of the prior occupation and dispossession of Aboriginal and Torres Strait Islander peoples in Australia. As Professor Daes has said:[145]

> In the culture of a nation, as in the psychology of individuals, the first step towards healing and reconciliation is honesty about the past.

The preamble to the constitution could set the constitution in context by referring to this history, and to the special status of the indigenous peoples as the 'first Australians', and also by describing the aspirations and the diverse cultural backgrounds of Australians today. ATSIC has put forward for consideration a preamble which includes these various elements.[146]

Secondly, we agree with the Constitutional Commission that s 51(xxvi) of the constitution should be amended so that there is an explicit power in the Commonwealth to make laws with respect to 'Aborigines and Torres Strait Islanders'.[147] The Constitutional Commission also recommended that s 25 of the constitution should be repealed because of its discriminatory basis.[148] Section 25 states that where a State law causes 'persons of any race' to be disqualified from voting at particular State elections, those persons will not be counted when calculating the population of the State or the Commonwealth. In our view, the provision is anachronistic, and should have been put forward for repeal at the time of the 1967 referendum.

Moving beyond the existing clauses of the constitution, we next consider the suggestion that a non-discrimination provision should be entrenched in the constitution. During the debates on the Native Title Bill, Aboriginal people recognised the importance of the guarantees against racial discrimination contained in the Racial Discrimination Act 1975 (Cth), but also their vulnerability as ordinary statutory provisions.[149] As Fr Brennan SJ has suggested, the principle could be included as part of a more general guarantee (against Commonwealth and State laws and practices) of

143 Note, for example, the potential impact of the High Court's decision in *Teoh v Minister for Immigration and Ethnic Affairs* (1995) 128 ALR 353.

144 *Op cit*, at footnote 10.

145 Daes, *op cit*, at footnote 1, p 61.

146 See Brennan, *op cit*, at footnote 28, pp 20–21.

147 See discussion above in text accompanying footnotes 35–47.

148 See, for example *The Position of Indigenous People in National Constitutions–Conference Report*, 1994, Canberra: AGPS, p 14.

149 See Brennan, *op cit*, at footnote 28, p 23; and Dodson, *op cit*, at footnote 56, p 12. The provisions of the Racial Discrimination Act were, of course, decisive in *Western Australia v Commonwealth* (1995) 128 ALR 1, in which the High Court held that the Land (Titles and Traditional Usage) Act 1993 (WA) was inconsistent with the RDA, and therefore invalid.

'freedom from discrimination on the ground of race, colour, ethnic or national origin, sex, marital status ... political, religious or ethical belief',[150] or sexuality, or age.

The components of constitutional change that we have mentioned thus far could be described as comprising a 'minimalist' position. Such change would not threaten traditional assumptions about the need to accommodate Aboriginal and Torres Strait Islander people within our existing system of representative government, in a way that is fair and non-discriminatory. We could add to this, two other possibilities: the reservation (by constitutional amendment) of a certain number of Senate seats for indigenous representatives,[151] and the enactment of a Bill of Rights.

It will be in considering the context of any Bill of Rights that Australian legal orthodoxy will face its greatest challenge. In recent years, various sections of the legal communities have become more supportive of the idea of constitutionally guaranteed civil and political rights.[152] However, not only is this a minority 'movement', but the issue of the protection of economic, social and cultural rights (particularly in the form of collective rights) has hardly been discussed. One model that does incorporate such rights is the Bill of Rights proposed by the Queensland Electoral and Administrative Review Commission (EARC). However, in contrast to the civil and political rights contained within the Bill, it is recommended that the special indigenous rights, and the economic, social and cultural rights, would be 'affirmed' rather than enforceable.[153]

We have discussed the nature of indigenous rights above, and have described them as various strands of the principle of self-determination. These rights could be set out in the constitution, or in a separate Bill of Rights or Bill of Indigenous Rights (whether entrenched or not).[154] They could also be set out in an agreement concluded between the Australian government (as representative of the Australian people), and representatives of the Aboriginal and Torres Strait Islander peoples.

The prospect of such an agreement – or 'treaty' or 'compact' – was under discussion at the time that the Constitutional Commission delivered its final report in 1988.[155] The Commission considered the proposal of an earlier Senate Committee that a new constitutional provision should be inserted, along the lines of the current section 105A, 'which would confer a broad power on the Commonwealth to enter into a compact with representatives of the Aboriginal people'.[156]

150 See, for example, the clause recommended by the Constitutional Commission in 1988, as set out in Brennan, *op cit*, at footnote 22, p 23.

151 As in New Zealand.

152 See, for example, Alston (ed), *Towards an Australian Bill of Rights*, 1994, Canberra: Centre for International and Public Law, HREOC; Wilcox, *op cit*, at footnote 108.

153 As Fr Brennan S J explains, it is instead proposed that the Bill would contain a clause stating that: 'The Parliament urges the Queensland community generally to observe (these) rights and encourages persons to assert the rights in ways that do not involve the legal process or proceedings', *op cit*, at footnote 28, p 28.

154 Opinion will differ on whether a referendum which concentrated on indigenous rights would have greater prospects of success than one which placed such rights alongside general guarantees of civil and political (and perhaps economic, social and cultural) rights.

155 For a brief description, see McRae, Nettheim, and Beacroft, *op cit*, at footnote 4, pp 317–19.

156 Senate Standing Committee on Constitutional and Legal Affairs, *Two Hundred Years Later....* (PP 107/1983), xii, 115, as cited in Final Report, *op cit*, at footnote 35, p 725.

The Senate Committee had recommended a draft provision which set out the subject matters that could be encompassed by such an agreement, and which stated that the Commonwealth would have power 'to make laws for the carrying out by the parties of any such agreement'.[157] The proposal was therefore that the Commonwealth could enact implementing legislation (which would bind both the Commonwealth and the States), regardless of whether it concerned subject matters, such as health and education, which were traditionally the province of the States.

The Constitutional Commission recommended against adoption of such an amendment. It considered that such an implementing provision could not be drafted until a particular agreement had been concluded, and it was known what the Australian people (in a referendum) would be approving.[158]

The Commission did not consider the suggestion that the full text of any agreement be incorporated within the constitution.[159] Nor did it discuss the possibility of *direct* constitutional recognition of indigenous rights: for example, the Canadian model.

In our view, further consideration should be given to the proposal that indigenous rights be accorded constitutional status. It would be necessary to examine many different issues – questions such as the interaction of collective and individual rights, the recognition of 'treaty' rights, and the extent to which indigenous rights can be limited by government action. We have touched on some of these earlier. We will mention now two other issues of central importance. First, should the indigenous rights be described in a way that is relatively detailed; or should we adopt an approach akin to that of Canada, which has simply recognised 'existing Aboriginal and treaty rights ...'?[160] If we adopted the latter approach, we would of course leave many questions of detail to be resolved by our courts. For example, we would not have specified whether such rights include rights to self-government, and rights to use land and resources in non-traditional ways.[161]

Secondly, how should such rights be enforced? There are various overseas models which may be thought appropriate. In Canada, indigenous rights are enforceable through the ordinary court structure. In New Zealand, the Waitangi Tribunal is a specialist body 'comprised equally of Maori and Europeans', in which 'Maori and European laws have equal standing'.[162] Its recommendations are not binding.

157 See text of the draft provision, as set out in Final Report, *op cit*, at footnote 35, p 726. Note the potential similarity with the broad scope of the external affairs power (s 51(xxix)).

158 See Final Report, *op cit*, pp 730–731.

159 See Final Report, *op cit*, pp 721, 725; para 10.438.

160 Section 35(1) Constitution Act 1982.

161 Fr Brennan SJ also suggests inclusion of a provision which would require our legislatures 'to legislate subject to Aboriginal law in circumstances when all parties are Aborigines who consent to Aboriginal law prevailing', *op cit*, at footnote 2, p 263.

162 See *The Position of Indigenous People in National Constitutions Conference Report* (above footnote 148) p 15. In any event, an additional mechanism could also be considered. This is Father Brennan's suggestion of a tribunal which would 'determine disputes between indigenous Australians and government when indigenous Australians are dissatisfied with government's attempts to accord them self-determination'. The tribunal's determinations would be non-binding, but it would provide a mechanism by which indigenous Australians could 'bring governments to account': see *Agreeing on a Document, op cit*, at footnote 97, pp 13–14.

It seems likely that a specialist tribunal could develop more culturally sensitive mechanisms for obtaining and evaluating evidence, than could the ordinary courts. On the other hand, a Commonwealth tribunal comprising non-judicial members could not make enforceable determinations.[163]

We are still a long way from debating such questions of detail. Indigenous peoples are still in the initial stages of considering the possibilities. The Council for Aboriginal Reconciliation and ATSIC have acknowledged that further public education and consultation with Aboriginal and Torres Strait Islander peoples is required.[164]

Constitutional change is of course notoriously difficult to achieve in Australia. It will occur only with bipartisan political support, and wide community support. It will not occur until a significant amount of reconciliation has already occurred in the hearts and minds of ordinary Australians. Consensus achieved by indigenous peoples during the native title discussions suggests that it will be possible to develop uniform principles to put forward to the Australian electorate.[165] But Australians will only endorse those principles if they have begun to believe the statement made in Article 3 of the Draft Declaration: that '[i]ndigenous peoples have the right of self-determination'.

163 See *Brandy v Human Rights and Equal Opportunity Commission* (1995) 127 ALR 1 in relation to the separation of judicial power which is implied in the Constitution.

164 ATSIC has suggested that formal processes should be set up within the context of activities marking the centenary of our Constitution. Such processes should concentrate on achieving bipartisan political support and popular support for the indigenous position, and on negotiating and drafting appropriate Amendments. '[A] special Constitutional convention (could) be held to consider proposed amendments': see CAR Report, *op cit*, p 177.

165 See the comments by Lois O'Donoghue set out in Brennan, *op cit*, at footnote 28, p 40; note the rather different emphasis of Michael Mansell on the same page. It has been suggested that an indigenous referendum should be held: *Conference Report*, *op cit*, at footnote 148.

CHAPTER THIRTEEN

RECONCILIATION

Irene Watson

The idea of reconciliation means to me a process of healing, ending opposition and commencing friendly relations. Nice idea but what does it mean for Nungas?[1] How can the healing not only begin, but be successful? Who needs healing and a healing of what? And who is to be reconciled? If we look to the Council for Aboriginal Reconciliation[2] for answers we will find they have a limited mandate: convening meetings and providing reports to the Federal government. At the end of the day we are still looking for the answers.

It is true that there is conflict in this country between indigenous and non-indigenous peoples, there are also peaceful relations amongst these groups. There are also both peaceful and conflict relations between and amongst indigenous peoples and their communities. But the greatest conflict arises between Nunga peoples and the state and federal government and a variety of trans-national corporations. So, when we speak of reconciliation it is fundamental to know who is to be reconciled and to what.

The 'conflict' that is to be reconciled has not subsided as a result of the Commonwealth government's recent reconciliation initiatives. The government established the following bodies: the Council for Aboriginal Reconciliation,[3] the Aboriginal and Torres Strait Islander Commission,[4] the Royal Commission into Aboriginal Deaths in Custody.[5] Nor has the conflict subsided since the High Court decision on native title,[6] or the Commonwealth government's response in the Native Title Act,[7] to be followed by the establishment of the Indigenous Land Corporation. The above initiatives have all been presented to the world as attempts by the Commonwealth government to ease the 'problem'.

Meanwhile, 'conflict' is continuing in many Nunga communities and in some circumstances conflict has been exacerbated by the above Commonwealth initiatives.

1 'Nungas' is an indigenous word which means indigenous peoples and is used in the southern parts of South Australia.

2 Council for Aboriginal Reconciliation Act 1991 (Cth).

3 *Ibid.*

4 Aboriginal and Torres Strait Islander Commissioner Act 1989 (Cth).

5 The Royal Commission into Aboriginal Deaths in Custody was established by the Commonwealth Government in 1987.

6 *Mabo v Queensland* (1992) 175 CLR 1 *(Mabo (No 2))*.

7 Native Title Act 1993 (Cth).

THE CONTINUING COLONIALISM

The above institutions were established by the Australian Government, imposed on Nungas unilaterally and are examples of the continuing colonial relationship between the Nunga Peoples and the 'Australian State'. They are colonial constructs which have been presented to the world as models of reconciliation and self-determination. I say this because, prior to the Invasion and colonialism of our laws, lands and peoples, in a land we now call Australia, hundreds of self-determining, peoples-nations existed in a state of independence and freedom from colonialism. We were the first of the first nations peoples to be living and practising self-determination. Self-determination inhered in the fact of our very existence. The deception of *terra nullius* was so widely spread and embraced by mainstream Australian society that it is largely responsible for creating a racist backlash. Australians had grown comfortable in the thought that the 'Aborigines' were contained by a legal theory – *terra nullius* – which held that we were peoples without any political rights or ownership of our territories. A fear spread across the country we now call Australia that the 'Aborigines' would claim all that belonged to 'them', and in the process block economic development and 'progress'. This fear was utilised by politicians who won parliamentary seats on a deliberate anti-Aborigine campaign. And as I write in August 1996 the Federal government presented a budget with major cutbacks to Aboriginal Affairs. All of this has occurred under the myth that *terra nullius* is dead; in reality the situation for Nungas is worsening.

So what is the 'conflict' or the 'problem'? In a nutshell, the 'problem' is the end result of more than 200 years of colonialism, resulting in dispossession of our traditional territories, and a struggle to survive past and continuing genocide and ecocide. The problem is, the problem is continuing. For Nungas genocide is a looming reality. We are just under 2% of the Australian population.

In thinking about reconciliation, colonialism must be addressed. Colonialism is the subjection of peoples to alien subjugation, domination and exploitation involving the imposition of social values and thoughts on the colonised peoples. The result is the subordination of indigenous peoples to the nation State. And against the pressure to disappear and become assimilated as one with the coloniser, Nunga peoples resist. This resistance is frequently unknown or seemingly invisible, I will not elaborate in this article on what is a huge and complex area of thought, but will simply state, that the resistance is against the stripping of our own indigenous perceptions of the world and the struggle for independence to be Nunga. The struggle is, to know the world through the eyes of our own Nunga beingness.

The perpetrators of colonialism have woven the deception that we have entered a post-colonial phase in world history. That is a lie. Whilst Nunga peoples remain enclaves of colonised peoples within the Australian State, we have not yet entered an era of decolonisation in this country. Australia is a State power that has derived its identity from unfettered colonialism. Nungas were massacred *en masse*, our lands were damaged, and the law of the land never acknowledged. This process has never ended, it has merely changed its face to meet contemporary practices.

A QUICK FIX OR THE FINAL CURE?

I do not see myself as representing the 'collective Nunga view', for it is the collective view that has been smashed by colonialism. Many of us are left with only the fragments of the past and in writing this chapter I do not claim to have laid out all the issues, questions and answers. Rather, I have looked critically at the idea of reconciliation and what that means from my own indigenous perspective.

Kevin Gilbert spoke of the idea of reconciliation and what the reconciliation process will become:[8]

> We have to look at the word 'reconciliation'. What are we to reconcile ourselves to? To a holocaust, to massacre, to the removal of us from our land, from the taking of our land? The reconciliation process can achieve nothing because it does not at the end of the day promise reparation for the taking away of our lives, our lands and of our economic and political base. Unless it can return to us these very vital things, unless it can return to us an economic, a political and a viable land base, what have we? A handshake? A symbolic dance? An exchange of leaves or feathers or something like that?

When I think about the reconciliation process, I am still left with the question: what will happen to the pain we still carry? When someone is murdered there is a process that is in place to right that wrong. In our tradition we call it 'payback'. But what is in place to right the wrongs that have occurred and are still occurring in indigenous Australia? A process of reconciliation is not that process. A 'let's be friends' approach is not a satisfactory solution for the family and victim of a murder or a rape. What is in place to ensure the perpetrator will not re-offend? Who will monitor the future struggle of Nunga peoples to survive? The colonial State? But what interest does it have in telling the truth? It has none.

To simply appoint another domestic tribunal or commission of inquiry to hear the stories of Nunga peoples is not the solution. Particularly when the Australian government is under no obligation to comply with recommendations for improvement and change. The recent Royal Commission into Aboriginal Deaths in Custody (RCIADC) is an example. The federal government revealed its propensity to hide behind the veil of federalism when it chose to do nothing about the current crisis confronting Nunga peoples. The federal government has failed to implement the RCIADC's recommendations and as a result incarceration rates of Nungas is increasing, as are deaths in custody.[9]

The RCIADC inquiry into the death of Malcolm Smith[10] referred to the removal of indigenous children under the assimilation policy as amounting to genocide. However, following the conclusion of the inquiry Nunga children were still being detained in juvenile institutions throughout Australia at levels incomprehensible to white Australia.

---

8 Gilbert, K, *Aboriginal Sovereignty: Justice, the Law and Land*, 1993, Canberra: Burrambinga Books, p 2.

9 For further discussion see Cunneen, C, and more recently in Bird, G, Martin, G and Nielsen, J (eds), *Majah, Indigenous Peoples and the Law*, 1996, Sydney: Federation Press.

10 Wooten, JH, Commissioner, 'Report of the Inquiry into the Death of Malcolm Smith', in *Royal Commission into Aboriginal Deaths in Custody*, 1989, Canberra: AGPS.

We were still left at the end of the inquiry asking the question – 'what and who is going to change this to make sure that it doesn't happen again?' – as we watch it happen again and again. Today our children are still removed from their communities. There is no evidence that this will stop in the near future. Meanwhile the Commonwealth government has established another inquiry to hear the stories of a past history of removal of Nunga children.

The earlier policy of removing Aboriginal children was used as a means of assimilating Aboriginal people into the dominant white culture. Under the States' Aborigines Acts children were taken away and placed in institutions, a practice continued until the late 1960s. The administrators of the time referred to this practice as a means of 'breeding out' the Aboriginal race. This is the story of the attempted genocide of indigenous peoples.

Article 11 of the United Nations Convention on the Prevention and Punishment of the Crime of Genocide 1948, of which Australia is a signatory, defines genocide as:

> ... any of the following acts committed with intent to destroy, in whole or in part, a national, ethnical, racial or religious group, as such:
> (a) killing members of the group;
> (b) causing serious bodily or mental harm to members of the group;
> (c) deliberately inflicting on the group conditions of life calculated to bring about its physical destruction in whole or in part;
> (d) imposing measures intended to prevent births within the group; and
> (e) forcibly transferring children of the group to another group.

It is (e) above that directly relates to the policies of the forced removal of Nunga children, which amounts to the crime of genocide. Even though the Australian government ratified this convention in 1949, indigenous children were still taken away under the assimilation policy up until the mid-1960s, a clear breach of the Convention.

This is our history. The important question for us is: 'Is history repeating itself?' Are there still contemporary forms of genocide still operating within society? And the answer is 'yes'. The practice of removing Nunga children from their families is now less overt but nevertheless it is still occurring through welfare policies and the juvenile justice system.

Our children are detained by the juvenile justice system at highly disproportionate levels to that of the general population. A recent study found that while the total number of children admitted to institutions had decreased, the ratio of indigenous to non-Indigenous children increased.[11] Nunga children are almost 20 times more likely to be held in detention than other children.[12] In Western Australia indigenous children comprise 57.9% of children incarcerated, yet they are only 2.7% of that state's juvenile population.[13]

11 D Report of the South Australian Office of Crime Statistics, April 1992.

12 Australian Institute of Criminology, *Persons in Juvenile Corrective Institutions* No 66, March 1994, compiled by D Dagger, and ed S Mukherjee, Table 9, cited in Aboriginal and Torres Strait Islander Social Justice Commissioner, 'Third Report 1995', Canberra: AGPS, p 14.

13 *Ibid*, p 15.

This situation is not likely to improve. Current trends exposed by the Aboriginal and Torres Strait Islander Social Justice Commissioner, reveal that the problem will reach crisis proportion in the future:[14]

> In six years, by 2001 there will have been a 15% increase in the number of Indigenous kids in detention ... in 16 years, by 2011 there will have been a 44% increase in the number of Indigenous kids in detention.

Indigenous children are being removed from their families through a process of criminalisation.

The welfare policies of the past still exist today but are more covert and invisible. The State and Federal governments have not considered the impact of genocide upon indigenous peoples and as a result have 'treated' Nungas 'equally' (post-1960s) with all other 'Australians'. However, there has not been any opportunity of healing for the thousands of indigenous families who have suffered as a result of colonialism. Colonialism has created dispossession and disempowerment, a huge inequality that has never been adequately addressed for the greater majority of Nungas. And until it has been repaired and compensated for we will always be disadvantaged by the equality equation. And in reality the expectation prevails that regardless of history indigenous peoples must get up and get on with their lives just like anybody else.

This mainstream approach neglects reality, a reality that we are the survivors of a holocaust. And yet the expectation remains fixed that we are all equal before the law when for example the courts determine what is 'in the best interests' of the child. In determining what are 'the best interests' of the child recognition of our history and our culture is frequently ignored. This has left families disempowered and disabled from being self-determining in the rearing of our children. And yet whilst the measure of 'equality' applies every social indicator is evidence of our inequality, we are the poorest; we have the poorest health, housing and education. Australian law may appear to promote progressive human rights laws, but Nungas don't share the experience of having those rights, the protection of our lands, culture, and very life is the least protected of any group in Australia.

The situation is more complex than that which I have indicated here, because we are not just reconciling individual grievances, but grievances against communities of peoples, ie the collective identity of Nungas. Therefore the redress should be for the betterment of the collective. However, Western legal thought struggles with the concept of 'the collective' and is generally backward in its recognition of the principle in law, in general, recognition of human rights is individual-rights-based.

So at the end of the day can we tell our story to a forum in which the coloniser is all powerful and accuse them of genocide whilst at the same time expecting the hearing to be impartial and fair? This scenario is not unlike the victims of the Holocaust appearing before the Nazis and accusing them of genocide. Should we expect domestic government inquiries to be anything else than an inquiry used by the State to whitewash its own colonial history? It is these same questions that have recently led to the

14 Aboriginal and Torres Strait Islander Social Justice Commissioner, Third Report, 1995, p 15.

establishment of the First Nations International Court of Justice (FNICJ). The court was established by the Chiefs of Ontario and the Assembly of First Nations, representing 640 First Nations across Canada. This court held its first sitting in Ottawa, during April 1996. It was created because indigenous peoples of Canada had lost faith in both the Canadian courts' and the United Nations' ability and lack of goodwill to bring about a just resolution to the continuing dispossession and genocide of the indigenous peoples of Canada. The establishment of the FNICJ is an act of self-determination, and affirmation of the inherent right to create and control our own indigenous institutions. It represents the first step in establishing an on-going mechanism for jurisdictional dispute resolution. The FNICJ assumes sovereignty and speaks in the language of first nations law – the laws of creation. The court holds central to its way of being a respect for the words of the elders.

This court would also have jurisdiction to hear the stories of conflict between the first nations peoples of Australia and the Australian State.

TERRA NULLIUS LIVES

In considering the depth of what needs to be reconciled we need to look at legal history and the creation of the Australian State. The myth of *terra nullius* described the land as empty of people or peoples who were without sovereign laws. This racist and imperialistic idea has over the past 200 years become entrenched in Australian law and governance and still remains firmly rooted today.

The High Court native title decision[15] was hailed as a true initiative in reconciliation, when it overturned the application of *terra nullius* to Australia's law of real property. However the High Court did not fully reject the *terra nullius* doctrine by going onto question the legitimacy of the British occupation of Australia. The High Court decided that the Invasion and the British Crown's acquisition of sovereignty over the Australian colony was an 'act of State' that could not be challenged in any Australian court.[16] The colonial history of dispossession and disempowerment of Nungas cannot be challenged in the Australian courts. The legal concept of *terra nullius* remains intact. A true rejection of *terra nullius* would have questioned the very legitimacy of the Crown's occupation of Australia.

Paul Coe challenges and questions the High Court decision as follows:[17]

> It is like the logic that went with the Third Reich when they started killing, when they started using force to imprison people to take other people's land and territory. And then to justify it in the name of the State so that the acts of State were above and beyond question ... They have not applied international law. They have not applied the decision [of] the Nuremburg War Crimes Tribunal [where] the allied powers ... said that an 'act of State' does not justify genocide, mass murder or using war to acquire territory.

15 *Mabo (No 2)* (1992) 175 CLR l.

16 *Ibid* pp 31–35 and 78.

17 Coe, P, '*Mabo* – Confirming Dispossession' in *Broadside,* 10 February 1993, p 9.

Human rights breaches by the Australian State against Nungas have not been enquired into in the same way that other international tribunals have heard crimes committed by States against humanity. And whilst it is said *terra nullius* is dead, it comes more than 200 years too late. The consequences of *terra nullius* surround us all. The continuing *terra nullius* is to be found over the greater proportion of the Australian continent and the Nunga peoples. The fantasy that *terra nullius* is dead is yet to become a reality for the few who are constructed by the High Court as the remnant traditional owners unaffected by *terra nullius*.

WHAT WAS REALLY STOLEN?

The native title decision is viewed mainly as a decision about the remnant 'native title' which may still survive invasion and dispossession. The land, however, was not lost, it remains beneath our feet, what was invaded and what we were dispossessed of was our sovereignty, that is, our ability to control what happens to the land and the people. The High Court decision did not improve our ability to regain self-determination. And for the small minority of Nungas who are able to establish that they have native title, they will continue to have limited power over the land and its peoples. The High Court decision does not recognise the peoples' sovereign right to determine what the future of the group will be. And a title that is recognised remains vulnerable and open to extinguishment. Questions as to jurisdiction and what can happen to the land and the people, remain open to negotiations with the State and other developmental interest groups. Whether a group is able to refuse intensive economic development on their lands in preference for a more ecologically sustainable lifestyle is not within the power of the community to decide, but remains vulnerable to the political power of the State and economic interest groups.

Before the invasion of our lands we were self-determining and independent; today we are captives of the colonial State. The High Court decision has not altered that fact.

A STEP IN WHICH DIRECTION?

Following the High Court decision on native title, the Commonwealth Government swiftly enacted the Native Title Act 1993, establishing the Native Title Tribunal. The tribunal was established to determine the existence or otherwise of 'native title'. Four years after the High Court decision there has not been one claim to native title recognised. The road ahead is not yet clear; the power of the State to extinguish native title looms. The Native Title Tribunal in a recent application determined that a pastoral lease extinguishes native title,[18] which was affirmed by the Federal Court.[19] The Waanyi people appealed to the High Court; however, the court failed to determine the

18 'Waanyi Claim' (1995) 4(1) *Native Title News*.

19 *North Ganalanja Aboriginal Corporation (and another) v State of Queensland (and another)*, 1 November 1995, Federal Court of Australia.

question of extinguishment of native title by pastoral leases.[20] This question is of fundamental importance, as the lands which may be successfully claimed as native title mostly lie in regions where a pastoral lease has been issued. If the courts decide that a pastoral lease extinguishes native title, or the Australian governments are successful in passing legislation not in contravention of the Commonwealth Racial Discrimination Act 1975, that allows for pastoral leases to extinguish native title; then the process of *Mabo* and the implementation of the Native Title Act would have been a completely farcical and cynical exercise. In many pastoral leases in South Australia the colonists made express provision for Nungas to camp, hunt and gather over the pastoral lease lands. However not all indigenous peoples in the past had the opportunity to assert their occupancy rights under pastoral leases. Many traditional owners were forcibly removed from the land, to be relocated onto concentration camps known as Aboriginal reserves; this control the colonists maintained through the Aborigines Acts. The occupancy rights under pastoral leases nevertheless remained intact. And now when the time has come for indigenous peoples to test those rights the State has added to the challenge the possibility of extinguishment of native title. It is this situation which illustrates best the shortcomings of the Native Title Act. Were we better off before the Native Title Act? And is this legislation going to be reviewed in the future as a contemporary form of dispossession?

Since the establishment of the tribunal no lands have yet been returned to traditional owners. We are still waiting to see the extent to which native title will be recognised by this new commonwealth body.

The concern over the land and its future is the most important concern. However one's ability to be a caring owner-custodian for the land is impossible if the traditional owners are to remain politically powerless. The power to determine future developments on land is retained by the colonial State; however, they would argue that the indigenous owners-custodians have a say. But the process in reality is guided by a monoculturalist and pragmatic view of the world and complex negotiating procedures whereby the 'best deal' and the minimal damage to land is the most that can be attained. And this exists even though the traditional owners might disagree, eg to the development of an extremely toxic mining development. This approach raises concern for the ability of future generations of traditional owners, to continue to live with and on the land, as developers continue to impose their agendas on Aboriginal communities. The number of applications made by development interests for determination of native title before the tribunal already exceeds applications made by traditional owners for a native title determination.

One may ask in whose best interest the legislation was enacted? The Commonwealth used the special measures provision of the Commonwealth Racial Discrimination Act,[21] to avoid challenges made pursuant to ss 9 and 10 of that same Act. A special measure taken for the sole purpose of securing adequate advancement of

20 *North Ganalanja and Bindanggu Aboriginal Corporation for the Waanyi People v State of Queensland and CRA*, 21 March 1996, full bench of High Court.

21 Racial Discrimination Act 1975 (Cth) s 8(1).

certain racial or ethnic groups … in order to ensure such groups ... equal enjoyment or exercise of human rights and fundamental freedoms'.[22] It is clear to me that the Native Title Act was not enacted for the 'sole purpose' of advancing the struggle for Aboriginal advancement, but was used to re-establish a stable stockmarket and business as usual.

WHO CAN SPEAK FOR THE LAND?

The Native Title Act has created conflict between the different indigenous peoples. During the initial negotiations, it was 'representative organisations' that negotiated with the Commonwealth government in the drafting of the Native Title Bill 1993. Involvement of a broad spectrum of traditional owners was not considered nor engaged in the process of negotiations. And, as a result, the breadth of the voices of traditional owners, the group with the most to either gain or lose from the Native Title Act went unheard. This omission is likely to cause conflict throughout Aboriginal Australia for some time to come, and in part has recently been exposed.[23] The negotiations were concluded in less than 12 months, and in light of two centuries of dispossession, the time frame is chronically inadequate. It cannot ever be said that indigenous Australia was freely and fully informed of the scope of the negotiations and their final outcome, the Native Title Act.

The 'representative organisations' who were involved in the negotiations for native title legislation, are some of the same 'representative bodies', named in the Native Title Act.[24] They are the organisations that are resourced to assist traditional owners in bringing native title claims before the tribunal. This administrative arrangement is creating new conflicts throughout indigenous Australia.[25] Traditional owners pursing a determination before the tribunal will be required to approach their named representative body for assistance in preparing their application to the tribunal. This approach is likely to limit the independence and autonomy of traditional owners, in the preparation of their applications before the tribunal.

A POLITICAL VOICE

Like my ancestors I am limited in my abilities to prevent the processes of destruction of our mother earth. The public media debate on native title illustrates the marginalisation of the Nunga voice. We did not hear the voices of the majority of traditional owners, what we did hear was the pressing need for economic development and the assertions that Aboriginal people were not opposed to these developments. The voice of pragmatism and compromise was deceptively presented as the voice of Aboriginal Australia. This was a lie.

22 Article 1(4) International Convention on the Elimination of All Forms of Racial Discrimination.

23 ABC Four Corners, 9 October 1995.

24 Native Title Act (1993) (Cth), s 202.

25 For further discussion see O'Grady, R (1995) 141 *Adelaide Review* 9.

Nungas in terms of military might are politically powerless; it is a lie to suggest that we have any real degree of self-determination through governmental bodies such as the Aboriginal and Torres Strait Islander Commission.[26] ATSIC was established unilaterally by the Commonwealth government. As the peak funding body for Nunga communities, ATSIC is able to control indigenous Australia through economic dependency, as did its predecessor the Department of Aboriginal Affairs. This control will be exercised with greater force in the future following the federal liberal governments budget cutbacks and their public support for a return to old policies of assimilation of the indigenous peoples.

The new ATSIC structure has further eroded traditional Aboriginal political systems. Whilst regional councillors are elected to ATSIC, the process of election is an alien concept to Nungas who in general used a consensus community model whenever making decisions that affected the future of the community. And further, in establishing ATSIC the Commonwealth imposed its own administrative boundaries upon Aboriginal Australia which mirrored old Department of Aboriginal Affairs arrangements more than it did traditional Aboriginal political boundaries. Through the establishment of ATSIC a representative model was created that has failed to reflect Aboriginal law and society in a culturally appropriate manner. It has subsequently left communities in conflict with one and another over disputes that are complex and difficult to resolve. The combination of limited resources and needy communities is a potion for conflict. Previously the conflict was between the old Department of Aboriginal Affairs and the Aboriginal peoples. The department was clearly identified as the colonial oppressor. And now the conflict is between communities and ATSIC, which is identified as being a model of self-determination. The difference being, prior to the establishment of ATSIC oppression was imposed, now, post-ATSIC, there exists the illusion of choice. In reality there is little difference.

Nungas who remain outside ATSIC are guaranteed marginalisation, unemployment, and the under-development of their families and communities. Nungas have been coerced into supporting ATSIC for reasons of survival rather than for freedom and independence. It is the pursuit of freedom and independence that I see as being compatible with any meaningful reconciliation.

ATSIC is another colonial construct that has been imposed. ATSIC is not a creation of Nungas, nor was it chosen freely and with consent by Aboriginal Australia to be its voice. Self-determination is what is created by the people for the people.

The recent United Nations endorsement of ATSIC as a non-governmental organisation (NGO) enables ATSIC to participate in UN forums. The recognition of ATSIC as being an independent body is a lie. The expectation of NGOs is that they be independent of government. ATSIC is a statutory body it is accountable to government, the minister responsible for Aboriginal affairs has broad powers to scrutinise and intervene; all of which indicates a lack of autonomy and independence from government. And further its chairperson is appointed by the federal government. It is

26 Established by the Aboriginal and Torres Strait Islander Commission Act 1989.

because of ATSIC's closeness to government, that conflicts of interest arise. And it is also because of that closeness to government that ATSIC cannot in truth ever be the free and independent voice of Nunga peoples.

CONCLUSION

Clearly reconciliation is about more than the institutions and issues I have discussed above. Reconciliation and healing is a global issue for all peoples who are thinking about the future of the planet. It is a process that requires facing the greater truths. Lies are obstacles and thus an enemy to the process of reconciliation.

In this short space I have examined lies portrayed as truth. These lies have become obstacles to the process of reconciliation and healing. They need to be removed, in the struggle to find the greater truths. For if we continue to allow these views to be nurtured and become known as reality, then we risk repeating a history of gross injustice to Nungas. We have already seen the damage come of *terra nullius*. Are we going to continue to deny that *terra nullius* still has a life in Australia? And are we going to also deny that this new life form lives in the name of an 'act of State'? Are we not to question the past? Are we going to allow the past to dissolve and therefore give permission to what the Nuremburg War Crimes Tribunal decided was a crime: for any State to justify acts of genocide in terms of a legitimate 'act of State'. Because this is what the High Court of Australia has done. And yet the Australian State has through myth and fantasy created an illusion of enlightenment and change. Nothing has changed, only the lies have become more difficult to detect. The danger with this is that it has made the position of indigenous peoples vulnerable to a new wave of racism. This racism will provide the fuel for trans-national corporations to plunder and destroy the last of pristine indigenous territories, culture and law. That is, unless the lies are revealed before it is too late. And then, in speaking in the language of truth, we may begin to venture along a path of meaningful reconciliation and healing for not only all peoples now, but for our grandchildren who are still coming to us.

INDEX